The Layers of
Magazine Editing

I am a lover of boats and communication;
and a lover of magazines as teachers.

Jon Wilson, editor, *WoodenBoat*

Layers
Layers
Layers
Layers
Layers
Layers
Layers
Layers
Layers
Layers
The Layers of
Magazine Editing

Michael Robert Evans

Columbia University Press
New York

Columbia University Press
Publishers Since 1893
New York Chichester, West Sussex

Copyright © 2004 Michael Robert Evans

Library of Congress Cataloging-in-Publication Data
Evans, Michael Robert, 1959–
  The layers of magazine editing / Michael Robert Evans.
    p. cm.
  Includes bibliographical references and index.
  ISBN 978-0-231-12860-5 (cloth : alk. paper)
  ISBN 978-0-231-12861-2 (pbk. : alk. paper)
  1. Journalism—Editing. I. Title.

PN4778.E93 2004
808'.0607—dc22   2003068834

⊛

Columbia University Press books are printed
on permanent and durable acid-free paper.
Printed in the United States of America

c 10 9 8 7 6 5 4 3 2 1
p 10 9 8 7 6 5 4 3 2

To Joanna, Dylan, and Miles—

honest critics, careful thinkers,

and the greatest family

a person could ever imagine

Contents

Preface   ix

Layer 1. The Big Picture

1. From Spark to Flame: How to Conceptualize
    a Magazine   3

2. Who Is Out There? Finding and Understanding
    Audiences   18

3. Hocus Focus: The Magic of a Clear Mission   40

4. Freedom and Responsibility: The Law and
    What to Do About It   64

5. Does Write Make Right? The Ethics of Editing   83

Layer 2. The Big Questions

6. The Plan's the Thing: Planning Issues and
    Working with Writers   109

7. Hands Off! First, Make Sure It Makes Sense   133

8. Editorial Muscle: Checking an Article's Fit and Tone   153

9. Beginnings, Endings, and All that Comes
    Between: Structure, Leads, and Conclusions   169

Layer 3. The Small (but Important) Stuff

10. How's That, Again? The Facts of Fact Checking   193
11. Word World: The Joy, Beauty, and Sheer,
    Staggering Unimaginable Grace of Grammar   209
12. Word World II: The Cutting Edge of Tricky Grammar   237
13. Dots and Squiggles: Spelling, Punctuation,
    and Other Proofreading Stuff   254
14. The Supporting Cast: The Other Little Things
    that Editors Do   281

15. The Business of Editing: How to Recognize
    Success Without Looking Overly Surprised   297
16. Final Thoughts: A Great Job and How to Get It   326

    Say What? Some Important Terms and
    What They Mean   339
    A Brief Bibliography   347
    Index   349

Preface

A good editor believes that he/she is really doing something worthwhile. He/she never stops looking for ideas and never stops thinking about what can be done to improve the magazine. He/she is always trying to make the next issue better— more entertaining, more useful, more informative—than the previous one.

Ed Holm, editor, *American History*

I was working as the publications editor for a private secondary school in Massachusetts several years ago. The school's administration had gotten into the habit of holding a brown-bag lunch once a month at which members of the faculty and staff would tell their co-workers what they really did all day. It was a great way to raise everyone's opinion of their peers and help us all get to know one another.

Eventually, it was my turn. I stood at the front of the room, while my friends and acquaintances ate their turkey sandwiches and twisted open their bottles of carbonated sugar, and I told them about the daily life of an editor. They listened politely, laughed at moments when I tried to be funny, and finished off their desserts.

Afterward, several of them came up to me and expressed amazement at the myriad facets of an editor's world. "I always thought," one friend commented, "that editors spent their days hounding writers for manuscripts and fixing obscure little grammar mistakes."

I assured him that if my days were like that, I would have thrown myself off a bridge long ago.

The purpose of this book is to show the complete magazine-editing picture. Editors work with people far more than they work with

> The editor's job has very little to do with working with text. It mostly involves managing the overall process, soliciting articles, and working with the organization. I thought editing was about working with words—but editors do very little work with words. Mostly we work with authors and ideas.
>
> **Sandra Bowles, editor, *Shuttle, Spindle & Dyepot***

words. We care about articles that are exciting, funny, shocking, surprising, and delightful far more than we care about sentences that meet arcane, dowager-driven rules of grammar.

Yet, in the public mind, magazine editors are not treated well. In one stereotype, we spend our days charming and chuckling at chic cocktail parties, shimmering under sequins and silk, sipping champagne, and swapping erudite witticisms pregnant with literary innuendo. We introduce the rich to the powerful, the beautiful to the daring. We drive expensive cars, frolic in upper-crust apartments, and never seem to sleep, and yet the publication comes out on deadline without fail, raising the cultural consciousness of all those who read it—or at least those who buy it and let it rest conspicuously on their coffee tables.

In another stereotype, we are the consummate word nerds. We toil like archaeologists over intricate manuscripts, muttering not-very-naughty curses as we ferret out dangling modifiers, crush passive sentences, and slay errors in noun–verb agreement. We delight in using *lay* and *lie* correctly, we take deep offense over construction that falls even slightly askew of parallel, and we crumble to near hysteria when we find otherwise promising texts riddled with misused *hopefullys*, misplaced participles, and malignant misappropriations of any slang coined since the Great Depression. If we get invited to cocktail parties at all—which is rare—you'll find us sitting quietly in a corner, pale and cheaply dressed, demonstrating to some poor, trapped soul that we are capable of forming the proper plural of any word that comes to mind.

In yet a third incarnation, we are arrogant, loud, power-hungry dynamos who bark at writers, intimidate secretaries, and scream into the telephone loudly enough to be heard without the benefit of actually dialing the number. We keep our sleeves rolled up, our chins thrust forward, and our beefy arms flapping in the air as we thrash and flail our way through conversations. We don't say "Good morning" or even "Hello," we walk quickly wherever we go (whether a crowd is in our way or not), and we interrupt people with such phrases as "I don't give a damn," "You got that right, buster," and "You have until Thursday—or else!" Our veins pulse with hypertension, our foreheads sweat from dawn until dinner, and our only real friends are antacids and scotch.

This book presents editing—and editors—in a more realistic light. We editors do enjoy the company of literary people, and we love to talk about article ideas and publishing challenges. But our social calendars don't fill up any faster than those of seamstresses or violin teachers, and when a fancy party does come along, we dust off our only dazzling suit and hope that people don't remember it from the last event. We do take great delight in the grace and elegance of well-written prose, but we also take our noses out of manuscripts long enough to raise children, pursue interesting hobbies, and keep up with professional baseball. And while we have been known to raise our voices from time to time, we don't enjoy confrontation unless it brings about the results we need to put out an impressive publication month after month after month.

As people, editors are pretty much like everyone else. But we do have fascinating jobs that are remarkably varied, intellectually challenging, and unusually fun.

Human beings are precious creations, brimming with color, complexity, and contradiction. In this strange and wonderful world we occupy, all people find themselves pressed into certain roles: parent, police officer, priest, partygoer. These roles give us certain tasks to accomplish, and they let other people draw certain assumptions about us. In general, these roles and assumptions enable us to function as a society—but they also rob us of some of our humanity.

Each of us plays numerous roles, and we "change hats" with a reasonable degree of swiftness and grace. Take me, for example. I am associated with quite a few roles:

man	son
husband	brother
father	Quaker
writer	environmentalist
professor	inexplicable Red Sox fan
American	and so on

Each of us has a similar list of roles we play, relationships we maintain, and expectations that we strive to fulfill. When I worked as an editor, that role was added to my list as well. But "editor" by no means described me, my ambitions, my worldview, or my hopes and dreams any more fully than does "brother" or "American" or any other label.

This is true for all editors. And yet, for the purposes of employment relations, an editor on the job is foremost an editor. We are asked to foreground that aspect of our lives while we are on "company time."

And so this book will teach you how to be an editor—which is somewhat, but not entirely, different from teaching you how to edit. Toward the end of this book, you'll learn how to keep your modifiers from dangling and your sentence structures parallel. Such knowledge is useful for editors, but it by no means represents the full compass of our skills and interests. In these pages, I will introduce you to scores of real-life editors who will talk about their real-life jobs. And as they will tell you, editing is primarily about people. Each human being we meet is a source of ideas, insights, and information that we don't already possess. Being arrogant serves no purpose; people tend to shy away from blowhards, and we want people to talk with us at great length. Being abrasive doesn't help, either. Nor does wallowing in superficial chatter or hiding from the world between the pages of a manuscript. Grammar is important, sure, but I'd take a truly dazzling but grammatically sloppy manuscript any day. I can fix grammar, but it's nearly impossible to inject life, passion, humor, and intensity into a moribund manuscript.

So we editors work with people. We work with writers, whom we encourage, challenge, and inspire. We work with publishers, with whom we negotiate over the very souls of our publications. We work with artists and photographers, circulation managers and advertising directors, graphic designers and printers and even copy editors.

I like magazine editing, probably because it suits my weaknesses as well as my strengths. As someone with an attention span measurable only by extremely sensitive equipment recently developed for SDI, one of the things I like best about editing is that I never have to do anything for longer than 27 seconds. Some editors complain about interruptions; I *love* interruptions. Without interruptions, I couldn't function.

Casey Winfrey, editor in chief, *American Health*

Above all, we work with readers. We struggle constantly to learn what they are thinking, what they want to know, and what really annoys them. They represent our very existence, and they decide whether we succeed or decay into miserable failure.

It is in this maelstrom of people that editors function, and we love it. When it all clicks—when a sparkling idea is researched thoroughly and converted into breathtaking prose, when the photos capture the essence of the topic and the cover art drives it home, when the layout and design create harmony on the page, when the printer gets it all on time and delivers it on schedule, when the readers take delight in receiving our latest issue and enjoy the time they spend with our handiwork, when the advertisers beam with satisfaction at the audiences we marshal with our talents—then we editors are the happiest people in the world. And when it doesn't all click, we still take comfort in the secure knowledge that we have jobs that we love, lumps and all.

What an Editor Really Is

Before we jump into specific questions about editing, it might be a good idea to talk about what an editor really is. An editor—despite the insistence of some—is not necessarily smarter than you are. She's not necessarily a better writer. She's not necessarily more experienced, older, wiser, or better looking than you, either. She has no secret stash of Good Judgment, no hidden reservoir of Deep Insight, no private supply of Extra-Strength Farsightedness.

She's just a person who likes to read a lot.

In fact, that's the best way to think about an editor. Not some Powerful Icon who jumps from Socialite Luncheon to Writer's Reception

> Most editors are not well paid. There are a handful of slots where the compensation is decent, but only a handful. Most of us ended up in this field not because we intended to become editors or expected to earn big bucks but because we were seduced by the idea that we would get to read all the time.
>
> **Diane Lutz, editor, *Muse***

in well-tailored silk suits, making career-crushing decisions about writers and articles. Just a reader. But a very important reader. An editor is the first person to see a manuscript before it will be scoured by a hundred thousand highly critical readers after it's published.

We'll define an editor this way: an editor is Reader Number One.

That's it. Nothing overly daunting. Nothing fiercely powerful. Just Reader Number One. Readers Number Two through Hundred Thousand will come later, but to begin with, writers have the luxury of trying out their manuscripts on one reader first.

That's quite a luxury. Writers get close to their material, and often, they get so close that they can't see some fairly major problems. But an editor, reading from a greater distance, can see things the writer misses. An editor can point out that the article's introduction is confusing or that the tone is inappropriate for the topic or that key information is nowhere to be found. An editor can explain that the article drags on too long or uses overly difficult vocabulary or fails to consider alternative points of view. An editor can mention that the ending isn't nearly as funny as the writer thinks it is or that the article jumps around from point to point haphazardly and without any apparent logic or that the terribly clever pun the writer offers in the lead is actually based on a limerick that most fourth-graders learn under the slide at recess.

Armed with that feedback, the writer can fix these problems before showing the article to the rest of the world.

So writers can benefit enormously from this helpful First Reader. But, of course, the editor isn't just any Reader Number One. The editor knows the tastes, desires, needs, and overarching worldviews of the rest of the magazine's readers better than anyone else. She knows their passions, their fantasies, and their sense of humor. And she can help the writer deliver an article that those readers will love.

Good editors take no delight in rewriting someone else's copy; if an editor has to make heavy revisions, then he has failed somewhere along the line. Perhaps the topic wasn't that interesting after all. The idea might not be right for his magazine. He left too little time for the writer to do thorough research. He failed to follow up with the writer during the research and writing stage. Or maybe he just chose the wrong writer for the job. Whatever the reason, he is now stuck with the job of dismantling and rebuilding an article that the writer was supposed to have delivered in good shape. This task does not bring with it feelings of power, importance, and superiority. It makes editors feel stupid.

So editors work hard to keep things from getting to that point. We try to find good ideas that our readers will adore. We try to assign those ideas to good writers. We try to work with those writers steadily—from assignment to article—to fend off any surprises, pitfalls, or colossal missteps. We're on the phone a lot, "chatting" with writers in a casual and cheerful way, all the while making sure that everything is on track.

And editors can never forget about their readers, either. In addition to working closely with writers and all the others, we do our best to keep in touch with readers. We can't possibly know who our readers are and what they want to read if we lock ourselves in small offices and ask our secretaries to screen out all those pesky calls from the General Populace. Instead, we read mail from readers, we make and receive telephone calls that let us hear what readers are thinking, we attend conferences and other meetings that let us have some nice face-to-face conversations over coffee and doughnuts, and we hold focus groups, conduct surveys, and take other steps to keep us abreast of the things that are on our readers' minds.

That's how editors spend their days—multiplied many times over. We work with readers. We work with writers. We work with other editors. We work with graphic designers, publishers, printers, proofreaders, photographers, advertising managers, circulation directors, marketing gurus, secretaries, interns, and the cleaning crew. And crammed somewhere amid all these meetings, phone calls, faxes, e-mails, voice mails, beeper signals, and lively lunches at inexpensive but clean restaurants, we find the time somehow to close the door, disconnect ourselves from the outside world, put our feet up, and read some good manuscripts.

This book answers fundamental questions about magazine editing, using the best experts in the world: magazine editors themselves. I contacted more than a hundred editors from all kinds of magazines—large and small, famous and obscure, sexy and mundane, profound and trivial—and I asked them to address some basic questions about audiences, missions, goals, and success. They were generous with their time and thoughts, and their responses give shape to the chapters that follow. They don't always agree—they are editors, after all—but they offer views into the realities of magazine editing that can't be found anywhere else.

I also offer my own thoughts and suggestions, based on my thirteen years of experience as an editor. I hope the information is helpful.

The book is organized into three "layers":

• The Big Picture (audience, mission, and so on)
• The Big Questions (sense, fit, tone, and such)
• The Small (but Important) Stuff (grammar, spelling, punctuation, and the like).

These layers are followed by a chapter about the business of magazine editing and, to wrap up, a chapter about the thrills of magazine editing and how to get started on your career.

The layers represent the fundamental philosophy of this book. Most magazine-editing textbooks get it backward, diving right into the trivia of grammar and punctuation before addressing the larger concerns of audience and tone.

Most editors don't work that way, though. They don't get manuscripts in the mail and begin searching for dangling participles. Instead, they read a manuscript and think about it, asking themselves whether it meets the readers' needs, whether it makes sense, whether it fits in with the rest of the articles planned for that issue. Grammar and other tweaks come last in the process, not first. There's no point in correcting the grammar of a paragraph if you're only going to delete it later because it doesn't make sense.

So this book journeys through the editing process the way most editors do: from the big questions down to the tiny ones. In so doing, it considers many of the facets of an editor's professional life—even though it is unlikely that you, a few relaxing weeks after graduation, will be called on to grapple with all of them. If you pursue a career as a magazine editor, you'll probably start as a fact checker or a copy editor. This book covers those jobs, but it doesn't stop there. In fact, it doesn't even start there. Eventually, you'll be promoted, and you'll need to know about some of the larger issues of magazine editing. This book covers those topics, too.

So to give you that complete picture, we'll look at how editors come up with ideas for magazines in the first place, how they define their audiences, how they determine their readers' needs and then strive to meet them, how they keep their magazine focused from issue to issue and year to year, and how they know whether or not they are doing a good job. Gradually, we'll work our way down to grammar and punctuation.

Some Notes on This Book

The research for this book took place over many years, and so not all the editors' affiliations are current. Some have gone on to other magazines. Some have retired. The affiliations mentioned in this book were accurate at the time the comments were gathered, and the wisdom offered by these editors remains on target.

It's also important to note that this book is centered rather firmly on a commercial, for-profit model of magazine enterprise. But as Jay Rosen, chair of the Department of Journalism at New York University, pointed out to me one day, the commercial reality is not the only reality. I offer the advice in this book because I want to help students secure editing jobs at magazines, and the commercial sector offers a large number of opportunities. But Professor Rosen is quite correct: there are other ways of looking at the world.

Acknowledgments

I'd like to thank Jon Dilts, Carol Polsgrove, and Paul Voakes for critiquing portions of this text and Grace Carpenter for tireless typing and transcribing. And special thanks to all the editors who took the time to send me their thoughts and ideas.

Future generations of editors will be indebted to these generous leaders.

Layer
Layer
Layer
Layer
Layer
Layer
Layer
Layer
Layer
Layer
Layer 1.

The Big Picture

Be fearless.

Margot Slade, editor, *Consumer Reports*

1. From Spark to Flame:
How to Conceptualize a Magazine

So. A woman marches into the room and plunks $250,000 onto the table.

"I have a job for you," she says without a smile. "I want you to take this money—a quarter of a million dollars—and use it to create a magazine. Any magazine at all. I don't care what it looks like. I don't care what it is about. I don't care about any of the decisions you make. I have just one demand. I'm going to return in five or ten years, and I'm going to want my money back—with interest. Deal? Deal."

And with that, she turns and walks out the door.

Once your pulse returns and you are again able to breathe, you realize that despite the remarkable opportunity that has been tossed your way, you face a considerable challenge. How will you go about creating a magazine from scratch? And one that will be commercially viable at that?

What on earth are you supposed to do next?

Few editors are handed such a delightful surprise, but by working through the problems inherent in this challenge, we can explore the situations that occupy most magazine editors' days. Contrary to popular opinion, editors don't spend the bulk of their time fidgeting with arcane rules of English grammar. They don't devote their lives to arranging words on a page. They don't grind away from nine to five trying to capture the most elegant way to describe the first lady's evening gown or the homeless man's shoes. They do those things, to be sure—but such tasks don't take up the majority of editors' daily schedules. Editors spend most of their time working not with words but with people. Editing concentrates on the magic of human communication, and so its primary attention is directed to the people involved in that communication.

Mercifully, that's the fun part.

In the Beginning

So—we have deposited the $250,000 into our shiny new bank account, and now we're sitting at our kitchen table wondering what to do with it. Sure, we'll have to hire some editors and writers, some graphic designers and photographers. We'll have to negotiate a contract with a printer and figure out how to distribute the magazine to subscribers and newsstand shoppers.

But first we have to decide what our magazine will *be*. What will we write about? What will we focus on? What will make our publication shine in the midst of a muddy morass of mediocre magazines?

It is said that magazines rank second in the Grand List of business start-ups and failures. Restaurants are first. In other words, except for restaurants, more magazines are born each year—and more magazines are buried each year—than any other business. The failures often follow a common theme. A magazine emerges with fanfare and enthusiasm, holding forth great promises of outstanding writing, riveting graphics, stunning photography, and solid editing. People buy copies off the newsstands because they are curious about the newcomer, just as people flock to the new restaurant in town just to see what it is all about. Some of the newsstand buyers become subscribers to save money and make getting the magazine more convenient. Armed with figures showing the rising trend in subscriptions and newsstand sales, the advertising team marches from one corporation to another, chatting up marketing directors and ad-placement specialists, lunching with vice presidents and managers, pushing demographic statistics in front of owners and CEOs. It is at this moment that the fate of the magazine is cast. If the circulation is strong, if the demographics are impressive, if the look and feel and the character and the tone of the magazine all seem right, then advertis-

Any start-up requires some money, but you don't necessarily need a lot.... *WoodenBoat* was started with only $14,000, one-third of it borrowed, [and it now has] a market value of perhaps $2–4 million. So, if the idea is really a good one, it has the ability to grow in value. In fact, if you're both impassioned and ambitious, you can create an extremely successful publication enterprise.

Jon Wilson, editor, *WoodenBoat*

ers smile and reserve full-page ads and double-page spreads with color pictures and expensive fold-outs. But if the numbers produce a shrug or a frown, the advertising dollars fall short of expectations.

At this point, some magazines vow to produce outstanding issues anyway, spending money to support the quality of the publications and hoping that the advertising will catch up. If the gamble pays off, a magazine can continue into the future without having tarnished its look—or its credibility. But if the gamble fails, the magazine empties its bank accounts and screeches to a shuddering stop. Such was the fate of *New England Monthly*, an excellent magazine that attracted top-quality writers, photographers, illustrators, designers, and editors. The magazine began with promise, producing issue after issue that offered readers tough reporting and engaging writing. (And boosting the career of Jonathan Harr, the eventual author of *A Civil Action*.) But, as editor Dan Okrent lamented to me one day, corporations in New York were unconvinced that New England was a community, and so they were reluctant to spend money pursing that community. The advertising dollars diminished, and the magazine eventually folded.

Other magazines fade out gracelessly. As income dwindles, a magazine's budget is trimmed, with less money available for top-notch writers and photographers. The cutbacks take the shine off the magazine's image, frustrating efforts to attract new readers and faithful subscribers. The circulation numbers begin to wane, reducing advertising revenue even further. The magazine's budget is scaled back even more in an effort to stretch the remaining revenue until advertisers and readers finally come to their senses. Talented employees are laid off. The quality of the paper is downgraded, so the magazine has a less sophisticated feel. The pay for writers is slashed, so only untested writers respond to the call. Less color is used throughout the magazine, issues grow thin and offer fewer articles, and photography and art are kept to a minimum.

With the reduction in quality comes another drop in circulation; fewer readers feel that the magazine is worth its subscription price. But still, the money continues to cascade out the door like sand through a sieve. Further cuts are inflicted on the staff. The magazine reduces the frequency of its publication from monthly to quarterly, or from quarterly to semiannually. The look and feel of the magazine continue to decline, making advertisers even more reluctant to buy ads in it. Desperation measures fail to reinvigorate the cash flow. The magazine's quality continues to plummet as good, hardworking employees are laid off. Eventually, the magazine declares bankruptcy—and its ability to influence the world comes to an end.

Eureka!

Magazines collapse for many reasons—indecisive leadership, insufficient capital, and so on—but perhaps none is as important as the initial idea. The best writing in the world won't salvage a magazine that focuses on a useless topic. The *Sandpaper Collector* has no chance of success if the number of sandpaper collectors in the country hovers around three. Bad writing can kill a good idea, but good writing can't save a bad one.

The process of thinking broadly about a magazine goes on for the life of the publication; it doesn't end once the first issue is on the stands. Editors think continually about the character of their magazines, the tone of their magazines, the content of their magazines, and the changing nature of their magazines—and they work hard to make sure that their readers' needs are being met.

But how can an editor tell whether the idea will fly or die, or whether the current idea is still standing tall or is getting weak in the knees? The answer lies in the rational decisions that people make.

National Geographic follows a 113-year tradition of exploring the world under the Society's mission: "For the increase and diffusion of geographic knowledge." The magazine and all aspects of the Society, including television, Web, and *Traveler*, *Adventure* and *World* magazines, view geographic knowledge in the broadest sense. The magazine fulfills this mission by mixing stories on Minor League baseball and stockcar racing in with more traditional historical and topical pieces. Also, since September 11, *National Geographic* aims to provide more stories contributing relevance and perspective to news events. We do this while working ahead under a longer planning time than most weekly news magazines and other magazines. Above all, the magazine stresses strong storytelling.

Peter Porteous, assistant editor, *National Geographic*

A classic Psychology 101 statement goes something like this: people spend money for two reasons only—to solve a problem and to enhance pleasure. That statement is a good beacon for those who want to edit magazines. If we don't enhance pleasure (say, by publishing funny spoofs of political bickering) or solve problems (say, by teaching readers how to dress well on a tight budget), we don't stand much chance of success.

That's what happened to the general-interest magazines—*Look* and the original *Life*, for example—that were so popular around the middle of the twentieth century. By reaching for audiences that were too broad, they were unable to deliver enough material to solve enough problems or enhance enough pleasure for each individual reader. The reader who wanted political articles found a better supply of them in *Time*, *The Nation*, and other publications. The reader who wanted sports information was happier with *Sports Illustrated* and *Field & Stream*. The reader who wanted fashion tips gravitated toward *Cosmopolitan*, *Vogue*, *Glamour*, and similar magazines. When television—the ultimate general-interest medium—came along, *Look* and *Life* and their counterparts lost their last unique angle, and advertisers departed in droves.

I encountered this problem personally when I became the father of twins. My wife and I, brand new to the child-raising business, decided to subscribe to a parenting magazine. We were looking for tips, tricks, hints, shortcuts—anything that would let us sleep an extra hour, worry a little less, maintain some semblance of order in our overrun little house, and file away into permanent memory all the moments of joy and beauty that were taking place around us.

But the magazines we looked at didn't do the job. Most of them were divided into sections by age group; each issue had one article about raising newborns, one article about six-month-olds, one article about one-year-olds, one about two-year-olds, and so on. So in any given issue, this fat and expensive magazine gave us just one article that mattered to our lives. And we could tell that unless we had more kids, that would never change. We would always care about just one article in each issue.

So we didn't subscribe to any of them. We bought a few good books, talked a lot to family and friends, and muddled through as well as we could.

American Archaeology is a popular archaeology magazine. I want it to inform and entertain a broad audience. My magazine has to be more sophisticated about archaeology than, say, a general-interest publication, and it has to present archaeology in a way that most everyone can understand.

Michael Bawaya, editor, *American Archaeology*

The problem was that the magazines we looked at were too broadly defined, too loose, too wide open. They weren't focused enough to help us.

The solve-a-problem-or-enhance-pleasure reality also means that we have to stuff our egos in a drawer. Putting out a magazine that features "whatever we happen to think is interesting this month" isn't likely to survive. Why should anyone trade their lunch money for a haphazard collection of articles that might—or might not—be useful or interesting to them? Potential readers are much more likely to buy magazines that they can count on, magazines that are clearly focused and that attempt to do something beneficial for the people who purchase them.

What this means to us is simple and painful. We might know in our hearts that a magazine about the interpretation of cloud shapes is just what this country needs. It would be riveting, engaging, dynamic. It would make people laugh; it would make people cry. We're just sure of it. And besides, our immediate circle of friends agrees that it would be a great publication.

So we cash in our savings bonds and launch *Water Vapor Wonderland*. And then, much to our astonishment, we discover that hardly anybody from Maine to California is willing to hand over the change in her pockets for our precious magazine. We love it, but it doesn't solve anyone's problems or enhance anyone's pleasure. Copies of the first issue dry up and die on the newsstand shelves. And then we quietly "suspend publication" and send our résumés to fast-food outlets and car washes.

So basing a magazine on our personal whims is probably not a great idea. What can we do instead? Smart editors turn not to their own psyches but to their readers. What audiences out there have

> *Car and Driver* is about 50 years old. It's a car magazine. The concept is simple: We test cars. We are the biggest car magazine in the world possibly because we are more honest in our opinions and more clever in the way those opinions are presented. So, we don't wonder once a month what the concept is. We know.
>
> **Steve Spence, managing editor, *Car and Driver***

needs that aren't being met? If you can find a good number of people who are not being served well by other magazines, you have an opportunity to create a winner.

Readers as Leaders

To pull this off, editors begin by asking themselves who could benefit from another magazine, and what would that magazine be about. When *Seventeen* was launched, the editors had a clear target: teenage girls interested in fashion, fitness, and fun. When *People* was launched, the editors had an equally clear quarry: readers interested in celebrities and other extraordinary people. When *Sports Illustrated* was launched, the editors courted people interested in sports and their relation to the larger world.

Not too many years ago, *Men's Journal* was created. The founding editor was Jann Wenner—who also had started *Rolling Stone*. At the time that *Men's Journal* hit the newsstands, very few magazines were aimed directly at men. *Esquire* is an outstanding magazine. *GQ* is consistently popular. *Heartland USA* covers a niche in the men's market well. But compared with the galaxy of women's magazines, the list of men's magazines was pretty short—especially if you eliminated the ones that carried pornographic photography.

That vacuum represented an opportunity. If someone could create an interesting, well-written magazine that dealt with issues that men cared about—careers, fitness, sex, relationships, money, sports, and the like—then success would be virtually ensured. Enter *Men's Journal*. A quick flip through the pages of the magazine will underscore the accuracy of the thinking behind it; the number of large, expensive ads is staggering. *Men's Journal* works because it targeted a segment of the market that was not overwhelmed with magazine titles.

Frances Huffman, the editor and publisher of U. *Magazine*, saw a similar vacuum on college campuses:

> U. *Magazine*'s primary philosophy is that it is for college students by college students. In addition to publishing the work of student writers, photographers and illustrators, we try to publish a cohesive package that appeals to college students and is written from the student perspective. We cover everything from campus news and student lifestyles to technology and entertainment—pretty much anything that students would be interested in.

In other words, Huffman keeps the readers' expectations foremost in her mind. She knows who those readers are—college students interested in campus news and student situations—and she makes sure that U. *Magazine* delivers the kind of material her readers want.

Editors who sign on at existing magazines have to understand the audience just as thoroughly. Magazines have to earn readers' loyalty over and over again, and that loyalty will evaporate quickly if editors start publishing material that falls short of readers' expectations. George C. Larson, editor of *Air & Space*, knows what his readers want, and he tries to deliver it in every issue:

> Way before *X-Files* brought the Cold War paranoia theme to television, we had sensed an upwelling of curiosity about the hyper-secrecy of that period. We launched a series on the Cold War that delved behind the scenes into personal experiences and tales from the hidden archives. An earlier perception about our audience's interest in far-out astronomy launched our series "Astronomy's Most Wanted" with six stories that right now are front-page.

By remembering why his readers buy his magazine, Larson is able to publish the fresh and engaging articles that keep his subscribers coming back.

The bottom line: magazines can survive only if they discern an audience that needs the kind of services that magazines can provide—and then deliver those services. If the audience is too broad, too small, too loosely connected, or too scattered, a magazine will have a difficult time enticing readers and pleasing advertisers. But if

> Never lose sight of who the readers are and what they want.
>
> **Jean LemMon, editor, *Better Homes and Gardens***

an editor can find an audience that needs something, and if that audience is cohesive and sizable and embraces the kinds of people that advertisers want to reach, the magazine has a shot at success.

Smart editors begin their thinking with readers. The topic comes second.

Topical Storm

With a prospective audience firmly in mind, editors must ask another question: What should my magazine be about? To put it another way: What does my audience need?

Sometimes, the audience needs information and inspiration about a social cause. Magazines have been launched to fight hunger, for example, or to minimize the number of fatalities on the highways. These magazines draw together readers who care about that cause, and the editors deliver the hard information necessary for effective action and the uplifting stories necessary for continuing motivation.

As founder, publisher, and editor of *Ebony*, I am pleased to say that *Ebony* came into being 50 years ago to celebrate Black excellence. In a world of negative Black images, we wanted to provide positive Black images. In a world that said Blacks could do few things, we wanted to say they could do everything. We believed in 1945 that Black Americans needed positive images to fulfill their potential. We believed then—and we believe now—that you have to change images before you can change acts and institutions. Without ignoring continuing problems, we wanted to highlight breakthroughs and to tell Black Americans that there is no defense against an excellence that meets a pressing public need. We wanted to focus on the total Black experience and celebrate Black women and men, youth and elders, workers and professionals, politicians and preachers as well as entertainers. The concept worked in 1945 and it is still working now.

John H. Johnson, founding editor, *Ebony*

Sierra is one of the prime magazines aimed at improving the environment, and editor Joan Hamilton relies on the talents and insights of her entire editorial staff to make sure that the publication's content is on target:

> We have editorial retreats about twice a year, and meetings once a week. Editors are expected to keep up on news in their field, through reading, telephone calls and travel, and bring fresh new ideas to our meetings. Editors of departments meet with me each issue to talk about what they have and how we should tailor it for our readers. Commissioned manuscripts are circulated to the entire staff for comment, before an editor and I decide how to shape them.
>
> We also put our heads together with freelance authors. They tell us what they want to write, and we tell them whether that subject and approach suits our readers. The best freelancers know our magazine well and consistently offer lively, appropriate ideas.

By surrounding herself with people who are knowledgeable and up-to-date on environmental issues—and by keeping current herself—Hamilton can count on editing a worthwhile and appreciated magazine each month. Because she knows that her readers care about the environment, she can use that topic as her guiding light.

Other magazines focus on hobbies or areas of personal interest. *Quilters Newsletter Magazine*, for example, has a clearly defined audience because it has a clearly defined topic; quilters want to read about quilts and quilting. *Shuttle, Spindle, & Dyepot* aims at readers interested in spinning and weaving. *MacAddict* targets Macintosh-computer users and gives them the practical information they need

---

Utne Reader was conceived as a general-interest digest of the "alternative" press, a filter designed to provide busy readers with the best material from hundreds of magazines they'd never seen or wouldn't have the time or energy to find. The editorial content focuses on personal growth and social change.

Craig Cox, executive editor, *Utne Reader*

to get the most out of their machines. As founding editor Cheryl England writes, "We have a central theme, which is to be the ultimate hands-on guide for Mac enthusiasts. At least 70% of the mag must fulfill that promise by bringing helpful advice or step-by-step articles or buying guides to our readers. The articles must all be accessible to the common person—not just the people in our office who get immersed in tech every second of every day."

The hobbies can be intellectual as well as material. *Naval History* targets people who want to learn more about seafaring ships of old (and not so old). Editor in chief Fred L. Schultz sums up the magazine's focus by pointing to advertising copy he wrote for the magazine:

> Embark with *Naval History* magazine on a dramatic bimonthly voyage above, below, and on the surface of the high seas, en route to hard-fought distant shores and exotic ports. Through gripping first-hand accounts, exhaustively researched—yet entertainingly written—narratives and interviews with notable naval veterans and the world's foremost historians, *Naval History* brings you the best in historical literature and art—from ancient Greek mariners through the Age of Sail to the World Wars, Korea, Vietnam, and beyond—all with a distinctly salty flavor.

Once again, a solid understanding of the reader leads to a solid understanding of the topic. *Naval History* readers aren't looking for the kind of how-to advice that you'll find in a magazine about photography or woodworking, but they do pursue a serious hobby—and they want information that will help them in that pursuit.

Along similar lines—but with a very different mission—some magazines strive to meet their readers' spiritual needs. *On the Line*, for example, considers both its audience and its religious mission in charting its course. As editor Mary Clemens Meyer notes, "The purpose of *On the Line* is to provide leisure reading for kids ages 9 to 14 (and up) that promotes Christian values. The magazine emphasizes God's love, the importance (worth) of each person, appreciation for people's differences, interest in many cultures, care for the environment as God's creation, Bible learning, and dealing with everyday problems."

Geography offers another means by which the common interests of an audience can be brought together. Nearly every area of the country has a regional magazine, from *New York* to *L.A. Weekly* and from *Florida Monthly* to *Alaska*. The editors of these magazines know that their readers care about the city or region: its history, its architecture, its nightlife, and its future. Tom Slayton, editor of *Vermont Life*, put it this way:

> There are two, perhaps three things uppermost in my mind as I plan the magazine. First, I know our readers want lots of beautiful pictures of Vermont. That is what the magazine is known for.
>
> Second, I try to have something in the magazine for everyone—active sports for the younger reader, history articles for the older reader, house-and-lifestyles features for women, outdoors/hiking articles for men, some topical articles for resident Vermonters and some articles (inns, places to go, travel pieces) for travelers and fantasy travelers.
>
> Third, I try to shape the magazine so that it conveys a distinctive sense of place: photos and articles that could have come only from Vermont. We often do town profiles because Vermonters love their home town and like to see it featured, and travelers like to know about interesting places to go.
>
> Also, we try to have stories from all geographic areas of Vermont. Realistically, this is impossible to do in any one issue. But over the course of a year, I like to touch as many geographic bases—north, south, Champlain Valley, Connecticut Valley, central Vermont—as I can.

In addition to those specific focal points, some magazines embrace a broader range of their readers' interests. Rather than zeroing in on one particular facet of their lives, these magazines strive to give readers useful and entertaining articles about several topics that might appeal to them. According to editor Brad Pearson, for example, *Heartland USA* "regularly includes an eclectic mix of short, easy-to-read articles on hunting and fishing, spectator sports (motorsports, football, basketball and baseball), how-to, country music, human interest, and wildlife." That statement, which also appears in the magazine's guidelines for writers, gives the editors the necessary direction to keep their 900,000 readers—described as "active, outdoors-oriented blue-collar working men"—satisfied.

So once a solid audience has been identified, editors try to figure out what those potential readers want to know. No one will read a magazine just to support the editor financially. They will read it only if it meets their needs. Magazines that do meet the needs of a large and well-defined audience tend to build strong subscriber bases, attract enthusiastic advertisers, and stay in business.

The Character Issue

However they determine what their readers need and want, some editors also rely on their own internal compasses to give their magazines character. The danger, some feel, is that excessive attention paid to readership surveys and focus groups could result in a confused, scattered, and boring publication. No one wants to read something that was edited by a committee.

At *Muse*, for example, editor Diane Lutz insists that a magazine with a strong personal identity will fare better than one shaped by a general survey of readers:

> In my opinion, the best magazines reflect the intellectual interests, personality and taste of one person or perhaps a few people who collaborate closely.
>
> I have never understood the notion that editorial policy could be determined by market research. This strikes me as akin to driving 60 miles an hour looking into the rear-view mirror. If readers are asked what they want, they usually list a few predictable and uninspired topics. They never list an author. They haven't given it much thought, after all, since they're not editors. A magazine that tried simply to meet their requests would be hollow and lack the uniqueness that attracts a loyal readership.

I think a magazine should reflect its editor's vision and personality. The best magazines always have. Punctuation is the least of it, but style is the essence of it—a style that suits the reader to a T. Keeps them reading.

Mimi Handler, editor, *Early American Life*

I assume our readers have a strong interest in American archaeology and that they prefer that their science be presented in a readable fashion. I also make the risky assumption that, if I think a story is interesting, many of them will, too.

Michael Bawaya, editor, *American Archaeology*

The editor selects the material not in the hope of pleasing marketing directives but rather in the hope of finding or creating a community of like-minded readers. Ideally the editor gives the readers not what they think they want but what they discover they want after reading the magazine. The editor sets taste, not follows it.

David J. Eicher, editor of *Explore the Universe* and managing editor of *Astronomy*, maintains a similar—but not exclusive—reliance on the universality of the editor's own tastes. He notes that *Astronomy* is guided "by numerous factors, from our own long experience in the field and knowledge of the article and illustration possibilities, to coverage of breaking news events and developments, to responding to reader requests and questions, to developing story ideas with science journalists and hobbyists." In short, editors talk to a lot of people, do a lot of reading, and then make the best choices they can.

The important thing to remember is that editors don't just dream up an idea and hope that people will like it—at least, the successful editors don't. Instead, they explore the needs and wants of potential audiences, especially audiences that are not well served by other

There are two schools of thought on the way to achieve editorial excellence.

1. Figure out what readers want and give it to them.
2. Take your own enthusiasms and passions and give them to your readers.

I think combining the two is the way to edit a magazine and achieve that elusive grade of "excellence."

Susan Ungaro, editor, *Family Circle*

magazines; figure out how to meet those needs and wants better than anyone else; and then put that plan into action.

If we want to repay that woman her $250,000—with interest—then focusing on readers and their needs represents our best chance at success.

2. Who Is Out There?
Finding and Understanding Audiences

Our readers love to know what to buy and how things work. They love to be surprised. They don't mind getting their hands dirty or saving a buck here and there, but they're not interested in learning how to make a masthead light from a mayonnaise jar.

Charles Barthold, editor, *Yachting*

Magazine editors create each issue to please—or at least satisfy—an audience that exists somewhere in the "real world." But sitting in an office, surrounded by filing cabinets, furniture, and photos of the family while staring into the blue glow of a computer screen, editors face some enormous challenges: How do you know who your audience is? How do you know who your audience should be? How do you go about defining your audience so that you get the readers you want?

The founding editor answers these questions at the beginning, and all the subsequent editors—of every rank—are responsible for maintaining, testing, exploring, supplementing, and tweaking that understanding. The goal is to develop and keep an audience that is focused, large, and active. Failure to pay attention to an audience often means that you don't have one.

For a magazine to be commercially viable, it must have a potential audience that is large enough to warrant strong advertising rates and

A good editorial staff must be constantly reading and talking with others on the phone.

Matthew Carolan, executive editor, *National Review*

We aim for the above-average (both in income and education), modern, middle-class woman, ages 30–50. We give her a good mix of both educational and entertaining articles, so she'll be smarter when she's finished.

Jill Benz, reader service editor, Ladies' Home Journal

sales, but defined enough to inspire members of that potential audience to buy the publication. If the target audience is too small, advertisers will ignore the publication. If the target audience is too broad, the publication will struggle to keep each reader satisfied.

A magazine for brain surgeons, for example, would have several advantages: the audience is well defined, the topics of interest are focused, and the readers are wealthy. But given the small number of brain surgeons in the country, a newsletter might make more sense than a magazine; few advertisers would be willing to pay a lot of money to attract such a small group. (I checked. There are about 3,000 neurosurgeons in the United States. Compare that with *Vogue*'s circulation of 1,136,000.)

A magazine for high-school students, however, would have a different set of advantages and disadvantages. The audience would be quite large, and the readers have more discretionary cash on hand than most people want to admit. But the audience would be so broad and diffuse that it would be difficult for the editors to offer a publication that consistently appealed to all the potential readers. Boys might like some articles that girls don't like—and vice versa. Seniors might be bored with articles that appeal to freshmen. Students in large city schools might feel put off by articles that are aimed at students in

We have a pretty good idea, from a variety of surveys as well as personal contacts, of who our readers are—although, since they're an extremely diverse lot, there's no such thing as "*the Sail* reader." They diverge geographically as well as in skill level and interests—racers and cruisers, weekenders, beginners, experienced, people who want to buy boats, build boats, and the like. It's a pretty extensive universe. And, of course, each of us on the staff has his or her own interests.

Amy Ulrich, managing editor, Sail Magazine

> In the case of *Field & Stream*, we know in our 100th year of publication that we are a hunting and fishing magazine. Our readers are not interested in mountain bikes, whitewater rafting, rock climbing, or hiking. They are interested in hunting and fishing, and if we give them anything but, they will tell us they are not interested by not buying the magazine.
>
> **David E. Petzal, executive editor, *Field & Stream***

small-town or rural schools. With few articles appealing to any one reader, the subscription rate would wane and the advertisers would be unimpressed at the dwindling audience size. Once the advertisers begin to leave, the magazine begins its agonizing death spiral.

So editors have to come up with an audience that is broad enough to be attractive to advertisers but narrow enough to capture readers. Some successful magazines offer insights into how this can work well. *Seventeen*, for example, is aimed at high-school students—but not *all* high-school students. Beginning with high-school students, the editors narrowed the audience further:

High-school students.

High-school girls.

High-school girls who are juniors and seniors. (It is true, of course, that people "read ahead," and *Seventeen* appeals to girls younger than seventeen. The target audience, though, is girls who are high-school juniors and seniors, and possibly some recent graduates.)

High-school girls who are juniors and seniors and who are interested in fashion, health, fitness, college, entertainment, and related issues. By inference, this compass excludes girls who are interested in topics that fall well outside these parameters.

> My favorite job as an editor is planning *Exploring* magazine. High-school teenagers are a fun bunch. They do neat things like inline skating, snowboarding, whitewater rafting, and scuba diving. The teen years are also full of cars, music, proms, movies, computer games, and SATs. We cover it all.
>
> **Scott Daniels, executive editor, *Exploring* and *Scouting***

We are a general-interest magazine. Our current audience is skewed slightly older, slightly more men, and better educated. They tend to be researchers—they're information hungry, and in some cases, information junkies. We like to think that we are approaching people who want to stay safe, be healthy, and protect their families.

Margot Slade, editor, *Consumer Reports*

With that defined, focused target audience in mind, the editors are able to come up with articles that will interest that group. One issue, for example, featured articles about a "pop sensation" and her relationship with a "heartthrob" (entertainment), the results of a teen poll about sexual issues (health), a young actress's search for the perfect prom dress (entertainment, fashion), and others. The audience is not so tightly defined, however, that it becomes too narrow for advertisers; educated, healthy high-school girls make an attractive market segment for quite a few companies.

So, What Do You Think of My Magazine?

How do editors target audiences that will propel their magazines to success? And how do they stay on top of changes in their audiences?

The simplest and most straightforward way editors learn about their audiences is by communicating with readers. Through letters, face-to-face conversations, e-mail correspondence, and other means of communication, editors can get a sense of who their readers are and who they aren't—and from there, make decisions about who they ought to be.

A proposed magazine about muscle cars, for example, might seek an audience of adult men who own or aspire to own such ma-

The median age of our readers is 56 years old. Of course, that suggests that references to Pearl Jam will be irrelevant, but jokes about Bogart and Hepburn are not. More important, our design and even our type-face choices must be mindful of the capacity of people in that age group to read the text....Every detail that we can gather about our readers influences dozens of decisions in each issue.

Scott Meyer, senior editor, *Organic Gardening*

chines—the "Tim 'the Tool Man' Taylor" types out there. By attending muscle-car rallies, participating in muscle-car chat rooms online, and writing to the major muscle-car hobbyists who buy and sell parts for these cars, an editor can get a sense of who these people are and whether they are numerous enough and passionate enough about muscle cars to fuel a new magazine. If the editor finds just a handful of dedicated muscle-car fanatics, a magazine on the topic might not work. If she finds an abundance of enthusiasts but discovers that they are irreconcilably split between Ford fanatics and Chevy chauvinists, she might conclude that too few would buy a magazine devoted to both makes. If, however, she finds a large and relatively cohesive group that is not being served sufficiently by existing magazines, she might take her $250,000 and create *Muscle Car Madness* in the hopes that her assessments were correct.

Communication with readers is a potent tool for gauging the attitudes and thoughts of a magazine's audience. Such connection provides not only information—they like the new column, they hate the humor pieces, and other opinions—but also a better understanding of the readers as people. Magazines compete for attention against the television blaring and flickering in the corner, the teakettle boiling on the stove, the kids wrestling on the coffee table, and the cat scratching on the arm of the sofa. By understanding the real-world demands that surround, infuriate, and excite readers, editors can do a better job of delivering material that will make the distractions disappear—at least for short periods of time. We want to create a continuous dream into which our readers can enter, leaving their real-world lives behind for a while. If we offer an article about Tahiti, our readers should *be* in Tahiti for the twenty minutes it takes to read the article. If we offer an article about profit-and-loss statements, our readers should inhabit a world of numbers and dollar signs until we let them go.

By learning all we can about them, we will be better prepared to guide them from their world to ours.

• *Mail call.* One method that most editors use for keeping in touch with their readers simply involves digging through the mail.

We editors are constantly reading reader mail. A huge part of my job is to look at reader mail to see what girls are talking about—what's plaguing them and what their concerns are, what they're looking forward to and what their fears are. *Cosmo Girl* is all about empowering teens. That's the key to us. So if we read that a whole bunch of girls are concerned about something, then we're going to try to figure it out. We create a book that deals with the five major aspects of a girl's life: her relationship with school, family, girls, boys, and herself. Every one of our stories satisfies one of those things.

Leslie Heilbrunn, senior editor, *Cosmo Girl*

Readers are often happy to write about themselves. Given the opportunity, readers and prospective readers write letters to editors that reveal their opinions, tastes, and needs. Savvy editors can use that information to shape their magazines for maximum impact.

Correspondence from readers is a tricky thing to gauge, though, because no one is certain how accurately it reflects the readership as a whole. One number tossed around suggests that for every letter a magazine receives, a hundred other people felt the same way but didn't bother to write. That figure is a guess, and some topics tend to stir up a greater response than others. It is also true that articles that anger readers are more likely to result in letters than are the ones that make people happy. (Negative letters don't always upset editors. As is often said, "At least it means they're reading the magazine.")

Tricky or not, reader mail is a powerful tool for gauging readers' attitudes. It is effectively free, it takes little effort to collect, and it almost always offers points and issues that readers are passionate about. You can't trust it completely, but it remains an easy and quick

If we aren't meeting readers' needs, they often let us know about it. We encourage our readers to keep in touch, and they do. Then, of course, we have to consider whether the needs being expressed are unique to one person or of enough interest to the general readership to pursue.

Amy Ulrich, managing editor, *Sail Magazine*

Read your mail. See what people are saying. Talk to the person that you think you'd like to have read your mag. (Want a women's mag for 40-year-old women? Talk to a lot of them about what they want to read.)

Cheryl England, founding editor, *MacAddict*

way to learn more about your readers. Craig Cox, managing editor of the *Utne Reader*, takes this path with vigor. He relies on letters, phone calls, e-mails, and other methods of contact to keep him up-to-date about the nature of his audience. A cheery note, a quick call—they add up to information that Cox can use in planning his issues.

• *Glad to meet you!* Another route for learning more about readers and their feelings is to attend gatherings at which you are likely to find some. For example, David J. Eicher, managing editor of *Astronomy*, attends conferences, "star parties," and other events at which he introduces himself and listens carefully to what people say about the magazine. Similarly, Rieva Lesonsky, vice president and editorial director of *Entrepreneur*, attends the magazine's Small Business Expos throughout the country, listening to what people say about themselves and the publication. Lesonsky also appears as a guest on several radio programs during which listeners call in with comments. "They help you know what the general audiences wants to know," she said.

• *All of the above—and then some.* For some editors, gathering anecdotal information about readers can become a passion, as Diane Lutz, editor of *Muse*, describes:

I am currently editing a children's magazine. I live with a child of the appropriate age, I read both children's literature and children's nonfiction whenever I have a spare moment, and I visit classrooms and listen to the kids talk about the magazine....I

The best magazine editors have a deep understanding of what their readers want and do. And the best way to find out is to get out in the world and participate in that special interest of activity.

Charles Barthold, editor, *Yachting*

Because of our clear focus, it's easy to stay on track. Plus, our editor in chief travels all over the country and the readers let her know if we've gone off the track. We take our readers very seriously and pay close attention to their needs and desires by reading their correspondence, answering their phone calls, and listening to them in person.

Linda Villarosa, executive editor, *Essence*

We stay focused on the readers' interest by reading their letters—we get about 70 to 80 in an average month and print 15 to 20—and surveying them twice a year. The editors often call readers who send letters and even visit some during trips to conferences. And we have regular correspondents around the continent who are in touch with gardeners in their areas.

Scott Meyer, senior editor, *Organic Gardening*

pay attention to this feedback and adjust what we are doing accordingly.

For these editors, contact with readers in any form is desired. They understand that by taking in all the comments, suggestions, complaints, and bewilderment that their readers offer, they can extract some helpful ideas for improving their magazines.

The tools we have to gauge reader interest are newsstand and subscription sales and reader mail. We should have reader research, but we don't. The other thing we have to do is get out of the office, and out of New York City, and hunt and fish. And while we are out there hunting and fishing, we make it a point to talk to other hunters and fishermen. The price of not keeping in touch with your readers is extinction. The most terrifying example of this is *True* magazine. At its height in the late 1950s, *True* was the pre-eminent men's magazine—a huge success with a readership comparable in size to *Look* or the *Saturday Evening Post*. Then, in 1970, its owners decided that it had to be hipper, trendier, and had to appeal to a younger audience. Within four years *True* had been sold three times, and by the end of the fourth year, it was history.

David E. Petzal, executive editor, *Field & Stream*

And the Survey Says...

The needs and interests of readers also can be explored through surveys. Beth Renaud, for example, uses them at *National Gardening* to "draw a bead on readers" and to augment information she receives through personal communication.

Such surveys ask about interests (How often do you go fishing?) and experiences (Have you ever traveled outside the United States?), and they gather demographic information as well (How old are you? Are you married? What is your income level?). Armed with this material, an editor can learn a great deal. If the intended audience comprises women between the ages of forty and sixty-five who enjoy crafts, for instance, an editor will want to know what percentage of these women work outside the home, do volunteer work at hospitals or animal shelters, go camping or hiking, and so on. An article on gathering the best pinecones for a homemade Christmas wreath might be appreciated by readers who like the outdoors—but if that group represents only a tiny minority of your audience, you wouldn't want to run such topics too often.

Similarly, if you're editing a magazine about decorating houses in stunning and elegant ways, you could send out a questionnaire that asks people about the decorating they have done, the kinds of decorating tips they would like to learn, the current hot styles in window treatments and upholstery fabrics, and so on. With such a survey, you might discover that the current "beautiful home" magazines have the market pretty well covered; everybody is getting what they need, and so your magazine had better do things in a unique and enterprising way. Or you might learn that those potential competitors are leaving out a group of readers—people, for example, who don't live in gorgeous mansions and who lack $20,000 decorating budgets. A survey might reveal that a lot of people want to know how to make their homes look dazzling without dropping half a year's salary in the process. If the results indicate that such a need is going unfulfilled, your magazine can seize that opportunity and satisfy that need.

Many companies will gather information about readers for you—for a price. (One company charges nearly $1,500 to do an online survey of 400 people, and the price tags can go quite a bit higher.) Joan Hamilton, editor in chief of *Sierra*, does some research on her own and also uses a syndicated research firm to bring home the data she needs. Understanding the results of a well-crafted survey, *Sierra* editors can make decisions about groups of readers and support those decisions with hard data.

A survey, for example, can tell an editor the kinds of topics that wealthy, seventy-year-old women would like to read about (how to make a quilt, a day in the life of the first lady, and such), and how much they would like to read certain kinds of articles (humor, exposé, personal experience, and so on). Do these women enjoy playing gin rummy at the senior center, or are they taking cruises up the Amazon? Are they more interested in funny articles about game shows, or exposés about scams aimed at the elderly?

When the results are in, editors look for strong indicators. If 60 percent of the respondents, let's say, indicate that they would "definitely" or "most definitely" like to read a magazine about vacation destinations that are safe for older women, the editor gets a clear idea of how to proceed. If the response is mixed or weak, however, indicating that these women share few interests or sufficient enthusiasm in any specific area, the editor would be well advised to seek out a different group to pursue.

Fred L. Schultz uses surveys to find out what readers of *Naval History* like and don't like—and who they are. David Eicher at *Astronomy* employs them as well. Jon Guttman, the editor of *Military History*, sends out surveys along with renewal forms four times a year. At *Vermont Life*, editor Tom Slayton takes surveys seriously:

> We do regular readership polls to determine the age, income level, gender, and interests of our audience. We do very focused polling in which we ask our readers to rate every story in each issue. Most of the time this confirms our own subjective perceptions, but there are surprises. The most popular stories are those that focus on specific Vermont places, Vermont people, and Vermont activities (maple sugaring, skiing, etc.) But we try to have items about contemporary Vermont—we have a piece in our winter issue about Jennifer Baybrook, a 19-year-old girl who's a national yo-yo champion. I like to have one or two surprises per issue for our readers.

Surveys come in several types, and editors choose among them based on the cost, the speed, and the need to hit a broad or a narrow target. One approach involves simply printing a lot of questionnaires, choosing a lot of addresses at random from phone books or other sources, and licking a lot of stamps. The advantage of this technique is that you'll end up with a sampling of the tastes of people from all walks of life: men and women, young and old, rich and poor, all different races and lifestyles and worldviews. The disadvantages, however, are numerous: you'll probably get a low rate of return, meaning that only a few people will bother to fill out the questionnaire and send it back to you. You'll also receive only a handful of responses from groups that really matter to you. If you are editing a "beautiful home" magazine for women, you might want a bunch of responses from, say, women between the ages of thirty and fifty—so all those responses you got from men, teenagers, ninety-year-old great-great-grandmothers, and other people outside your audience range might amount to nothing more than wasted paper and squandered money.

So you might want to target your survey more tightly. This approach involves sending the survey to people from a specially prepared list of names and addresses. Lists are for sale everywhere. (If you ever want to test that notion, just enter a sweepstakes and see how quickly your mailbox fills up with junk-mail offers for cheap cookware and introductory credit cards.) These lists come with cross-referenced information attached to each name, so you can request a list that contains *only* women between the ages of thirty and fifty. You can even fine-tune it further, cross-referencing that list with subscription lists for other magazines, with ZIP-code profiles, with credit-card purchases, and so on. Properly tailored, a targeted list should let you send your questionnaire only to women between the ages of thirty and fifty who subscribe to high-end travel magazines (they like the elegant life), who live in certain ZIP codes (they own nice houses and so probably want to make them beautiful), and who drive expensive cars (they have money). Armed with that information, you should be able to target your potential readers well. They still might not return many of your questionnaires, but you can be sure that every one you receive represents a good potential subscriber.

And as anyone who has ever sat down at the dinner table can tell you, surveys don't have to be done by mail. For a fee, companies that own large phone banks will hire starving college students and harness them to conduct your survey by telephone. The advantages of

We have a good feel for our readership that is based on constant marketing research. Our marketing department surveys a set of readers after every issue, and from this feedback, we are able to determine (to a point) how the readership feels about the magazine. The feedback doesn't dictate what we do, but it provides a certain guidance. It also helps us to know where there are problems and allows us to respond with creative solutions.

Jackson Mahaney, associate editor, *Endless Vacation*

this approach are a higher rate of return—some people are still too polite to slam down the receiver—and the opportunity to pick up additional information that the interviewees offer ("Well, now, if your magazine told me how to keep my house looking great even though I own three Saint Bernards, then I'd be interested"). These phone-bank companies also can complete the survey in a relatively short span of time. The main disadvantage—aside from annoying a lot of people at dinnertime—is cost. A thorough survey conducted rapidly over the telephone and analyzed in a rigorous and accessible manner can cost thousands of dollars.

Surveys work in other ways as well. Sometimes, editors survey their own subscribers, but other times they might survey people of the right age group, sex, or other characteristic who have not subscribed yet. This approach can yield valuable information: Why don't these people subscribe? What about the magazine turns them off? Is it too expensive? too boring? too bizarre? What can the magazine do to attract these potential subscribers—without changing so much that its soul is lost?

Some editors also conduct surveys of prospective advertisers in an effort to determine the needs those companies are trying to meet. If a car company is pursuing the same sorts of people as your magazine, you can learn a great deal by working with that company. You'll be able to discover the information that the company already has about these potential customers, and you'll be able to target your magazine to attract that company's advertising dollar. *Entrepreneur*, for example, conducts advertising studies to determine what its audiences want—and what its advertisers want as well.

Traditionally, we have had a very high readership and a renewal rate among the highest in the industry. We study our audience a lot, both the magazine subscribers and those who visit our Web site. We have a large circulation and marketing staff to focus on this area. We also test the market and evaluate our audience by sending out direct-mail solicitations for items like books and special issues.

Peter Porteous, assistant editor, *National Geographic*

In an interesting variation, Brad Pearson, editor of *Heartland USA*, notes that the majority of his "900,000-plus subscribers" come from a database provided by one of the magazine's primary advertisers. "Over time," Pearson said, "this advertiser has gleaned a lot of information about the men in their database—information that has helped us know our readers better."

Surveys have the advantage of speed, breadth, and loads of information, and many magazines rely on them to remain up-to-date on readers' thinking. Crafted and interpreted well, they can give editors a clear sense of broad questions about the audience and specific questions about particular articles. They are flexible and powerful tools.

But they aren't perfect.

Keeping in Focus

Although useful, surveys don't offer the whole story. The wording of the questions, for example, can lead to dramatic shifts in the responses. Imagine the difference between "tell us which story was the least offensive" and "tell us which story was the most outstanding." The latter, of course, implies that all stories in the magazine are outstanding, but some are more so than others. Depending on the respondent's reaction to that implication, some answers might be more prevalent than would be found with the first question.

Surveys offer you responses only to the questions they ask and the comparisons among those responses. They can't tell you anything about information that the person who wrote the questionnaire overlooked. A survey might show that 88 percent of respondents from a carefully selected, targeted sample say they would subscribe to a magazine about bird-watching, for instance. But maybe half of these people would be interested only if it were priced at $12 a year or less. Or maybe they'd be interested only if it offers detailed information about birds in their areas, suggesting that a zoned format might be important. Or maybe they'd be interested only if the magazine combines bird-watching with exotic travel; instead of reading about the cardinals of Indiana, these potential readers might want articles about the rare birds of the Galápagos. Without knowing this additional information, you might steer your magazine off course.

To get this kind of qualitative information in a more systematic way than readers' mail and conversations can offer, some editors turn to focus groups. In a focus group, a dozen or so people who are randomly selected from within certain parameters are brought together in a room. Typically, the participants sit around a large table, nibbling on cookies and sipping coffee, while a moderator asks increasingly specific questions in an effort to spur the dialogue in the desired directions. The moderator might, for example, begin with general questions about reading habits and tastes, and then guide the conversation toward books and magazines about bird-watching. Once the participants have had a chance to talk at this level, the moderator might ask more pointed questions about specific bird-watching magazines already on the market. One participant might complain that *FeatherSpotter* has become really dull lately, with boring articles about ordinary birds. Another might praise *Friends of the Condor* for its bold environmental stance. Another might long for a magazine with a little more humor and a lot less material on migration patterns.

The questions and responses continue, covering such topics as the selection and impact of articles, overall impression, and even the look of the publications being discussed. When the agreed-on time is up, the participants are thanked—and often paid a modest sum—and then sent on their way. Throughout it all, editors lurking behind an observation mirror are taking notes and thinking about how to shape the proposed magazine. And a video camera is recording all the comments and expressions, so anything that is unclear can be checked later.

Focus groups can give editors a sense of readers' satisfaction level with their publications and their competitors'—and of some worthwhile directions a new magazine might take. Because the groups are usually small, this approach doesn't offer the broad overview that a

> We make sure our magazine serves the readers by keeping in touch with them through monthly surveys, focus groups, and reader letters.
>
> **Jean LemMon, editor, *Better Homes and Gardens***

properly framed survey can give, but it can provide depth and specificity in a way that surveys can't match.

At one publication where I worked several years ago, the editors decided to use focus groups to make sure we were understanding our audience properly. We hired a company to conduct several focus groups that consisted of subscribers, nonsubscribers, and—perhaps most important—former subscribers. The moderator screened possible participants from several demographic lists and from our subscriber database. The chosen ones were invited to participate, and those who declined were replaced by others from the same lists.

The participants were settled around a conference table in a small, fluorescent-lit room with not terribly subtle two-way mirrors. The guests were told that there were people and cameras behind the mirrors, and microphones were placed down the middle of the table. The participants seemed self-conscious at first, but then they relaxed and opened up with enthusiasm.

We learned a great deal that day. The primary reason people dropped our publication, for example, was that they felt it no longer provided them with information they needed in their lives. They turned to us not for entertainment or human-interest pieces but for hard news they could put to good use. As they concluded that we weren't offering enough of that kind of material any more, they turned their attention—and their subscription money—to other outlets. With the benefit of that information, we were able to make some adjustments to help keep our current subscribers and perhaps reattract some of the ones we had lost.

Focus groups are far from conclusive tools that give editors a clear sense of direction. Often, the participants disagree about the fundamentals, including why they read the publication at all. Editors who use focus groups must be prepared to sift through the responses and then, without flinching, make the tough decisions that will please some people and alienate others. Still, focus groups can provide valuable qualitative information that such impersonal tools as surveys can't capture.

Alternative Means

As popular as meetings, surveys, and focus groups are, some editors prefer other ways of getting the information they need. These approaches vary widely and often are based on an editor's own attitudes toward research methods. Some editors distrust surveys, for example, knowing that the wording of the questions can skew the outcome. Others distrust the findings gleaned from casual conversations, knowing that the sample size is small and that people often exaggerate their views once they finally get a chance to vent them. So these editors search for other ways of finding an audience that will be large and faithful.

Some, like *U. Magazine*'s editor and publisher, Frances Huffman, define their audiences by how their magazines are distributed:

> *U. Magazine* is distributed at 275 four-year colleges and universities throughout the nation, including religious colleges, private liberal arts schools, historically black colleges, and major research universities, so we know that our audience is very diverse. In keeping with the statistics on campus enrollment, our readers are generally age 18–24, but we also have some nontraditional student readers and faculty readers.

On the Line functions in a similar manner. Published by a Mennonite publishing house, the magazine is distributed through bulk subscriptions to Mennonite churches, shedding at least some light on

As to how we determine who makes up our audience—we don't. Oh, the guys in marketing have done "studies"—they used to send out questionnaires to, oh, a thousand readers with a one-dollar bill attached—and we'd get an idea of the age, income, etc., of the reader. But as editors, we just try to produce stories for automobile enthusiasts in a lively and entertaining and informative way. Guys (and a small percentage of women) buy car magazines because they want to know what's new, and what we think of it. It's that simple.

Steve Spence, managing editor, *Car and Driver*

the readership right away. Anyone is welcome to subscribe to *On the Line*, and the magazine does have individual subscribers, but in general, the readers share an interest in articles that reflect a Mennonite perspective.

In other words, the editors of these two magazines—as well as editors at *Heartland USA, National Geographic, National Wildlife,* and several other publications—know their audiences because they have a clear grasp of how their magazines are getting into people's hands. The means of distribution defines the audience.

Other means of clarifying the audience profile include conducting marketing studies, competition analyses, and other techniques designed to convert messy attitudes into neat and easy-to-digest numbers.

However they go about it, most editors strive to gain and continually refine an understanding of their audiences. Whether they rely on the magic of numbers or the quirkiness of personal communication, these editors attempt to get a sense of the people who read—and who might want to read—their magazines. By understanding these audiences, editors can gain a greater comprehension of the needs, desires, and curiosities that their magazines can meet. That knowledge allows them to choose articles and shape stories in such a way that readers will be consistently delighted.

To Thine Own Self Be True

Some editors damn the torpedoes and steam ahead on the confidence that their own tastes and outlooks will be of sufficient interest

I assume that the readers are like us, with the same tastes and interests. We aren't putting out a mass magazine, whose readers can be known to the editors only through focus groups and demographic research.
William Whitworth, editor, *The Atlantic*

We watch reader mail and occasionally do an informal reader survey, but we mostly trust our own gut to sense what's interesting to people out there.
George C. Larson, editor, *Air & Space*

In this age of special-interest magazines, every publication has a target audience, and part of the task of conceptualizing the magazine's focus and learning how best to serve the needs of the readership will be achieved through the use of reader surveys and close attention to reader correspondence. But more important, I feel, is one's internal sense as an editor (and a reader) of what will interest people. A good editor will not simply be knowledgeable about the material that provided the focus of his/her magazine; he/she will be dedicated to it and will regard himself/herself as something of a missionary who is seeking to find and share with readers the best possible selection of topics for articles and the best writing on those topics that can be assembled, within the limitations of the available resources.

Ed Holm, editor, *American History*

to others that an audience will form. *MacAddict*'s Cheryl England holds to that approach:

When we first started *MacAddict*, the audience was, well, me. That's not very scientific. The best I can say here is to have someone on staff who has a real feel for the person who cares about the subject—and you don't get this through research studies or other dry things. I think editors lead readers. You

Most magazines continually research their audiences through focus groups and surveys. One magazine [I know of]…has a whole staff doing nothing but research. That much study, it seems to me, reveals a high level of insecurity on the part of the editors, and insecure editors seldom produce a good magazine—no matter how much information they have about their readers. We do very little research, partly because we're cocky but mostly because it's expensive and highly subjective even under the best of circumstances. When we think we need to look at some reactions to new material we may hold some focus groups or show things to local classrooms, but mostly we just read our mail and trust our instincts about what is interesting and what kids can understand.

Gerry Bishop, editor, *Ranger Rick*

The nice thing is that our readers aren't much different from me. Most guys, and I would say all of our readers, want to improve their lives, get fitter, look better, eat healthier, love more, be happier, be more productive, enjoy their families, be challenged at work. Those desires are part of being a man. Now, not every story in the magazine is for every reader. Some readers hate our sex coverage—and they let us know about it. But the majority love it and would miss it if we acted on the desires of a vocal few. As an editor, you have to think of the majority of readers, and stay true to your mission no matter what kind of letters you get.

Jeff Csatari, executive editor, *Men's Health*

need to pay attention to what they say in order to look for common themes, but don't take EVERYTHING they say at face value.

Doug Moss—the founder, publisher, and executive editor of *E/The Environmental Magazine*, which focuses on environmental issues—trusts his own instincts and goes after people who don't necessarily agree with him:

For example, a horse-riding enthusiast magazine will find people already into that subject and then get them on the rosters so as to build an ad base. We need—to some extent—to do the

When I inherited the editorship of *Ranger Rick* in 1987, after the 20-year reign of the founding editor, much of the publication's identity was already in place—a colorful, entertaining, educational, scrupulously accurate, friendly magazine that tried to inspire an understanding and appreciation of nature and wildlife and thereby develop a conservation ethic in children aged 6 to 12. During the past eight years, this identity has not significantly changed. However, due to an increase in the number of other high-quality, highly entertaining children's magazines, as well as the explosion of other kinds of entertainment for children of this age group, I've seen the need to make *Ranger Rick* increasingly attractive to an increasingly distracted audience. Subjects such as plants, for example, which used to be covered regularly because we felt they should be covered, have a very hard time finding a slot in today's *Ranger Rick*—unless, of course, those plants prey on insects, grow to extraordinary sizes, poison people, or defend themselves in amazing ways. In other words, with so many other things for kids to be entertained by, and with so many kids being far more busy than they've ever been before, we keep reminding ourselves that every piece in *Ranger Rick* must be a star performance, and that we do not have a captive audience. We must concentrate on producing a magazine not for those who love nature and who would read anything about it they can get their hands on, but rather for reluctant readers who are only marginally interested in what we have to say. That is the only way we know to reach as large an audience as possible with the most interesting material we can produce.

Gerry Bishop, editor, *Ranger Rick*

same to survive financially, but our aim is really more to grab onto those NOT already members of the choir. That's how we have impact....

In a way, we buck the mainstream magazine trend (build an advertising base around thin editorial material) by starting with a different mission in the first place: to smarten-up (rather than dumb down—sorry, I can get cynical about these things) the masses about issues they may not yet realize are important to them. Commercial magazines usually define a market that already exists, then try to milk it for as much circulation (read: ad revenue) as possible.

The editors at *International Wildlife* pursue a similar approach:

International Wildlife readers include conservationists, biologists, wildlife managers and other wildlife professionals, but the majority are not wildlife professionals. In fact, *International Wildlife* caters to the unconverted—those people who may have only a passing interest in wildlife. Consequently, our writers should avoid a common pitfall: talking only to an "in group." *International Wildlife* is in competition with television and hundreds of other periodicals for the limited time and attention of busy people. So our functions include attracting readers with engaging subjects, pictures and layouts; then holding them with interesting and entertaining, as well as instructional, text.

The Demons of Demography

Demographics generally refers to the basic breakdown of a group of people. How many are women? men? old? young? black? Hispanic? American Indian? homeowners? apartment dwellers? upper class? middle class? lower class? And so on.

This information can be combined to create interesting data. For example, let's say you ask about your readers' income levels, and you get a breakdown that looks like this:

$10,000–20,000	8 %
$21,000–30,000	15 %
$31,000–40,000	22 %
$41,000–50,000	24 %
$51,000–60,000	18 %
$61,000–70,000	7 %
Over $70,000	6 %

In addition, half your readers say they would like to earn more money. And two-thirds of them say they want more vacation time.

Now you can learn some interesting facts. By bringing certain pieces of the survey together, you might learn that few of your readers who make less than $30,000 a year want more money—but most of the people who make more than $50,000 want a raise.

And the people who want more vacation time are scattered evenly throughout the income levels, as well as the sex, urban/rural, and age categories.

As an editor, you can use this information to make decisions about articles. "How to Ask Your Boss for a Raise" might be interesting, but only your wealthiest readers are likely to care—and they make a lot of money already. But "How to Negotiate an Extra Week of Vacation" would be useful for a larger segment of your audience. (Assign it to a freelancer. You don't want your staff to get any ideas.)

Understanding Understanding

Back to that incredible $250,000 loan. The core challenge is that our benefactor wants her money back—with interest. We could follow our hearts and publish *Matchstick Aficionado*, but we might not get the readership we need to stay afloat. It could be that there just aren't enough matchstick lovers in this world to support a major magazine. Go figure.

Or we could follow our observations about the marketplace and publish *Breathing Today*. Everyone, after all, has to breathe, so our audience base should be huge! But the need for information might not be great enough to keep the publication alive; most people have the "inhale, exhale, repeat" thing down pretty well. In other words, while the breadth of breath is great, the shortness of breath is a problem.

So we had better do some work to figure out what the people out there might want or need. It's been said before: people spend money only to solve problems or increase pleasure. If our publication doesn't meet at least one of those goals, people probably aren't going to support us with their subscriptions. Whether we rely on our own tastes or put our trust in the hands of marketing maestros, our ability to continue publishing will depend on our ability to ascertain what people want and need.

3. Hocus Focus:
The Magic of a Clear Mission

It's *Esquire*'s role to provide the spark that comes from contact with exciting writers, new ideas, new personalities, fresh takes on more familiar figures, the inside story on what's really going on. Besides the distinctive journalism, we should be pointing you to the best new books, offering ideas about sex and relationships, cars, travel, food, booking the right hotel in Venice, handling an IRS audit—A Book of Life for successful men and women who share their lives.

Edward Kosner, editor in chief, *Esquire*

A good, clear focus is essential for a magazine—imagine if *Field & Stream* had instead been *Field & Scream*. With focus come readers, but when focus is lacking, interest is lacking.

This emphasis on a tight focus makes sense when we look at our own lives. We have jobs or go to school. We have families—parents and siblings, or spouses and children. We like to do things: play in a band, read literature, whack a tennis ball, paint with oils on canvas. We know we should sleep more, get more exercise, spend quality time with people we love. And the television claws at our eyes, luring us into the artificial worlds of half-hour sitcoms and hour-long adventures.

So where in this blizzard of activity and demands do we find time to read magazines? We fit in such reading when we can: over a bowl

If the magazine is focused and consistent, it's because I'm working with some of the best writers in the world, because I have surrounded myself with editors who are smarter than I am, and because we are never satisfied. We are always scouting and critiquing ourselves. And I seek criticism and comment from outsiders whose judgment I value.

William Whitworth, editor, *The Atlantic*

The *MH* formula has been quite consistent over the years, and we've been successful because we stick to our core. It's what the readers want. Fitness, weight loss, nutrition, weightlifting, stress reduction, health, guy wisdom. Those are our core topics. We don't deviate much from those. When we have strayed, our readers let us know—especially our newsstand buyers. We have a panel of readers who fill out a survey each month, ranking their favorite departments and features and commenting on what they don't like and what they'd like to see more of. We take their opinions very seriously—and it has paid off. Again, we stick to our core. We make sure each issue has those key elements. Even in our Malegrams department, we make sure we cover our core topics. It ensures that there is something useful in the magazine for every reader, whether he wants to lose weight, build muscle, or improve his sex life.

Jeff Csatari, executive editor, *Men's Health*

of Cheerios at breakfast, on the sofa before the next rerun of *Seinfeld*, in bed at night before turning out the light. (Oh, all right—we might as well admit it. A huge percentage of magazine reading takes place in the bathroom as well.)

With our leisure reading time so precious, we aren't going to gamble it on a magazine that might or might not give us something relevant to our lives. As mentioned in chapter 1, most general-interest magazines have been driven from the landscape, pushed back by the evolutionary pressures of tightly focused, "niche" publications. These niche magazines have the advantage of predictability. If I want to read about cars, I'll pick up *Car and Driver* or *AutoWeek*. If I want to read about makeovers and the secrets to luring men, I'll pick up *Cosmopolitan* or *Glamour*. If I want to read about music and musicians, I'll pick up *Rolling Stone* or *Spin*. I don't want to risk wasting my time and money on a magazine that might not give me what I want. There are some general-interest magazines left in this country, but they are scarce—and they restrict their range by focusing on a highly specific audience. In general, general-interest magazines are gone.

So a magazine editor has to figure out how to focus her magazine tightly, so readers can know, in advance, what to expect from the publication—and so they can know that the magazine will offer in-

First, you need to create a unique mission. This, essentially, is *Popular Science*'s mission statement: "As the What's New Magazine, *Popular Science*'s vision is to be a relevant, practical, and entertaining survival guide for a technologically inundated society. It is a window on the worlds of science and new technology, and the products that grow out of those worlds." Corollary to that first rule:

Q: Why is a magazine like a steamship in the Arctic?
A: Ships and magazines are big, and they don't turn too well or rapidly.

So if you want to head in a new direction (that is, fulfill a new mission), you'd better make darn sure it's correct before you go. And watch for icebergs!

Mariette DiChristina, senior editor, *Popular Science*

formation and entertainment that suits their lives. If a magazine attempts to offer interesting articles about celebrities *and* golf *and* woodworking *and* astronomy *and* cooking, few people are going to read it. Those who are interested in golf might not be interested in astronomy or cooking. Those interested in celebrities might not care about cooking or woodworking. So the focus has to be tight to capture the attention of a sufficient number of readers.

Steady as She Goes!

Editors also must figure out how to keep their magazines focused over time. Just as the initial scope of a magazine must be tight, the nature of the magazine should not wander from issue to issue, year to year, or decade to decade, unless the editors make a conscious decision to alter it.

This consistency can be harder than it seems. A thirty-year-old editor might launch a magazine aimed at thirty-year-olds, featuring articles about the entertainment, politics, and life situations that interest people of that age. But when that editor turns forty or fifty or sixty, how can the magazine remain constant? When the editor has children, everything in his life will change—but the magazine has to maintain a steady course. Suddenly, at age forty, with kids in school, the editor who once cared only about music videos, muscle cars, and

You'd think that a 50-year-old magazine founded on a principle as clear and simple as organic gardening would be immune from identity crises. But the truth is, *Organic Gardening* has been variously a forum for unconventional social and medical opinions, a homesteaders' handbook, a vehicle for political advocacy, and a lifestyle journal. The magazine has always been strongest—in terms of circulation and profit & loss—when it has been a guide for helping amateurs grow food and flowers without pesticides and synthetic fertilizers.

Scott Meyer, senior editor, *Organic Gardening*

beer might find himself caring more about educational policies, minivans, and fine coffees. But if the magazine "ages" along with the editor, the thirty-year-olds will stop reading it—and the forty-year-olds might still think of it as a magazine for younger readers. So the publication could find itself without an audience, without an income, without a means of staying afloat.

Similarly, an editor might develop a passion for amateur radio and sign on at a magazine that focuses on that hobby. But then, as time goes by, amateur radio might take a back seat to a new hobby—flying model airplanes, raising draft horses, bungee jumping, or something. The editor probably can't scoot from one magazine to another as her interests change. So how can the magazine remain enthusiastic about amateur radio when the editor is spending her spare time flinging herself from bridges with elastic cords tied around her ankles?

Mission Control

The answer to both concerns—tight focus and consistency over time—lies in a clear understanding of a magazine's mission. The magazine has to have a solid reason for its existence—otherwise,

Study the long history of the magazine, know its well of potential topics very thoroughly, rotate the proper subjects in and out at logical times, and hire an outstanding copy editor and supporting editorial team.

David J. Eicher, managing editor, *Astronomy*

> As far as conceptualizing the magazine, we have a main purpose that we abide by throughout the book: All articles must inform, entertain, and/or provide helpful information to black women.
>
> **Linda Villarosa, executive editor, *Essence***

readers will drift away, complaining to their friends that they just don't get what *Everything Monthly* is all about, anyway. That reason for being must be well defined, concise, and easy to grasp. With such a mission, the magazine stands a chance of achieving a tight focus and keeping it steady over time. At the *Utne Reader*, for example, Craig Cox relies on "a simple and clear mission and a commitment to serving the readers, not our egos."

Successful editors are able to state their magazines' reason for existence in just a few simple sentences. Those who need overly complex phrasing or seemingly endless run-ons—"We do this, and we do that, and we do this other thing, and we also do a little of that stuff sometimes"—are putting out a magazine that will baffle and discourage its readers.

Good magazines have simple, straightforward missions. In fact, these missions are often so clear that readers can figure them out from the magazine's content and tone alone. For example, without reading its mission statement, I'd say that *Maxim* exists to give young men entertaining information about sex, women, and beer. *People* is published to offer its readers information about celebrities and other interesting folks. *Model Railroader* provides its readers with useful and interesting information about the hobby of HO- and N-scale trains. Try it with your favorite magazine. The odds are good that if you can't state the magazine's purpose in a single, clear declaration, it's not your favorite magazine.

So a clear, solid mission gives the magazine the focus it needs. It also solves another problem—making sure that everyone on the staff envisions the magazine in the same way. For example, take *Esquire*, whose masthead lists staff members in the following positions:

editor in chief	designer
deputy editor	art assistant
editorial director	director of photography

design director
editorial products director
fashion creative director
executive editor
articles editor
senior editor
managing editor
literary editor
Web editor
research editor
three assistant editors
five editorial assistants
special assistant to the
  editor in chief
deputy art director
assistant art director

associate photo editor
photo coordinator
senior fashion editor
market editor
editorial production director
editorial production associate
editorial production coordinator
two associate copy editors
assistant copy editor
two associate research editors
six writers at large
eighteen contributing editors
food and travel correspondent
and a whole lot of other people
  on the publishing and
  business side of
  the magazine

How do all these people end up with the same vision for *Esquire?* As editors and writers come and go, how do the new people learn about the magazine's mission? How can *Esquire* stay consistent with all these different people putting together the magazine's content and appearance every month?

Disaster awaits the magazine if all these people don't hold a roughly similar vision for *Esquire* in their minds. Imagine what would happen if the managing editor thought that *Esquire* should be an entertainment magazine for college-age guys, while the articles editor thought it should be a fashion magazine for middle-age men. Or if the deputy editor thought that the magazine should be serious and hard-hitting, while the director of photography thought it should be punchy and just a little bit zany?

One of the most important tasks that a magazine's editor has is keeping everything in focus—working with the authors, his editorial staff, and his art director to achieve a presentation of words, images, and design that pulls together, with each element supporting the others. This is a difficult task.

Ed Holm, editor, *American History*

What if the half of the writers at large considered *Esquire* a travel magazine, while the other half thought of it as a health-and-fitness publication?

You can see the mess that *Esquire* would face if its editors and contributors weren't in general agreement about the nature of the magazine. One minute you'd be reading a funny article about the hottest skateboard styles, and then you'd turn the page and see an informative piece about vests that hide bulging waistlines. You'd read an exposé about the hidden charges you'll encounter at five-star hotels in Paris, and then you'd find a wacky article about James Bond's women. No two articles would make sense together—and the magazine as a whole would not appeal strongly enough to any particular group of readers.

One way that editors can avoid this debacle is with a written mission statement, which spells out what the magazine does and what it stands for. Many magazines have mission statements. Some magazines frame them and hang them on the office wall, for the staff to read and remember. Some put them in editor's handbooks or other in-house material. Some publish them right in the magazine, where readers can see them as well.

The advantages of a mission statement are potent. It lets all editors read—and reread—a concise description of what the magazine wants to be, so there is little chance that some editors will think of the publication one way and the others will have different ideas. Combined with other tools, a mission statement can reinforce success and thwart danger. "We have an editorial statement that keeps us on target, clear guidelines for each department, and occasional reader surveys to see how we are doing," says *Sierra* editor Joan Hamilton. "Several editors comment on manuscripts at each stage of the editorial process, acting as surrogate readers, letting the editor and author know when material isn't clear, accurate, or compelling."

I read the magazine's mission statement four or five times a month—even though I have it memorized.

Hank Nuwer, editor in chief, *Arts Indiana*

First, of course, is the formulation of an editorial philosophy or mission statement. Ours is as follows: *Mature Outlook* is a special interest magazine for 50-plus men and women who have a real zest for life and who share a curiosity for the many and varied pursuits available to them. It fulfills their needs by supplying upbeat contemporary coverage of such topics as travel, health and fitness, food and nutrition, money, and people. Each article inspires its readers to live life to the fullest.

Peggy S. Person, associate editor, *Mature Outlook*

Done properly, a mission statement isn't an anchor that inhibits creativity and squelches innovation. Rather, it is a foundation that can keep the magazine on course while also keeping it fresh and exciting.

Mission statements can be long and involved, such as the statement for *National Geographic Traveler*:

National Geographic Traveler aspires to live up to its tagline: "Where the Journey Begins" and to be *the* source for the active, curious traveler. One who is more inquisitive than acquisitive. Every department and article is designed to inspire readers to pick up and go—and to provide them with the tools and orientation to do so. Our stories and special sections all combine the Society's storied expertise with an insider's point of view.

National Geographic Traveler's mission is to employ storytelling and you-are-there photography to inspire culturally aware readers to travel; and to provide the deepest, most reader-friendly service information to enable you to go places wisely and well. The magazine carries the authority that comes

By having a clearly defined mission, we are able to keep focused on what our readers expect to find in the magazine. The editors are kept in constant touch with their markets and abreast of the sociological trends, enabling us to publish material that reflects what's happening in the bridal marketplace as well as the economic and cultural changes that affect the way couples plan weddings today.

Cele G. Lalli, editor in chief, *Modern Bride*

with being the flagship travel magazine of the National Geographic Society, which has not only traveled the globe but also groundbreakingly explored it for 113 years. Ask us "Who knows the world better?" And with clear-eyed honesty we can say: "We do."

National Geographic Traveler eschews fashion and fluff in favor of visceral photography and articles flavored with personality, passion, perspective, and a strong sense of place. Our voices are those of writers who love to travel—not correspondents who travel as a means to write.

Traveler cares about fine writing—contributors include Paul Theroux, Jan Morris, Arthur Golden, Bill Bryson, David Halberstam, Elizabeth Berg, Ray Bradbury, George Plimpton, Jimmy Breslin, Rick Bass, James Fallows, Maeve Binchy, Tom Robbins, Frances Mayes, Bill Broyles, and Salman Rushdie.

In keeping with our heritage, we showcase some of the world's finest photographers and photos—Jim Richardson's provocative Edinburgh coverage, Theo Westenberger's *Communications Arts*–winning take on Venice's Carnivale, David Alan Harvey's you-are-there rhapsody on Tobago, Macduff Everton's breathtaking Beijing.

We present news—"Smart Traveler" regularly beats newspapers and other magazines on travel trends and topics—from the safest airline seats to hot ski trends to an investigation on travel-tax rip-offs. And Jonathan Tourtellot's probing pieces on "The Two Faces of Tourism" and "The Tourism Wars"—part of a series on the future of tourism—is the kind of reporting that illustrates we offer more than just advice on places to go.

We care about serving our readers with information that empowers—our map-enhanced TravelWise sections give you a ticket to the open road, telling you what you need to know before you go. These detailed, timely mini-guides offer nuts-and-bolts information on how to make the most of your time in the field. Not only do we offer actionable destination information, but we serve up travel-related products and resources, insights from fellow travelers, accessible (and surprising) travel opportunities; and travel advocacy (we specialize in issues related to sustainable tourism).

And our special surveys—"The Faces of Australia," the Essential National Park series, the Insider Guides to major cities—are built not on unreliable reader polls but are developed with on-the-ground insiders who have real expertise.

Traveler is a traveler's magazine. It's the travel magazine readers keep. The magazine that propels you from the armchair and into the field.

That mission statement gives you an extraordinarily thorough understanding of what kind of publication *National Geographic Traveler* is and what it strives to give to readers. Most mission statements, however, are short and to the point, like this one for *Lake Superior Magazine*:

> *Lake Superior Magazine* will work to be the eyes, ears and voice of Lake Superior and its peoples. Through quality writing, graphics and photography, we strive to surprise, inform and delight our readers.

A good mission statement explains not only what the magazine does—but also what it doesn't do. Compare the mission statements of *National Geographic Traveler* and *Lake Superior Magazine* with that of *Endless Vacation*: "RCI's *Endless Vacation* magazine provides informative, do-able vacation ideas for timeshare owners." *Endless Vacation*'s mission statement carves out a specific territory for the publication. "What it means is that we try to provide our readers with re-

Outside is a monthly national magazine dedicated to covering the people, sports and activities, politics, art, literature, and hardware of the outdoors. Its readers share this general interest but are otherwise diverse—from the extremely active mountain-biker to the occasional backpacker to the armchair traveler. We aim to entertain and inform and challenge them all, with the highest-caliber writing on outdoor events, activities, and travel destinations; informative seasonal pieces; sports and adventure-travel stories; profiles of engaging outdoor characters; service pieces on travel, fitness, and equipment; and investigative stories on environmental issues and policy matters affecting the outdoors.

Greg Cliburn, executive editor, *Outside*

> We think of ourselves as the essential magazine of country living. The litmus test is the word *country*—does the content have a meaningful and particular interest to people who live in the country, and (in some cases) does the action occur in the country? We're also a North American magazine, and have intentionally kept our focus on what's happening in Canada and the U.S. We always keep the magazine's focus in mind while assigning articles. We view an article as a contract with our reader. What should we be providing the reader? Once we determine what an article should contain—what our contract with the reader is—we make that clear in our assignment letter to the writer.
>
> **Karan Davis Cutler, managing editor,** *Harrowsmith Country Life*

alistic travel goals, destinations that they can easily travel to and enjoy," said associate editor Jackson Mahaney. "The mission statement guides the concept of the magazine. We are not a magazine for esoteric travel, difficult and adventure travel, or destinations that require a great deal of expense. The mission statement also helps to keep us focused."

Mission statements are essential tools for magazines—and for editors. For magazines, mission statements provide coherence among the editors, a well-defined and tight focus, and a clear direction despite the distractions of time, whims, and fads. For editors, mission statements provide a reliable insight into the character of the magazine and the important tasks at hand. They can guide editors through the marshy tundra of freelance submissions and off-the-wall ideas, offering a beacon by which effective navigation can be managed. If every article that you publish can be traced back to a part of your magazine's mission statement, you will go far as an editor.

The Collective Mind

In addition to putting the mission statement in writing, many editors rely on the editorial team to keep the course straight. If an editor suggests an idea or approach that seems out of line, the other editors chime in with corrective cautions. At *On the Line*, for example, editor Mary Clemens Meyer relies on her fellow editors to watch out for missteps. "My supervisor and consulting editor also keep an eye on things," she said.

Much like a drummer's "independence" (his ability to keep separate beats with his hands and feet), an editor has to be able to split his or her awareness, keeping focused on the issues currently in production, while also making sure that future issues will continue to interest our readers. Teamwork is all important in accomplishing this. When I lose perspective (either short term or long term), I can count on my associates to set me straight. At our magazine, editing is not a "my-way-or-the-highway" situation.

Brad Pearson, editor, *Heartland USA*

This teamwork approach has some advantages. It puts the magazine's mission up to a collective interpretation, rather than funneling all views of the magazine through one editor's wording of a mission statement. If your editorial team works in relative harmony—and especially if turnover is low, so editors have time to gain an in-depth understanding of the magazine's character and history—then many minds can maintain an agreed-on focus.

Teamwork also leads to creative tension, a healthy and useful factor in a busy magazine office. As long as the tension is kept at tolerable levels—as long as people don't end up feeling hurt, threatened, frustrated, or exhausted—lively and respectful disagreement can keep the spark in an editorial staff. The articles editor, for example, might want to tackle a project that falls right at the edge of your magazine's general scope. The photo editor loves it; any chance to get creative and energetic photos into the magazine is treasured. But the managing editor isn't so sure—the article might turn off more

It's talking, talking, talking, as in other kinds of human relationships. It's talking things out and bringing them to articulation....I think it's a process question more than anything else. I would never give any rigid or codified rules that you could put on a plaque, other than the dictum of process. Once you have that in place and the writers and editors know that it is their obligation to raise questions with the people in charge—and to talk them through before making a decision—then people will ultimately be on a sound footing. ,

Alice Chasan, editor, *World Press Review*

First, we had a very clear and strong vision to begin with. Any Mac mag, for example, can run an article on a new version of the Mac operating system. But when we do an article on the Mac OS we always ask ourselves what the article will contain that makes it a *MacAddict* article, not just any old Mac article. The original vision was to be candid, a bit wacky, completely supportive of the Mac, and always incredibly helpful (for example, including very clear step-by-step articles on how to do something cool with your Mac). The magazine is targeted to an individual—editors are hired not only for their editing and writing skills but also for their passion for the Mac. We then encourage them to write articles they or their friends would like to read.

Cheryl England, founding editor, *MacAddict*

readers than it turns on. And so the debate begins, with suggestions and modifications to the idea coming from all quarters. Eventually, as a group, you polish the idea until everyone feels comfortable with it. Or you flog it until everyone is tired of the concept and even the articles editor doesn't want to do it anymore. Or—the least desirable outcome—the staff remains divided, and the editor in chief has to make a decision that will delight one group and miff the other. Still, as long as the ground rules of respect and courtesy are maintained, even this outcome tends to generate new ideas, new perspectives, and new enthusiasm.

This approach has dangers as well, however. Perhaps the greatest danger is that a strong personality will dominate the group for a while, persuading the other editors into following a particular path. Then, when that person leaves—or another strong personality joins the group—the dynamics shift, and different priorities surface. Such dramatic changes can wreak havoc on the harmony of the editorial group, and they can cause the magazine to veer sharply in one direction and then in another as the persuasive people move about. The

Every Tuesday, the senior editors come together to conceive of our feature articles. It's really a brainstorming session in which we work as a collective to come up with ideas.

Linda Villarosa, executive editor, *Essence*

net result can be readers who like a magazine for a while but then drop it when its character changes. Without consistency, readers will turn elsewhere for the information they need and the entertainment they seek.

Another danger is that factions can develop. I've never had to work in such a place, but I've known people whose offices operated like Europe during World War I. "Camps" and "cadres" develop, leading to debates that make the Democrats and Republicans seem like the best of friends. The boundaries often are drawn along lines of risk taking: the innovators and tinkerers on one side, versus the "if it ain't broke don't fix it" crowd on the other. The end game in this situation often involves bitter feelings, Machiavellian power brokering that distracts everyone from the actual task of putting out a magazine that readers will love, and ultimately mass resignations and even lawsuits.

When it works, it works well. When it doesn't, the results can be grim.

Instincts and Experience

Some editors—especially those who have built their magazines around their own views of the world—don't rely on mission statements or the editorial team for maintaining their publications' focus over time. Instead, they rely on themselves. With their long track records in the business, their acute understanding of their audiences, and their proven ability to deliver articles month after month that thrill, inspire, horrify, or otherwise engage their readers, they are confident that they will be able to spot the right ideas—and the

All material purchased for publication is not consistent in quality, no matter how discriminating the manuscript evaluation process is. That is where the editor plays a major role. He or she can and must set an editorial standard and hold everything that appears in the magazine to that standard. If a manuscript is still hopeless after undergoing the editorial process, the editor must have the confidence to pull it and publish something else. I believe that loyal readers can spot uneven editing a mile away.

Fred L. Schultz, editor in chief, Naval History

wrong ideas—with a reasonable degree of precision as the years go by.

The strengths of this approach can be powerful. A magazine that reflects the personality of a dynamic, engaged, passionate editor can be a joy to read. It can enliven our minds, stimulate our senses, challenge our assumptions, and embolden our spirits. It also can upset and even infuriate us, which some editors do just to keep their readers moving forward.

The dangers of this approach are different from those in the teamwork model. Factions and camps won't develop as easily because the editors knew what they were getting into when they signed on. If they couldn't stand the editor, or if they didn't like the direction in which she was taking the magazine, they wouldn't have agreed to work there.

Rather, the primary danger lies in "focus drift." As mentioned before, the editor is bound to go through some significant life changes during his five, ten, maybe even twenty years of editing the magazine. He is likely to pick up and drop various hobbies, develop passions for different kinds of writing and different topics, and become concerned about different issues—not to mention get married, have kids, buy a house, and plan for retirement. Editors who lack significant self-awareness run the risk of dragging the magazine behind them as they grapple with different opportunities and challenges over time.

One editor I know, for example, founded a regional magazine but became increasingly interested in business as time went on. This shift was only natural—he had to make payroll, develop a business plan, hire marketing and ad-sales people, and make an endless series of business-related decisions to keep the magazine afloat. These decisions—and their roots, their ramifications, and their strategic importance—became fascinating for him, and the magazine began to feature more and more business articles with each passing issue. Readers who wanted a broader range of articles dropped their subscriptions in favor of magazines that covered the region more thoroughly. And readers who were interested in business articles were slow to perceive the magazine's new focus—and so they didn't subscribe in any great numbers. Ironically, by drifting toward business, the magazine eventually went out of business.

Monitor Wizards

Another tool in the editor's arsenal for keeping her magazine focused and consistent involves paying attention to the publication's central topic. By monitoring the core subject as it evolves in the real world, the editor can make sure the magazine is keeping up. She also can make sure that the magazine isn't wandering too far afield.

For some magazines, this means keeping a close eye on the changing needs of readers. A magazine like *Seventeen*, for example, isn't publishing the same kinds of articles that filled its pages thirty years ago. The interests of teenage girls have changed during that time, and the magazine has grown right along with them. "Sex and Body," for example, is a regular department, whereas such topics were handled in more subtle ways decades ago.

But just because *Seventeen* has evolved to keep up with the changing interests of its readership doesn't mean that it is wandering without a mission. In fact, it's quite the opposite. *Seventeen*'s mission is to deliver to teenage girls the kind of information that they find fun and useful in their lives. As girls change, the magazine must change to remain true to its mission.

For other kinds of magazines, monitoring the landscape might involve keeping track of changes in the central issue itself. As the nature of the information changes, so must the publication.

For example, *Gambling Times* didn't have to worry about online gaming a decade ago. Back then, "online" meant you were waiting for your turn to play the slot machines. Now online gaming is a huge business, replete with clicks-to-riches success stories, endless debates about systems that even the odds, and the occasional scam that bilks people out of their savings and racks up illicit debt on their credit cards. So these days, *Gambling Times* covers the online gaming in-

---

The original concept for *Better Homes and Gardens* was developed by its founder 73 years ago, and every editor since has followed the path. This is a magazine that's very tightly focused, even though it deals with several major editorial subject areas. There is a common thread: home and family!

Jean LemMon, editor, *Better Homes and Gardens*

National Review is the oldest conservative magazine in America. It is now a biweekly publication, devoted to covering the news from a conservative point of view, which means, in short, an emphasis on limited government, individual responsibility, free markets, and traditional moral values.

Matthew Carolan, executive editor, *National Review*

dustry just as vigorously as it does the regular casino and racetrack scene.

Editors keep up-to-date with their topics in a variety of ways.

• *Freelancers.* Most editors rely heavily on freelancers to find new and interesting ideas. It can be difficult for an editorial staff—trapped in isolated, insulated offices from 9 to 5 each day, five days a week—to learn about all the different facets of, say, organic gardening. So editors scour the piles of mail they get from freelancers in the hopes that a fresh idea will spring out and delight them. It's a low-odds game—most of the material editors receive from freelancers is useless because it is off-target, vague, tired, or otherwise substandard, but from time to time, an on-the-ball freelancer spots an idea that is just right for a particular magazine. The best freelance ideas are those that reveal new, unexplored areas of a magazine's topic and zero in on unique and compelling stories that show that new terrain to readers.

• *Industry contacts.* Whether your magazine focuses on mountain biking, child rearing, or martini mixing, chances are there's an industry that makes products essential to your readers. And most of the businesses in those industries would love to tell you about their new products and services. In fact, they probably employ public-relations professionals whose job it is to keep you and your competitors up-to-speed on the latest developments.

The first line of contact is the press release. Nearly every publication in the country receives torrents of press releases from companies interested in gaining some free publicity. Like freelance material, most of the press releases are worthless; they amount to little more than desperate attempts at self-aggrandizement ("PhlemCo an-

On an ongoing basis, we are fed an enormous amount of newsletters, press releases and queries from freelance writers—and, in addition, of course, we read and watch the news ourselves—which collectively keep our "ear to the rail" as to what's important to cover under the broad umbrella of environmentalism (and we define it very broadly).

Doug Moss, founder and executive editor, *E/The Environmental Magazine*

nounces a new way to ship cough syrup!"). Nobody cares, and only the most misguided editors routinely put this kind of material into their publications.

But some press releases offer truly new and interesting information, so savvy editors dig through the mailbag in search of solutions to their readers' problems. Remember—that's one of the two reasons people spend money. (The other is to enhance pleasure.) So if a product, a technique, or an idea has been developed that will save your readers time, money, headaches, or anguish, that press release can serve as the seed for a new and useful article.

Industry contacts take other forms as well. Some PR people make the rounds, meeting with editors on a regular basis to discuss possible article ideas. Some editors achieve the same face-to-face contact by attending trade shows and other gatherings where businesses offer information. (Editors also get information about readers this way, as we saw in chapter 2.) Editors also, from time to time, get free samples of products. While this is a good way to learn about the new stuff, it does raise some interesting questions about ethics and the appearance of bias (see chapter 5).

• *Personal action.* Editors also acquire current information about their topics by getting out and doing the things their magazines cover. Editors at *Organic Gardening* get their hands dirty by raising toxin-free vegetables. Editors at *Field & Stream* stalk pheasants when they get a chance. Editors at *Massage Magazine* get and give massages; editors at *Cigar Aficionado* light up from time to time; editors at *Baby Talk* know what raising a child is all about. By taking an active part in the interests they share with their readers, editors learn—and remind themselves—what it takes to do the things they advocate on their pages. And through this close contact with their

> Here at Cowles, we publish several dozen special-interest magazines on themes that range from history to dolls to bowhunting to vegetarianism. All of the senior editors are people whose primary interests and skills relate to the topics covered by their magazines—and the younger editors are developing their skills and interests along those lines as well.
>
> **Ed Holm, editor, *American History***

subject matter, they stay abreast of new developments and changing priorities.

Competition

Good editors also read their competitors' publications. In part, they do this to generate a sense of superiority ("I can't believe they published *that!*"). They also do it to find good writers who might be lured away with the right offer. But mainly, they read their competitors' magazines to make sure that they aren't missing anything, to check out any new topics that they haven't thought of yet, and to continually improve the quality and reach of their own magazines.

And there's another reason that editors scope out their rivals. Magazines target specific audiences whose members have a common bond: an interest, a life situation, a problem. But magazines that merely mimic existing, successful publications aren't likely to gain an audience. Why should someone switch to *Socks and Shoes Monthly* if it comes across as nothing but a knock-off of the highly successful *Shoes and Socks Monthly*? To gain readers, magazines have to offer something new, special, and unique.

And so editors carve out niches in the marketplace by paying attention to what everyone else is doing. By checking out the compe-

> I keep up with the latest in teenage popular culture. I read *Sassy, Entertainment Weekly, Car and Driver, YM, PC Computing*—all these help keep me current.
>
> **Scott Daniels, executive editor, *Exploring* and *Scouting***

> One of the ways we carve out our editorial niche and refine our coverage is to constantly analyze the competition. We try to find the points that distinguish our editorial and to play to those strengths so that we do not become a carbon copy of other magazines for the senior market.
>
> **Peggy S. Person, associate editor, *Mature Outlook***

tition, an editor can sharpen her magazine's focus in a way that draws readers away from the other titles crowding the newsstand.

Knowledge of the competition also lets you discover what you've missed. If your magazine caters to unusually bright children, for example, you have to know what similar magazines are publishing. That article about the new digital cameras for kids might count as a scoop for your rival, but at least you can get going on a similar piece—done in your own magazine's style, of course—that will help you catch up. In general, competitors' articles that make you laugh or shake your head are no big deal. It's the ones that make you *wince* that serve as wake-up calls.

Reading your rivals also allows you see what they are doing badly. If a topic is being covered, but not well—that's an opportunity for you. If a question is going unanswered—that's a chance for you to deliver important information for your readers. If certain aspects of a topic have been rendered in bizarre or bewildering ways—that's a sign that you should publish a clear, well-grounded article on the topic.

Similarly, by checking out the competition you can find out what has been overlooked. The digital-cameras-for-kids idea was brilliant, but what about camcorders? Maybe your magazine should cover ways in which kids can make movies. So editors read not only for what's there, but also for what isn't there. Sometimes, it's in the dark gaps between stories that the best new ideas emerge.

And editors read the competition to find out what is being done to death. Every category of magazines has its own list of over-flogged topics, but editors who don't read other publications run the risk of missing that saturation and tossing yet another article onto the bulging heap. The writers' guidelines that many magazines publish offer clear language about which tired topics to avoid. For example:

• *Arizona Highways*: "We do not want a rambling series of thoughts or vignettes, diary entries or a travelogue (a piece that begins in the morning, goes hour-by-hour through the day and ends in the evening). We want a story that opens by introducing us to a story line or theme, then develops the tale and finally concludes. We want an ending, a logical conclusion to the story we are telling. Just stopping the story won't do."

• *T'ai Chi*: "Try to avoid profiles of teachers that focus just on their many skills and accomplishments. Interviews with teachers or personalities should focus on their unique or individual insight into T'ai Chi Ch'uan, internal martial arts, qigong, or Traditional Chinese Medicine rather than on their personal achievement or ability, although their background can be woven into the article."

• *Florida Sportsman*: "We avoid boat racing, sailing, narrative adventures and 'celebrity' or 'hero' articles in which an individual is the story's primary focus."

• *Moment*: "We receive many more articles than we are able to publish, particularly about certain subjects, such as the Holocaust and Israel. We're more likely to use an article if it is not on these subjects."

Editors use the incoming stream of freelance submissions—and their own sense of saturation—to determine when enough is enough, but they also have to look around. If a particular topic has appeared several times in *Cosmo*, *Glamour*, and *Elle*, the editors at *Vogue* might think twice about assigning it to their own writers. In fact, some editors are required to analyze the competition as part of their employment duties. At *Popular Science*, for example, editors meet about once a year to discuss large and small issues that affect the course of the magazine. At one such meeting, the editors gave presentations about their favorite magazines. "In this way, we entertainingly taught each other a lot of lessons about what we like in magazines—and, consequently, what we'd like to see in *Popular Science*," said senior editor Mariette DiChristina. "We did some practical exercises, too—such as working in teams to develop ideas for a special, single-topic issue, which we then presented to the group as a

Based on what I was seeing other people publish and what I read about kids' attitudes about the environment, I decided about a year ago that kids were becoming saturated with information about environmental problems and their responsibility in helping correct those problems. I became convinced that we were doing a disservice to children by further burdening them with gloom-and-doom articles about dwindling rainforests, the extinction of species, the threats of ultraviolet radiation, and global warming. My directions to the staff were that we would play up the wonders and beauty of wildlife and the natural environment, would try to get kids outside to better appreciate their surroundings, and would cover only those environmental problems that are directly relevant to kids' lives, seem manageable, and in fact are already being solved. We sensed a decline in optimism among kids, so we decided to do everything we could to reverse that trend.

Gerry Bishop, editor, *Ranger Rick*

whole. In the past, we've also analyzed our competitors in various subject areas, and then given presentations on these analyses to each other. We have also discussed where we've been and where the magazine is going."

Enter and Sign On, Please

For editors joining the staffs of existing magazines, consistency of focus is essential on two levels.

First, you have to be able to understand your magazine's mission and deliver material that suits it. If you don't understand the magazine's mission—and so end up accepting material that falls outside that mission—you will have a hard time defending your decisions to your boss and an even harder time defending yourself to your readers. (Tragically, we don't often get the chance to defend ourselves to readers. Instead, the readers just slink off and give their subscription money to someone else.)

Blunders are especially difficult to avoid when you're presented with an article or idea that you think is *great*—but that doesn't quite fit your magazine's mission. If your grasp of that mission is shaky, or if you allow yourself to be swayed by tangential factors that have nothing to do with the reasons that your readers pick up your maga-

> Once you've set your mission, you have to fulfill that every month (or week or whatever) with every feature, every news item, every photo or illustration, in the book.
>
> **Mariette DiChristina, senior editor, *Popular Science***

zine every month, you might be tempted to send off a glowing letter of acceptance to the writer. Your boss, however, might see things somewhat differently, and then you'll find yourself defending an article that really belongs in another magazine.

Only by knowing your magazine's mission—and keeping your mind on it while you're considering proposals and deciding what to include in the part of the magazine you control—can you help the editorial team hold that mission steady.

Second, you have to understand the magazine's mission to help the publication grow. Remember, a mission statement is not intended to freeze the publication forever; it is intended to make sure that any changes in the magazine's focus are deliberate and well considered. After working at your new publication for a while, you might come to the realization that the mission is a bit outdated, tired, or irrelevant. And so you might come up with ideas for how to inject some new life into it. This thinking and these ideas are signs of leadership and vision—attributes that tend to get you promoted. But you won't be able to offer your suggestions for improvements unless you understand the mission in the first place.

So as a new editor, you would be wise to take these steps:

• Get to know the magazine's mission, even if no written mission statement exists.

• If a written statement exists, get a copy and keep it in sight. Put it on your bulletin board. Frame it and hang it on the wall. Type it into your computer's screen saver. But keep it in front of you. Then, for every major decision you make, ask yourself what facet of the mission you are serving. If you can't see how your impending action will support the magazine's mission—don't do it.

• Figure out how the various parts of the magazine work together and how each serves the magazine's overall mission.

How do I keep it focused? Years of practice.

Jon Guttman, editor, *Military History*

How does your part of the magazine or your task (fact checking, for example) fit in?

• Listen for disagreements among the editorial staff about interpretations of the magazine's mission. Talk to the editor in chief or take other steps to make sure you are following the best path.

• Read back issues of the magazine, starting a few years before your arrival, and pay attention to the trends.

• And give yourself time to learn about your magazine. It won't all come at once.

4. Freedom and Responsibility:
The Law and What to Do About It

Congress shall make no law respecting an establishment of religion, or prohibiting the free exercise thereof; or abridging the freedom of speech, or of the press; or the right of the people peaceably to assemble, and to petition the government for a redress of grievances.

The First Amendment of the United States Constitution

While we're thinking about the Big Picture, we should take some time to consider the laws that govern what magazine editors can and cannot do with impunity. The "press" is specifically mentioned in the Constitution, and the protection that flows from the one sentence that makes up the First Amendment gives editors some terrific responsibilities. By understanding at least the basics of communications law, we can go a long way toward keeping our publications—and ourselves—on the right track.

This is not to say, however, that all articles have to be watered down, meek, timid, and cowardly, just because we're worried about the law. "I love you, you love me" is great for purple dinosaurs, but journalism has a mandate to protect society from abuses, to ferret out and expose wrongdoing, and to keep a watchful and critical eye on the government. That responsibility makes journalism a rough business at times; there might be instances in which you have to hurt someone. If a member of Congress is taking bribes from an oil company, it is perfectly valid for you to bring that truth to light—even if it means hurting the legislator. If a corporation is running sweatshops that force workers to put in long hours for low pay, you might decide to blow the whistle—even if it means harming the corporation and its stockholders. If a con artist is fleecing the elderly out of their life savings, you might have to call attention to his actions—even if it means sending the swindler to jail for decades.

The trick is to make sure that you don't hurt people unnecessarily or unintentionally. And it's very important that you understand your legal footing before you take steps that might upset someone.

Basically, the laws that affect magazines fall into two overall categories: libel and invasion of privacy. To be sure, there are other ways in which editors can run afoul of the law, but these two areas represent the bulk of an editor's legal concerns. We'll discuss them in a moment.

But First, This Word...

Talking about the law requires us to understand a few important terms, so let's get those out of the way first. We don't have to worry about bizarre Latin phrases like *habeas corpus*—which, by the way, means "you have the body"—but we do have to understand the legal meaning of some key concepts.

• *Libel.* We'll get to the actual meaning of libel in a moment, but first we should clear up a common confusion. *Libel* refers to the laws that we're about to discuss, which have to do with damaging someone's reputation in print or on the air. *Liable*, which sounds very similar, means "responsible for," as in "My son broke the window, so I'm liable for the damages." It also can mean "obligated to" or "likely to," as in "Now that she's been offered a big raise, she's liable to turn down that other company's offer." These terms are not interchangeable.

• *Sue.* In casual conversation, we use a kind of shorthand that can be confusing when we are trying to be precise about the law. You'll often hear people say, "You could be sued for that!" The fact of the matter is that you can always be sued for anything under the sun. Nothing is preventing people from suing you for breathing their air, looking at them in strange ways, talking too loudly, or occupying an unfair portion of space on this planet—except that such lawsuits would be a waste of their time and money. "Suing someone" merely means that you filed the right paperwork. Obviously frivolous claims (the previous sentence included) will be dismissed early, but in general, the system is designed to let people air their grievances in court. Suing someone is really quite easy.

So when someone says, "You could be sued for that!" what they really mean is that you could be sued *and you stand a good chance of losing*. Nothing in the law is automatic—that's why we have judges and juries—but "You could be sued" generally means that you are heading down a dangerous legal path.

• *Slander.* You'll sometimes hear the word *slander* used when talking about damage to reputation. Slander and libel are not the same thing. *Libel* refers to damage to someone's reputation as a result of a statement that is broadcast or published. In other words, a comment fixed in a medium. *Slander* refers to damage to someone's reputation as a result of a statement that is spoken. So if I stand up in a restaurant and shout, "This chef has leprosy!" I might be sued for slander (especially if the chef is leprosy-free). But if I publish an article in a magazine that says that my neighbor beats his wife, I might be sued for libel (especially if he doesn't).

• *Burden of proof.* If you publish an article that calls your neighbor a drug addict—and she sues you for libel—then the burden of proof might fall to you, especially if the article is not considered to focus on a matter of public concern. In other words, you must be prepared to prove that she *is* a drug addict; she might not have to prove, initially, that she isn't. So she could take you to court, sit back, and let you try to prove to a jury that she really is an addict. If you fail to prove it, you're likely to lose—even if you *know* that your neighbor is mainlining heroin every night. If the burden of proof is yours, you have to make a convincing case.

If you are able to offer a reasonable case that your neighbor is an addict, or if the article is deemed to focus on a matter of public concern, the burden might shift to her—now she might have to refute your claims with proof of her own.

• *Malice.* In common usage, *malice* means "evil" or "nasty." A malicious person does things just to hurt other people. In publications law, *actual malice* has a more precise definition. The main meaning is that you knew something was false, but published it anyway. If you know that a certain candidate for sheriff never touches alcohol, but you publish an article that says he's a drunkard—then you're acting with malice. If you know that a billionaire CEO has given millions of dollars to charity, but you publish an article that says she spurns all requests for contributions—that's malice. If you know that a local banker has been entirely faithful to his wife since the day they met, but you publish an article that says he has three girlfriends and a mistress—it's malice once again.

Generally, we're expected to publish the truth as we know it.

There's a second flavor of malice, which involves reckless disregard for the truth. *Reckless disregard for the truth* means that you had serious doubts about whether something was true or false, but you published it anyway without bothering to check it out. So if I hear a rumor that Jane is embezzling money from her company, and I publish an article that repeats that rumor even though I strongly suspect that it's false—that's reckless disregard. If a candidate for mayor tells me that his opponent is an ex-con and did hard time for carjacking, and I publish an article about it even though I think it's not true—it's reckless disregard again. If my stockbroker advises me to dump my shares of SludgeCo because the CEO is about to be indicted for money laundering, and I ignore my disbelief and run the article anyway—I'm acting with reckless disregard for the truth.

Whether the problem is actual malice or reckless disregard for the truth, we leave ourselves open to trouble if we flirt with it. We are expected to publish the truth as we know it, and we are expected to know the difference between rumor and fact. Journalists have to support their claims.

• *Negligence. Negligence* refers to doing something that a reasonable person would not have done (or not doing something that a reasonable person would have done). If you leave a loaded gun lying around your living room, and someone gets hurt, you probably will be charged with negligence (among other things) on the grounds that reasonable people don't leave loaded guns lying around.

As a magazine editor, you might be considered negligent if you publish a story without bothering to verify it. In other words, you hear a rumor and run it because you are lazy or short staffed, without making sure that the rumor is true.

You also might be considered negligent if you fail to determine whether it was Paul Robinson, Sr., or Paul Robinson, Jr., who robbed a bank, for example, or if you assumed that kidnapper Lucy Kramer of Springfield was a citizen of Illinois when in fact she was a citizen of Massachusetts. (The Lucy Kramer of Springfield, Illinois, will not be amused.) Careless but harmful errors fall into the category of negligence.

Ouch! My Reputation!

So what, exactly, is libel? Generally, libel is injury to reputation. If you publish something—text, photos, or cartoons, for example— that causes someone to experience disgrace or ridicule, you run the risk of losing a lawsuit and having to shell out some serious money.

This law is based on the notion that our reputations are valuable, even in the literal dollars-and-cents meaning. If I have a reputation as a strong and competent manager, I might get a great job. If you publish something that ruins that reputation, I might not get that job. So I'd be out a lot of money (and stability and further enhancement of my reputation and other benefits) just because you decided to trash my good name.

Furthermore, the law figures that our reputations are something that we build or cultivate throughout our lives. My reputation is the result of my actions—good and bad. The Founding Fathers believed that people should be free to build whatever reputations they were capable of creating. It's part of that "life, liberty, and pursuit of happiness" thing. Being a journalist doesn't give us license to tear down the legitimate reputations that people build for themselves.

So while the media are protected to a large extent by the First Amendment, editors aren't free to publish anything that crosses their minds. We have to make sure that we aren't libeling someone, or we risk finding ourselves on the wrong end of a very expensive lawsuit.

My Bad!

The vast majority of libel suits result from ordinary, routine articles, not O. J. Simpson–type coverage. When editors handle "big" stories, they know that their actions will be scrutinized and challenged, and they are careful to avoid any slip-ups. (And if they choose to commit libel in pursuit of a greater good, they do so with their eyes open.)

It's when we're doing a profile about a sweet little old lady and her muffin-tin collection that we sometimes drop our guard, and that's when mistakes often creep in. So smart editors give every article some legal thought, checking for anything that might be libelous.

For eight years, for example, I wrote a syndicated newspaper column called "Finders." It helped people find old friends and missing relatives. People would write to me, Dear Abby–style, and I would publish their letters after I edited them. Because the letters contained personal information, I checked each letter carefully for anything that might upset someone or reveal information that otherwise would have been private. Picture something like this:

> Dear Finders,
> I am looking for my best friend from college, Sheila Hoberman. Sheila and I spent two weeks one summer on a cruise ship, exploring the islands off the coast of Greece with our boyfriends. That trip created some of my fondest memories, and I would love to reminisce with Sheila again.
> Sincerely,
> Dolores Bloomfield

Most "Finders" letters were longer and more detailed than that, but you get the idea. When I would get a letter like that, it would seem just fine on the surface: a woman searching for her former best friend so they can share some nice memories once again.

But wait: this letter tells the world that Sheila spent two weeks on a cruise ship with her boyfriend. What might that revelation do to Sheila's reputation? A lot of people might not care—but she might. Her husband might. Her parents might. How might she feel about that information being published in a newspaper column that has more than a million readers? What if she feels that I have damaged her reputation by publishing this information?

If she feels that her reputation has been damaged, she might sue me for libel. Even if I win the lawsuit, it would cost time and money—and the lawsuit itself could hurt the credibility of my column.

So I was careful to remove statements that might cause someone to believe that I had harmed his or her reputation. In this case, I would publish that Dolores and Sheila went on a two-week cruise around the Greek islands, but the reference to the boyfriends would be dropped.

Another of the small but dangerous blunders that editors can make involves incomplete information. In cases like these, magazines publish information but don't identify the person clearly enough to avoid misunderstanding. In one small Midwestern newspaper, for example, an article was published that identified a person—I'll use the name Jim Smith, just to be safe—who was convicted of molesting children. In the same town was a podiatrist whose name was Jim Smith. Because the newspaper did not identify the molester beyond those two words—Jim Smith—the podiatrist was concerned that people would think he was the villain. He threatened to sue the newspaper for libel, arguing that the newspaper's failure to include the molester's middle name, age, and address allowed people to think that *he* was guilty of molesting children. He pointed out that as a podiatrist, he depended on his reputation to build up a patient base in town, and that the misunderstanding that the newspaper allowed would cause people to leave his practice and find another foot doctor. The error was small—the editor just missed the fact that the identification was incomplete—but the impact to the podiatrist's livelihood could be huge. His lawyer called the editor a few days later.

(In the end, because the editor realized that he was at fault, the newspaper avoided the lawsuit by giving the podiatrist acres of free advertising, in which he could tell the world that the Jim Smith convicted of molestation was someone else. It was an expensive decision, but it was better than being sued—and the newspaper stood a very good chance of losing and being forced to pay an enormous settlement to the podiatrist.)

Complete but incorrect identification also can get you into trouble. Bob Braun does something terrible, for example, but your writer didn't ask about the spelling of his surname and types it as "Brown." When you edit the article, it doesn't occur to you to challenge the spelling of the last name, especially since Brown is the typical spelling. Then Bob Braun goes to prison, and Bob Brown goes to his attorney. Oops.

Libel also can result when sources pursue hidden agendas. A source might tell your writer that two certain people are getting married. That's great—if it's appropriate to the story, in it goes. Then you discover, after the article is in print, that these two people actually hate each other—the "engagement announcement" was some kind of evil joke. The source will be laughing mightily, but you'll be left to deal with the angry phone calls.

At a newspaper where I worked as an editor, we had to give code numbers to the funeral homes so we could be sure that a call about somebody's upcoming funeral was legitimate. Too often, publications receive phony funeral announcements and obituaries as pranks.

Because small things can cause enormous amounts of trouble, good editors check each name, description, fact, and other snippet of information carefully. And they challenge their writers to do the same: Did you check the spelling of that name? Did you look up his address? Did you confirm that it is the son—and not the father—who was convicted? By keeping an eye on the little things, big problems can be kept under control.

En Garde!

For a libel lawsuit to succeed, three things have to happen:

• *Publication.* For libel to result, the comment must be published. The term *published* is shampooed and combed and puffed and glazed enormously in court proceedings, but basically it means that the comment was rendered in such a form that others can read or hear it for some time. The word *others* runs into legalistic coiffery a lot also, but basically it means an audience of at least one person. The degree of the damage often varies with the size of the audience, of course. If I hurl evil lies about someone in a letter to my mother, I have damaged his reputation (in my mother's eyes, at least). But if I print those lies in a magazine with 150,000 loyal readers, the damage may well be greater. Either way, publication has happened—but the scope of the damage might be different.

The still-settling area of online journalism law is a prime area for debates about the meaning of the word *publish*. If I publish something in my magazine, it's pretty obvious: we wrote it once and then made 100,000 copies for distribution around the country. But what if I publish something in an online magazine? In that case, I'm not making any copies at all. I post the article to the Web, and then 100,000 people take a look at it. How is that different from my writing a letter to my mother—and then she passes it around to 100,000 close friends?

One of the advantages of print journalism is that it has been around for hundreds of years, so a lot of the kinks have been worked out. Online journalism is still so new that many of the terms and definitions haven't been settled yet.

• *Identification.* The person whose reputation you sully must be identifiable. If I publish an article that says that "one guy at Woodstock had a big butterfly tattooed on his butt," the guy in question won't win a libel suit against me. I haven't told people who he is, so his reputation can't be damaged by the article. As long as he keeps his pants on, the tattoo will be his little secret.

But if the article names him—"At Woodstock, Frank Franconio mooned the cops during the Jimi Hendrix set and revealed a giant butterfly tattooed on his butt"—the first requirement has been met. I identified him to the world. It won't matter to a jury, most likely, that there are fifty-seven Frank Franconios in the United States. In fact, the article could be seen as damaging the reputation of all of them, since everyone who knows a Frank Franconio will assume that he's the one with the butterfly on his backside.

It's important to note that merely eliminating a person's name is not enough to protect us from a charge of libel. If an article indicates who the person is, with some specificity, then he has been officially identified even without a name. Referring to the CEO of Boeing, for example, is a clear identification, even though he hasn't been named. Descriptions, jobs, locations, and other factors can be used to make a solid identification in the absence of a name. As long as people can figure out whom I am talking about, the identification has been made—name or not.

• *Defamation.* Even if a person has been clearly identified, libel results only when the person has actually been damaged. Miffing someone, hurting his feelings, offending her, upsetting him, ticking her off—all these are considered part of sharing the planet with other people. We're all expected, by the law, to have a relatively thick skin. (This is one of the reasons that the *Saturday Night Live* gang can make fun of people. Up to a certain point, we're just supposed to laugh along with it.)

So publishing something that wounds someone's sensibilities isn't necessarily libel. The person has to suffer actual damage to his repu-· tation. Calling someone "chubby" in an article might upset him, but has his reputation actually been harmed? Do people trust him less? Has he become the butt of jokes around town? Do people think less of him? That would be a difficult case to make. If he really is chubby, then people already knew that about him—and the article didn't reveal any secrets. If he isn't chubby, then readers will dismiss the article as clueless.

But if I print that someone is a drug addict, that's more serious. People might think less of her. They might not trust her as much. Her reputation might be seriously damaged—and possibly without hope of repair.

Sometimes, the damage to reputation will carry a price tag, which makes the lawsuit even more dangerous. I print that Helen Bell is a Communist—and she loses her job. Or I print that Clarence Taylor beats his grandmother—and his wife leaves him and sues for alimony. In cases like these, the plaintiff (the person who feels wronged) might be able to convince a jury that my article resulted in damage to her reputation and cost her a lot of money, which could be very damaging and expensive to me and my publication.

Other times, the damage is less specific, but it might still be assumed to be there. If I can show that *Abuse Professors Weekly* has harmed my reputation, I might receive compensation even if I can't point to a specific instance in which my wallet was hurt by the action. If the article is a matter of public concern, though, I'll have to show some actual injury to get any money.

In short, cases that involve matters of public concern—generally meaning actual news coverage as opposed to entertainment pieces, human-interest features, and the like—require the injured party to demonstrate several things: publication, identification, defamation, actual malice or negligence (depending on the laws in question), actual injury, and falsity. Then the journalist is given a chance to defend herself, citing truth, fair comment, qualified privilege, or any of several other possible defenses.

In cases that do not involve matters of public concern—my column about finding people, for example—the wounded party would have to show publication, identification, and defamation. Then it's up to me to defend myself.

These various facets of libel law are important for editors. Avoiding any of the pitfalls can keep us out of trouble. Making sure the person can't be identified, for example, can keep the lawyers at bay. Taking care not to damage a person's reputation can keep you out of court as well. And, of course, choosing not to publish will always keep you safe—but the mandates of your job might make that step inadvisable.

D-Fence

If you find yourself on the wrong end of a libel lawsuit, you still can come out on top. There are several things you can do to defend yourself. These defenses are built into our legal system to allow publishers and broadcasters to pursue legitimate stories vigorously, without being handcuffed by massive fines every time they do. Nearly all editors know these defenses, because it's only by knowing them that they can function effectively.

• *The truth.* There's an old saying in publishing that "the truth is the ultimate defense." That's not 100 percent accurate, but it's pretty close. If you can prove that what you published is true, you're off the hook. The theory is that if your statements are true, the person damaged his own reputation through his own actions; you're just the messenger.

So if you publish an article that calls your neighbor a drug addict, you might damage her reputation. She might find it harder to get a job. She might find it harder to get a mortgage. But if she really is a drug addict, she really harmed herself. The article isn't at fault.

Two warnings:

1. As with any legal case, the reality matters less than the jury's *perception* of reality. In other words, simply being true isn't enough. The statement has to be *provably true* to serve as a defense against a libel charge.

2. It is very difficult to prove a negative. Proving a positive statement can be pretty simple: a photo of your neighbor

with a needle in her arm will go a long way toward convincing a jury that your claim is valid.

But let's say that someone runs for mayor as a member of the Bull Moose Party. She is nominated by the party, and she launches her campaign for the position. You publish an article that argues that she is, in fact, not a member of the Bull Moose Party. You bask in the glow of a successful and significant bit of investigative journalism.

But then she sues you for libel, alleging that you damaged her reputation and made it nearly impossible for her to be elected mayor. The burden of proof, remember, is yours. How are you going to prove that she *isn't* a member of the Bull Moose Party?

You could produce a list of all the members of the Bull Moose Party and show that her name isn't there. But that won't slow her down. "Secretarial oversight," the candidate says. "They made a mistake."

You could put the chairman of the party on the stand and have him testify that she is not a member of the party. "How would you know?" the candidate replies. "You sleep through all the meetings."

And so it goes. Proving a negative can be extremely difficult, making the burden of proof burdensome indeed.

• *Privilege.* Another way to defend yourself against a libel suit is to demonstrate that you acted with privilege. In this case, *privilege* means that you are protected from a libel suit because you met certain specific criteria.

There are two kinds of privilege: absolute and qualified.

Absolute. Some people—legislators, judges, participants in a court proceeding, and so on—are free to communicate in their official capacities without fear of libel. Even if their comments are "published" in a transcript or another record, they're protected. The rationale, of course, is that people must be free to speak openly and plainly in certain legal and official circumstances. So a senator can stand up on the floor of the Senate and say, "I support this bill opposing the mistreatment of animals because my brother-in-law mistreats animals—and we need tools to make these people stop!" The brother-in-law won't get very far in a libel lawsuit against the senator because the senator was making a statement in her official capacity in a public proceeding.

Absolute privilege covers officials for the most part. It doesn't do much for journalists, but they benefit from qualified privilege.

Qualified. The term *qualified* means that the protection can be lost if you don't do everything the right way. In other words, you're protected—but you have to work to maintain that protection.

To maintain this qualified protection, you have to ask certain key questions:

1. Does the information come from a privileged source? Those senators and judges are free to speak their minds in the legislature and in court, and magazines are free to publish the things that they say. That nasty brother-in-law probably won't win a libel suit against you if you quote the senator accurately.

2. Is the report fair and accurate? If you misquote the senator, you could find that your privilege evaporates in a hurry. But if you quote a privileged source accurately, you should be protected. The thinking is that if a judge says something in the courtroom, the public has a reasonable desire to know what he said—and so journalists have a reasonable mandate to report it.

If the material you publish comes from a privileged source and is accurate and fair, you should be protected from charges of libel under qualified privilege—even if the statement turns out to be false.

Evil, or Clumsy?

Different kinds of people are granted different levels of protection under the law. In other words, you can publish comments about some kinds of people with a fair degree of freedom, but you have to treat others more carefully.

• *Public officials.* Public officials are literally elected to public office (mayors, senators, presidents) or appointed to public office (cabinet members, Supreme Court justices).

To win a libel case, public officials have to prove actual malice. Remember, that means that they have to convince a jury that you knew the story was false and published it anyway or that you acted with reckless disregard for the truth.

As you might imagine, that's a tall order. It is very difficult to prove what someone knew. But it is possible; witnesses who heard you say something, memos you wrote to other editors, and other kinds of evidence might prove that you knew that the article was false. That's the kind of material that public officials have to present to prove your mind-set—and to win the case.

The thinking here, of course, is that people who want to hold such a powerful and visible position as mayor or Supreme Court justice have to tolerate journalists and others printing negative things about them. Furthermore, people should be relatively free to discuss public officials—in person and in print—without worrying about a lawsuit. That kind of discussion is essential in a democracy. There's a fine line between insult and damage to reputation, and the law errs on the side of the media in these cases. Editors have the greatest freedom to publish material about public officials. (In chapter 5, however, we'll talk about ethics.)

• *Public figures.* Public figures are "household names" who don't hold public office but who deliberately "thrust themselves into the spotlight" in other ways. Movie stars, the leaders of local or national organizations, corporate CEOs, television personalities, and other people who call attention to themselves are public figures. Even some prominent magazine editors can be considered public figures.

The same sort of thinking that applies to public officials pertains to public figures. They chose to take center stage, and so they have to put up with a fair bit of backlash. To win a libel case, they, too, must prove malice.

• *Private individuals.* Private individuals occupy the rest of the world—everyone who isn't a public official or a public figure is a private individual. This category is for you and me.

The law figures that because we aren't thrusting ourselves into the spotlight, we have the right to be protected from the media. Magazines can't publish things about us unless they are darned sure those things are true.

So in most states, private individuals don't have to prove malice, which is very difficult. Instead, they have to prove only that a magazine editor acted negligently, doing something that a reasonable person would not have done.

This is not true in all states, however, so it pays to know your local laws.

With all these categories, there are shades of severity. The head of the sewer commission in your town is technically a public official, but he isn't as public as the president or even the mayor. A jury is going to want to offer a bit more protection to the poor sewer guy than it would to a Supreme Court justice.

Similarly, the CEO of General Motors probably is a public figure, but the CEO of Busy Bee Housecleaners likely would be regarded as a bit more private. As in all facets of the law, nothing is rigid.

With the offense and the defense lined up, the game is played. They accuse. You defend, using as many of the arguments just outlined as possible. The side with the stronger case (usually) wins in court.

But, of course, the message is deeper than that. As mentioned earlier, lawsuits are expensive; they take time, require effort, and cost money. Smart editors pay close attention to the material they publish, so they are surprised by lawsuits as infrequently as possible— and so they're prepared for the ones they can anticipate.

Eeek!

Other laws also are based on the idea that ordinary people should be allowed to go about their lives without unwanted intrusions from the media. If I want to sit in my own living room, eat potato chips, drink cherry cola, and watch some cheap and silly game show on television, that's no one's business but my own.

If the media were to intrude on my private life and print text or photos that shattered the privacy to which I am entitled, they could be guilty of *invasion of privacy.*

It's the laws concerned with invasion of privacy that let us putter along without worrying about journalists embarrassing us. If we are in some place where privacy can reasonably be expected, then we are supposed to be left alone.

But what if I'm outside, cutting the grass or working in the garden or sitting on the porch? Do I have any expectation of privacy then? I am, after all, out where passersby can see me easily.

That depends on what I'm doing. If I'm just digging in my potato patch, the media really should leave me alone. A famous case some time ago involved a seriously obese woman who was sitting on her porch. The afternoon was unbearably hot, and this woman—who obviously lacked air-conditioning in her house—was trying to stay as cool as possible by sitting on a rocking chair, on her porch, wearing a thin cotton dress.

A newspaper photographer had been given an assignment: show, in a single photo, how hot the day was. He drove down the street, spied the woman, and pulled over. He rolled down his car window—he had air-conditioning—and took the picture without getting out of the car. He drove off, and the photo ran in the next edition of the paper.

The woman sued for invasion of privacy. She argued that she had a right to sit on her porch and sweat without making the front page of the newspaper for the accomplishment. She was unaware that the photographer had taken the picture, and she was embarrassed at the thought that the entire town was laughing at her size, her shoddy dress, and her sweat.

The photographer argued that he had been on public property—the street—when he took the picture and that anyone driving or walking by would have seen the same thing.

The woman won the case. The judge decided that her right to privacy protected her from being held up for ridicule by the local newspaper. Sure, anyone passing by would have seen the same image, but there's a big difference between a few pedestrians or passing cars and the entire circulation of the newspaper. Furthermore, newspaper photos carry connotations that can add to the insult.

The key to the case was the lack of newsworthiness. If you are sitting on your porch and your house catches on fire, the local photographers have the right to snap that picture and publish it. House fires are newsworthy. People sweating on porches are not.

What this means to us is that if our writers or photographers bring us material that reveals information (or images) about someone that she would rather keep private, we had better be able to argue that the material is an essential part of a newsworthy story. Otherwise, we are going to find that exposing that material to the world constitutes invasion of privacy.

Of course, the definition of the word *privacy* changes as we go up the food chain. If I'm outside cutting my grass while wearing a goofy-looking T-shirt, the media really should leave me alone. I'm allowed to look silly if I want to. But if the starting quarterback for an NFL team is doing the same thing—and a photo of him runs on the cover of *Goofy Quarterbacks Quarterly*—then most courts, I suspect, would chalk it up to the price of celebrity and not find the publication guilty of invasion of privacy.

Especially potent in this thinking is the willingness and vigor with which someone thrusts himself into the public spotlight. If a person passes out press releases, speaks at press conferences, and pickets city hall, he probably is going to be considered more of a public figure than the poor person who happened to be involved in a car accident.

Another important consideration: to avoid invading someone's privacy illegally, you have to stick to the newsworthy topic. If the woman who was sweating on her porch had been involved in a public effort to promote diversity in the schools, that prominence doesn't give the media the right to dig through her garbage and report on how many double-meat pizza boxes they find there. Journalists could gather information about her educational background, the schools her children attend, and other relevant material, but because she thrust herself into the spotlight doesn't give the media access to every facet of her life.

The Other Things that Can Get You

Libel and invasion of privacy aren't the only legal missteps that journalists can make. They're big, and they get the most attention, but they aren't the only ones. There are several other laws that editors should watch.

• *Trespass.* Being journalists doesn't give us the right to trespass on other people's property. Even if I think that my congresswoman is taking bribes from the Mob, I don't get to sneak into her yard at night and listen through her windows.

Generally, the law says that we are allowed to go anywhere the public is allowed to go. So if I hear something in the grocery store and use it in an article, that's fine—anyone is allowed to be in the grocery store. If I ride in an elevator with someone and learn some bit of news that I want to use in an article, that's fine. Even if I'm walking down the street and I see something through a window, that's fair game. As long as I was standing on public property, I'm all right. (This is true as far as trespass laws are concerned. Don't forget that you could still get in trouble under the invasion of privacy laws.)

I was doing some research once into an illegal dog-fighting operation. I knew that the supposed ringleader had a lot of dogs in his backyard, but I couldn't see them. He had a high wooden fence that blocked all view.

But then I noticed that a two-story hotel occupied a nearby lot. I entered the hotel and found a second-story hallway window that allowed me to look down into this guy's yard. There I saw dozens of emaciated, scarred dogs—and I called the authorities. (I also wrote up my research.) I was not in danger of trespass accusations because I got a look into the yard from a vantage point that was open to the public.

• *Harassment.* In these days of cheap and offensive "gotcha" journalism, it seems that harassing people is just part of the job description for journalists. I've seen reporters chase people down hallways, block possible informants' cars from leaving parking lots, and otherwise badger potential sources or subjects—all the while with cameras clicking and tape recorders humming.

This approach, of course, is both obnoxious and worthless. It is aimed more at a feeble attempt to impress readers and viewers— "Look at me! Aren't I a tough journalist!"—than at a serious effort to gather important information.

It also can be illegal. People have the right to move about freely, eat in restaurants, drive through parking lots, and go about their everyday lives without being accosted by journalists every step of the way.

But that doesn't mean that we have to be overly timid, either. There's nothing wrong with approaching someone who might have useful information and asking her a few questions. She might threaten to sue for harassment, but she won't get very far if we're just doing our jobs.

A few things to remember, however:

1. You have to be working on a legitimate story. You can't ask this person a thousand questions just to upset her.

2. You have to choose the time and place well. Launching into a tape-recorded interview with someone just when her daughter is saying "I do" at the altar might well be regarded as harassment. We can be persistent and even aggressive, but we can't destroy people's lives unnecessarily.

3. You have to know when to stop. If you've approached someone three times for a quote, and each time he told you to leave him alone, two things should come to mind. First, you aren't going to get the quote. Second, you could be successfully sued for harassment if you keep it up.

Sword and Shield

Generally speaking, the law protects journalists more than it restricts them. We have a constitutional right to freedom of the press, meaning that Congress is prohibited from passing laws that impinge on that freedom. (Granted, Congress has passed a bundle of laws that do restrict that freedom, but for the most part journalists have the right to do their jobs.) We have shield laws that allow us to go about our business without looking over our shoulders all the time. And we operate under an overarching attitude that a free press is not only healthy but essential for the fair and open operation of a democratic society.

But there are laws that magazine editors have to understand and uphold—or risk being involved in devastating lawsuits that can mean the end of their careers and the bankruptcy of their publications. These laws are relatively fair, and they aren't hard to follow. They exist to protect people from overzealous or unscrupulous journalists who are after cheap fame, a tough-guy reputation, or the pursuit of a personal vendetta—rather than the pursuit of important journalism that illuminates facets of society and promotes debate and discussion.

As long as our skills are sound, our conduct is professional, and our aims are true, we should have little trouble with the law.

5. Does Write Make Right?
The Ethics of Editing

I don't think ethics, as such, is on the mind of editors. They are too busy trying to get the magazine out. But it comes up every minute of the day.

Victor Navasky, publisher and editorial director, *The Nation*

Compared with the law, morality is far less clear, far more subjective, and far more important. It's relatively easy to tell the difference between legal and illegal, but it's far harder to tell the difference between right and wrong.

In *Absence of Malice*, an excellent movie about a newspaper reporter, an editor observes that he knows how to tell the truth and he knows how not to hurt people—but he doesn't know how to do both at the same time. He's right: when you do something as important and as public as journalism, people get hurt. Careers can be ruined. Marriages can be destroyed. People can be embarrassed, humiliated, or even driven to desperate acts—all by the words published on a printed page. The trick for editors is to pay enough attention and anticipate reactions well enough to avoid hurting anyone unintentionally.

Basically, ethics boils down to systems of tensions. If I'm forced to choose between helping Fred and helping Ethel, there is a tension in that decision. Which one should I choose? How should I decide?

In the absence of tension, decisions are easy. If I have to choose between helping Fred and *hurting* Ethel, tension doesn't enter into the picture. I choose to help Fred, and I sleep well at night.

Similarly, if I have to choose between publishing an article that will hurt Fred and not publishing the article at all, I'll choose to skip the article and keep Fred happy and healthy (unless Fred is doing something that should be exposed). No problem there.

But decisions are rarely that easy. Often, we have to choose between two things that are both wholesome or between two things that are both harmful—with no way out of the either/or dilemma.

Sometimes, decisions boil down to a "hurt–hurt" choice. At one newspaper where I worked, for example, the editors faced a thorny decision. A beloved minister in town had just been charged with molesting children. He came to the paper, admitted to the crimes, and told us that he was going to plead guilty and serve his sentence. He only asked that we not write about it, to spare his family the humiliation and grief.

That's a classic journalistic dilemma. If we chose to publish the article, we would hurt this minister and his family. But if we chose to drop the article, we would hurt our readers and the community, by not giving them important information about a serious problem. What if others had been molested by this man? What service would we be doing for our readers if we let this crime go unreported? And what about all the people whose crimes we did report? Why should they appear in the paper if this man's crimes were kept quiet?

It was a difficult decision, because this minister was so admired in town. But it was a clear decision. Our duty was to our readers and our community. We published the article.

Things can get even thornier than that. Our instinct tells us to opt for the path of lesser injury, but even that isn't as straightforward as it sounds. What if Rosencrantz is a felon who will be hurt a *lot* if I publish the article, but Guildenstern is a kind and generous pillar of the community who will be hurt a *little* if I don't publish? In other words, what if I face this choice:

- Hurt the bad guy a lot, or
- Hurt the good guy a little.

Choosing the option that causes less pain means that I should hurt the good guy a little. But I don't want to hurt good people. So maybe I should choose to hurt the bad guy a lot. But is that reasonable? And who am I to make these decisions?

It does get complicated.

Before we look at some paths through that maze, it makes sense to consider why we care in the first place. What difference does it make if people get hurt? Why should we worry about people's feelings? Who cares if someone loses a job or a spouse or a life?

There are practical answers to those questions, and there are human answers to those questions.

On the human side, we care because we share the world with thinking, feeling, spiritual beings who don't deserve to be treated badly. Most people have a vision of the kind of world they want to live in, and it usually has something to do with people getting along reasonably well. The stereotype of the hard-nosed editor aside, most magazine editors I know would feel awful if they hurt an innocent person. It violates our sense of justice and fair play.

On the practical side, we care because it's in our best interest to do so. If our readers get the sense that we're trampling people unnecessarily, they'll come to the conclusion that we are mean-spirited, nasty people. And who wants to subscribe to a magazine put out by despicable thugs? Our subscription base would dwindle down to the handful of surly louts who get a kick out of undeserved abuse, and they probably don't represent a population large enough to keep our magazine afloat.

Meanwhile, of course, advertisers would flee as well. Few companies want to advertise their products in a magazine that generates anguish and anger.

So we'd lose the respect and attention of our readers, and we'd lose our advertising base. In exchange, we'd be left with the unpleasant feeling that we've become the kind of people we ordinarily would detest.

Not worth it.

So for human and practical reasons, it makes sense for us to take steps to ensure that our magazine does not hurt people unnecessarily. And that means taking a good look at ethics.

Gray Matter

Technically, *ethics* means "the study of right and wrong." More loosely, it refers to the rightness or wrongness of a particular action or decision—for example, the ethics of publishing pornography.

In the world of magazine editing, ethics comes into play mainly at two times: at the time the information or material is gathered, and at the time it is published. We'll start with the first.

We've all seen or heard about the overaggressive television reporter, zooming up to the site of a train wreck and racing up to dazed people who have lost loved ones and a lot of blood. "How do you feel right now?" the reporter asks, sticking a camera and microphone in a poor victim's face.

That sort of thing really does happen, although perhaps not as often as people think. Magazine writers—and the editors who send them on assignments—have to think carefully about how to get the necessary information without stepping on people's toes (literally or figuratively) in unfair or unnecessary ways. So the tension is between (1) getting the information and (2) being nice to people. If we swing too far in the nice direction, we tend to publish very little—and the material we do publish tends to be bland and uninteresting. If we swing too far in the "get the information at all costs" direction, we tend to upset readers and lose advertisers. Somehow, we have to figure out how to balance those two poles.

There are several ways of thinking about the ethics of information gathering. A lot of people, for example, fall back on the Golden Rule: Do unto others as you would have them do unto you. In other words, treat people the way you would like to be treated. If you would be hurt or offended by a reporter's intrusion, the odds are good that other people would be, too—and perhaps backing off is the right idea. Part of the magic of magazine work is that you can always get most of the information later.

But the Golden Rule brings another tension with it: What if being nice to people means that I don't get some important stories? The tension then is between (1) being nice to people and (2) advancing my career. Aggression is often rewarded in journalism, and the people who get the story at any cost are likely to be seen as tough and successful journalists.

As happens often, decisions like these boil down to your own moral compass—and the amount of anguish you can tolerate. It's not the sort of thing that people can teach you.

On the publish-or-not side of ethical editing, things actually get trickier. Once you have information or images in your hands, the decision to publish can be quite difficult. For example, scores of editors faced tough choices after the terrorist attacks of September 11, 2001. A lot of pictures were available that showed the horror of the attacks, and editors had to figure out which images were necessary to convey that horror and which went too far. How can we find a way to make such decisions? And how can we find a way to make the smaller, but still important, judgments that pull us in multiple directions every day?

Fortunately, there are some generally accepted ways of considering these dilemmas that can help you figure out what to do. These approaches won't get anyone off your back, you understand—editors have to deal with critics all the time, and being able to point to a philosophical model doesn't keep people from screaming into the phone at you—but they can help you choose a path and stick to it.

So let's say that you're faced with a difficult ethical decision. One of your writers has uncovered evidence that Glowing Products, a major manufacturer of cosmetics, has been testing its products on animals, even though the company insists in all its advertising that it does not. The company president calls you, assuring you that the firm is changing its testing procedures and will not use animals in any of its future testing. She asks you not to run the article.

Dilemma. You know that an article about the testing could do serious damage to Glowing Products—possibly even putting the company out of business. It seems a shame to publish an exposé that could cost all those people their jobs, especially when the president has promised that the testing will stop. And if Glowing Products really does stop testing its cosmetics on animals, it could function as an industry leader and convince other companies to do the same. Inflicting damage on the firm by publishing the article might even persuade other companies to abandon the humane treatment of animals, noting that Glowing Products was slammed just as it was improving its procedures. "So what's the use?" they might ask.

But...If you kill the article, aren't you letting Glowing Products off the hook? The company lied to its customers, and your readers would want to know that. And why should you trust the president? Once you scuttle the article, how will you know that Glowing Products has really stopped testing its cosmetics on animals? And don't your readers count on you for full, fair, and accurate information? What would they think if they learned that you had this information and didn't publish it? Readers who use Glowing Products shampoos and moisturizers might be furious to find out that they have been supporting a company that tests its products on animals—and that you could have brought that to light.

This is just the kind of ethical bind that editors face regularly. Working through some thinking in advance can help enormously when the real thing hits.

Editors (and others) think about such situations in a number of ways.

• *The Golden Rule again.* If you were the president of Glowing Products, how would you feel about this article? Would you consider it fair and reasonable, or would you think it was a vicious attack on an otherwise decent corporation? What if you were a typical reader? How would you feel then?

The Golden Rule works rather well, but it isn't perfect. No two people think exactly alike, so you can't be sure that the person you're dealing with sees things the same way you do. I'm often astonished at people's reactions. For example, when someone dies, I tend to assume that his widow, parents, or friends would like to be left alone for a while. But often, relatives and friends are pleased to talk to writers because they want the deceased to be remembered. They want to know that the person's life mattered. Attention from the media is far better, in some people's eyes, than uncaring silence.

So while I am a big fan of the Golden Rule, it isn't absolute.

• *The Golden Mean.* The famous Greek philosopher Aristotle, who basically was the first person to think of everything in the entire planet, argued that extremes are bad. His rule for ethical decision making focused on the middle ground, the mean between the extremes. The middle ground, he argued, is the best, the safest, the most reasonable choice.

Take our Glowing Products example. One extreme might be to make the exposé your cover story, complete with an unflattering picture of the company president looking shocked and evil. Add a saucy cover blurb:

Bunny Killer!

And a zinger of an explanation:

**Thought your Glowing Products moisturizer was kind to animals?
Think again!**

And drive it home with an inset photo of a sweet, innocent-looking
rabbit with the words

Oil of Betray!

splashed across the image in blood-red letters.

That would do a good job of representing one extreme. You've
done your best to discredit the company, infuriate its customers, and
incite the anger of animal-rights activists everywhere. You even
threw in sarcasm and a snotty tone for good measure.

The other extreme is to publish an upbeat, positive article about
Glowing Products and the steps the company is taking to be a good
global neighbor. Ignore the evidence that your writer has gathered,
and mislead your readers into thinking that Glowing Products is
every bit as honorable as its own public relations would have customers believe.

Aristotle would tell us that both extremes are bad and that the
best approach lies directly between them. Publishing nothing
doesn't feel like the midpoint—it seems closer to the Glowing Products side—so he would want us to publish something. But nasty photos and biting comments on the cover is the other extreme, so we
can't go that far. One possible midpoint is to publish a balanced,
well-documented article that lays out all the facts, including the
president's promise to change the company's ways, and let readers
think things through for themselves.

The Golden Mean is a pretty good guide, but, of course, it isn't
perfect either. The midpoint, for example, depends entirely on the
extremes that you choose. If you decide that the scathing cover represents one extreme and that publishing nothing represents the
other, you might conclude that publishing a fairly harsh article—but
keeping the nasty pictures off the cover—might be a good midpoint.

• *A multipart approach.* Philosopher Sissela Bok offers a multipart
strategy for evaluating ethical dilemmas. First, she invites us to
consider our feelings—a departure from the more objective approaches. What *feels* right? What strikes us as wrong? Which option will let us sleep at night, knowing that we did our best?

She also suggests that we consult experts in the field. Talk to lawyers, counselors, priests, journalists—anyone who can provide some expertise on the matter. In short, she instructs us to become aware of all the possible perspectives and ramifications of the decision.

And she wants us to talk to the very people involved in the decision. Talk to the Glowing Products president. Talk to readers. Talk to the advertising department. Talk to animal-rights activists. Ideally, get them all in the same room together and have a big, open discussion on the issue.

After going through these steps, you probably will develop a sense of what ought to be done. Not everyone will be happy with your call—this process doesn't absolve us of editorial responsibility—but you can at least argue that you made the most informed, thoughtful decision possible.

• *The categorical imperative.* The categorical imperative comes to us from the famous German philosopher Immanuel Kant. Unlike Bok, Kant believed in absolutes. The *categorical* part of his categorical imperative means "absolute" or "total," just like when politicians *categorically* deny the latest allegations slung against them.

Imperative carries further absolutes. *Imperative* means "compelling without exception," like an imperative sentence: "*Go!*" There's not much room for discussion.

So Kant wanted a way of looking at ethical dilemmas that would not allow for any wiggle room. He wanted a black-and-white, totalizing formula that would guide us in any circumstance.

The categorical imperative works like this. You choose one of the options before you—say, publishing the nasty exposé as your cover story—and then assume that everyone is free to make that choice under similar circumstances. In other words, if it's acceptable for you to publish a nasty exposé on the cover in this case, then it's acceptable for everyone to publish nasty exposés on magazine covers whenever they run across some wrongdoing.

Then you have to ask yourself a key question: Would this lead to an absurd situation? By *absurd*, Kant did not mean "weird," "unpalatable," "disgusting," or "difficult." The bizarre and the appalling were fine by him—they did not suggest that something shouldn't be done, because such perspectives are so subjective. By *absurd*, he meant "logically self-contradictory."

Here's an example. Let's say that your best friend spends $100 and gets the ugliest haircut imaginable. She looks like a poodle that had a bad run-in with a greasy power sander. She walks into the room, beams a great big smile at you, and asks, "What do you think of my great new 'do?"

You have two options. You could tell her the truth, hurting her feelings and possibly damaging your friendship. Or you could lie and tell her that it's a bold and daring new look that makes her seem thin and attractive. Which do you do?

Time for the categorical imperative. If you lie, you are in essence saying that it's all right for people to lie in an effort to preserve friendship. But what happens if everyone goes around lying to their friends? It wouldn't be long before we all figured out that we couldn't count on our friends for honest evaluations. So the world would be filled with people lying to their friends, and the friends wouldn't believe a word of it. That leads to a logically self-contradictory spiral: What is the point—or even the meaning—of lying if no one is going to believe us anyway? We have an absurd situation.

Now try the flip side. If you tell your friend the truth, you're saying that everyone should feel free to be honest with their friends. People would discover that honest friends can help them maintain a desirable image by pointing out disasters and embarrassments. Some friendships might crumble in the face of the honesty, but the true friendships would in fact become stronger. Nothing absurd here.

So Kant would say that lying is wrong. Lying, if everyone does it, leads to an absurd situation, which is unacceptable. So he thinks that you should stiffen your spine, brace yourself, and tell your friend—as kindly and gently as you possibly can—that she looks like a sewer rat that swam through some Nair.

In the Glowing Products example, Kant would argue that helping the company cover up its animal-abusing past is wrong. When your readers discover that you can't be trusted to deliver truthful reporting, they'll stop believing your articles at all. And if they don't believe your articles, it doesn't matter what you say about Glowing Products or any other company. That's an absurd situation. So Kant would say that honesty is mandatory.

The categorical imperative has the advantage of a relatively high degree of objectivity, but it is a bit rigid. If you follow this approach, and it says that a particular course of action is wrong, you're supposed to accept that directive no matter how you feel. That's why Bok and others worked personal feelings into their equations. Rigidity can sometimes cause problems.

• *The greatest good.* Another approach to ethical decision making also relies on something like an objective formula. This approach, called utilitarianism, asks one simple question: Which solution would bring about the greatest good for the greatest number of people?

This approach tries to boil ethics down to a mathematical process. Simply by assigning "Pleasure Points" and "Pain Points" (my terms), we should be able to do the math and come up with the optimal solution.

Following the Glowing Products example: ignoring the evidence and printing nothing would bring about some good for Glowing Products and its employees. They would be able to continue doing business, earning their paychecks and receiving benefits. So let's give each of the, say, 500 Glowing Products employees 5 "Pleasure Points," for a total of 2,500 points to the good.

But the customers of Glowing Products, who have been attracted to the company's lipstick and eye shadow at least in part because of the company's claim that it does not test products on animals, would be horrified if they ever learned that they had been duped. They would be sickened at the thought that for years they were contributing to the mistreatment of animals—and that you could have prevented it. So let's give each of the 500,000 customers 3 "Pain Points," for a total of 1.5 million points to the bad.

Subtracting the 2,500 good points from the 1.5 million bad points gives us a grand total of 1,497,500 points to the bad—not exactly "the greatest good for the greatest number of people."

Now let's look at the situation if you publish the article. The company goes out of business, and the 500 Glowing Products employees are now out of work. Let's give them 20 "Pain Points" apiece, for a total of 10,000 points to the bad.

But the 500,000 customers are pleased to learn that the company's secret is out and that such evildoers are no longer in business. Each gets 1 "Pleasure Point." (It would have been more, but they are still horrified that they had been duped.) So we have 500,000 points to the good.

The 500,000 good points minus the 10,000 bad points leaves us with 490,000 points to the good. Obviously, this is the better of the two choices.

Like the others, this model is valuable but not perfect. For example, we have to make up the number and value of the "Pleasure Points" and the "Pain Points" in each case; other people might assign far different amounts. The model is dangerously subjective, despite its attempt to rely on cold, hard math.

And, of course, utilitarianism heavily favors large majorities. Under this approach, gladiator battles are a good idea. A lot of pain for one person is offset by a little bit of pleasure for a whole bunch of (very sick) people.

Interestingly, however, this is the approach that most influences our judicial system. If we catch someone who has been robbing pedestrians, what should we do with him? If we throw him in jail, that will cause him a lot of pain. But it will bring relief and a greater sense of safety to everyone else in town. All those "Pleasure Points" outweigh the perp's "Pain Points," so it's off to the slammer for him. This approach allows us to justify causing pain to someone who has been disrupting the social fabric of the community.

• *The good of the group.* Communitarianism is very similar to utilitarianism, but it has one major difference. In communitarianism, the good of the group outweighs the good of the individual. That sounds a lot like the utilitarian model, but they aren't the same.

Under utilitarianism, each person's pleasure or pain is weighed equally, regardless of who he or she is. The president's pain is the same as the street sweeper's pain. The queen's pleasure is no different from the bank robber's pleasure.

Under communitarianism, who you are *does* matter. If you are a member of the community in question, your situation counts for a lot. If you are not a member of the community, your situation matters far less.

For example, let's say that the United States is feeling nervous about some faraway regime that isn't playing ball by our rules. Under utilitarianism, we might refrain from a military solution, on the theory that a whole lot of misery and death for Them would not be off-set by a small increase in security for Us.

But under communitarianism, the good of the group is para-mount. So if we define the "group" as the United States, then Bombs Away! Whatever we can do to help our own group is good, even if it means harming the other group.

There are probably as many systems for ethical decision making as there are philosophers in the history of the world. Which one should you choose and use? That is, of course, up to you. Find a way of thinking about ethical dilemmas that feels comfortable to you, and use it as needed. Be prepared for people to disagree with your judg-ments anyway, of course. People will even disagree with the ap-proach you have chosen to help you solve the dilemmas. But consis-tency will help your position to some degree—as will patience, clear communication, and the foresight to work out some of these con-cerns in advance.

Situations

It is impossible to anticipate all the challenging situations that mag-azine editors are likely to face during the course of their careers, but a few dilemmas do seem to crop up on a recurring basis. Some of them are easy. It is never acceptable, for example, to deliberately dis-tort information or someone's position on an issue. It's all right to use technical means to enhance the clarity of a photo, but it is never all right to use technology to make a photo misleading or inaccurate. Never publish other people's material—ideas, quotes, text—without proper credit. Avoid racial and other slurs, as well as stereotypes that paint a race, a sex, a religion, or another characteristic with broad and inaccurate brush strokes. Never put someone unnecessarily at risk just for the sake of getting a story. Never allow your own bias to diminish the fairness of your story.

But, of course, most of the dilemmas that editors face involve tan-gled, complicated situations that defy simple answers. That's why we still face them. While a lot of thought has gone into these challenges, few hard-and-fast rules have emerged. In general, editors tend to err on the side of being nice human beings—but that tendency is by no means universal.

There are certain things that would never occur for you to do because they are not ethical. You don't make up quotes, for example. You don't steal other people's work or plagiarize. And then there are all of the places where there are difficult lines to be drawn. You start out with the presumption that you don't want to invade people's privacy. But if you're dealing with a public figure, where their private and public lives are intermixed, where do you draw the line?

Victor Navasky, publisher and editorial director, *The Nation*

Here are some common dilemmas.

• *Pseudonyms*. One of your writer's sources provided essential information for an article—but she has asked you to keep her name out of the article. Should you allow the use of a pseudonym?

Pseudonyms, or made-up names that hide the identity of sources, almost always reduce the credibility of an article. If you use a real name, readers generally believe that they could track this person down and verify the information if they wished. They hardly ever do, but that's not the point. The belief is there that the information is real.

But with pseudonyms, that verifiability is gone. And in its absence come suspicions that maybe you made up the whole story, which is a good reason to avoid the use of pseudonyms.

There are circumstances, however, in which pseudonyms are necessary. Sometimes, the source's life (or health, marriage, or job) would be in jeopardy if his name were revealed. Or the source might be able to provide additional information later—unless people know that he was talking to the press. Or the article might include information about activities or behaviors that the source finds too embarrassing to admit publicly.

We could be justifiably slammed if somehow the correspondent managed to slip through a piece that brought only the perspectives of the pro-government publications or only of the opposition.

Alice Chasan, editor, *World Press Review*

Somewhere in all this, editors have to decide when to allow pseudonyms and when to refuse the request—understanding that refusing the request means that the information provided by the source cannot be used.

Most editors base that decision on several factors:

1. How valid is the rationale for the request for a pseudonym? If the source's life might be in danger, that's one thing. If the source merely doesn't want people to know that he spent his last vacation at a weight-loss camp, that's another.
2. How important is the information to the story? If it is essential, perhaps the request should be granted. If it is tangential, or if it can be obtained from another informant, perhaps this source isn't really needed.
3. How important is the story itself? If your writer submits a guide to the ten best beaches in Florida, you might be less tolerant of pseudonyms than if she submits an exposé of the inner workings of a gun-smuggling operation.

Two caveats:

1. Pseudonyms always should be clearly labeled: "Mary Jones (not her real name) became addicted to crystal meth at the age of 17...." Readers deserve to know when the information they are reading is not entirely accurate.
2. Sources can be kept anonymous from readers, but they should never be kept anonymous from the editor. The only way you can be sure that sources are real is to require your writers to give you their full names and contact information.

• *Undercover work.* When is it acceptable to "go undercover"—in other words, to use deception—to get a story?

We allow people to use a pseudonym. But if a person is telling us to run an article under his or her own name, no one knows more than that journalist. It would be condescending or patronizing of us to assume that we know more than he or she does.

Alice Chasan, editor, *World Press Review*

Given that the whole point of journalism is to present the truth, lying to get a story might seem like a bad idea. And generally, it is. People for the most part have the right to know when they're being watched, interviewed, photographed, or otherwise recorded for an article.

But at times, deception is the only way to get the story. If your writer wants to expose ongoing health-code violations at a meat-packing plant, for example, he can't exactly walk in the front door, announce that he's a reporter for your magazine, and then ask questions about the meat-handling procedures. Such honesty often leads to dishonest answers. So instead, he might have to apply for a job at the plant and work there for a few weeks, gathering evidence for his article. That approach is deceptive, to be sure, but it might be the only way to expose the wrongdoing.

When should editors allow undercover work? The usual guidelines are similar to those for the use of pseudonyms. Undercover work should be avoided completely unless it's the only way to get the information, the information is essential to the story, and the story is worth the deception.

• *Gifts and favors.* A far fuzzier problem centers on people who offer gifts, favors, and other gestures to editors and writers. The situation is fuzzy because it is so difficult to draw clear boundaries between acceptable and unacceptable behavior.

If you're editing a car magazine, and a car manufacturer offers to give you a free SUV if you publish flattering reviews of his products—that's an easy call. As tempting as the vehicle is, you decline the offer.

But what if your writer is interviewing someone over lunch, and the source picks up the check? Was the source merely being nice, or was she trying to curry favor with your writer in the hopes that the article would present her (or her position, her company, and so on) in a positive light? Does it matter if the lunch was a couple of hot dogs? What if it was a couple of steaks, a few martinis, and some cheesecake?

What if your writer receives a gift from a source? If the gift is a nice but inexpensive pen, is that acceptable? What if the gift is a free trip to Hawaii?

Reasonable policies become difficult to find and even harder to enforce. On the one hand, you don't want to be rude to sources who are trying to be nice to you. On the other hand, you don't want to feel indebted to a source, because that feeling might translate itself into biased coverage. And on the third hand (hmmm...), you don't want to give the *appearance* of impropriety, even if the gift had no influence on the article.

Publications that have policies about gifts generally ascribe dollar limits. It's fine to accept a $5 lunch from a source, for example, but an $80 pearl necklace is way over the line.

• *Payment for interviews*. The flip side of the problem of gifts and favors surfaces when sources insist on payment for interviews, information, or assistance. Instinctively, the answer is a resounding "No way!" but the situation might not always be that clear.

For example, if an article fulfills a fundamental part of your magazine's mission, and the only way to get it is to pay someone for an interview, pragmatic concerns bump right up against idealistic platforms.

Refusing to pay for interviews and information becomes increasingly hard as other publications give in to such pressures. If all the good sources and interesting stories are flocking to your competitors because they pay for information, you might find that it gets uncomfortably lonely on the moralistic high ground.

And refusing to pay can become difficult to defend in the face of certain economic arguments. You are willing to pay your writer for writing the article. You will get paid for editing it. Your magazine will make money from subscribers, newsstand shoppers, and advertisers. Why should the source—the person with the information on which the entire enterprise is based—be the only one to operate for free?

Of course, there are good arguments against paying sources. When information becomes a commodity at the source level, the validity of that information can become suspect. How do we know that sources aren't amplifying their information in an effort to buck for more bucks? Journalists are always skeptical of information and sources, and they always check things out in other ways, but the situation becomes even more skewed when money enters into the picture. Furthermore, no one wants to become part of a system that encourages people to do outrageous things just to make money from the rights to the story.

Where should you come down in this dilemma? Kant would tell you to refuse to pay. Other philosophers would tell you to operate less rigidly, allowing payments under certain specific circumstances. Your position is yours to decide.

• *Cooperation with law enforcement.* Let's say that your writer interviews a drug dealer. The writer knows who he is, and you know who he is. But the article disguises the dealer's identity.

The next sound you hear is a knock at your door. It's the police, and they want the name of the dealer described in the article. Should you give them the information?

There are moral and practical factors to consider in this situation. On the moral side, you have an obligation to the source. You agreed to keep him anonymous, and giving his name to the police would violate that agreement. Furthermore, revealing his name would most likely result in his arrest—pretty harsh treatment for helping you with the article. Of course, the guy *is* a drug dealer, and most people would agree that drug dealers should be arrested and tried in court. Should you protect someone who is causing harm to people?

On the practical side, if you give his name to the police, it won't be long before people come to realize that they can't trust you to keep them anonymous. The success of future articles might depend on your willingness to stand up to the police; if potential sources believe that you will turn them in, they won't talk to you about anything.

Furthermore, it is the mission of journalism to function at arm's length from government and law enforcement; our "watchdog role" suggests that we keep our distance from the people and systems we are covering. Finding drug dealers is the job of the police. Why should we do their job for them?

In addition, the use of journalists to get information for law enforcement is often merely a convenience. If your writer could find this drug dealer, why can't the police find him? Why do the police need journalists to find the bad guys?

This maze of questions is difficult to navigate, and editors have responded in different ways at different times. As a general rule, though, most journalists refuse to release information or other material to law enforcement except under severe circumstances.

> We frequently reject advertising that contradicts our mission, though it would make us more profitable.
>
> **Scott Meyer, senior editor, *Organic Gardening***

• *Other dilemmas*. Editors face an enormous variety of ethical dilemmas during the course of their careers. Should we allow advertisers to influence our editorial decisions (about which, see chapter 15)? Should we identify the victims of rape or other sexual crimes? How should we handle the interviewing of minors? And so on.

Most editors find ways to field these crises that allow them to sleep at night. And from time to time, we make some pretty spectacular blunders. When that happens, we try to learn from the mistakes and move on. As the saying goes, good judgment is the result of experience—and experience is the result of bad judgment.

For further guidance on ethical dilemmas, check out the Poynter Institute (www.poynter.org) and the Society of Professional Journalists (www.spj.org).

Balancing Act

The kind of ethical decision making just described represents only one of the facets of morality that editors face. When faced with making choices that will hurt someone, editors try to act in accordance with some kind of defensible principle. But there are many other, less pointed ways in which unfairness can creep inside a magazine's covers.

For instance, if editors aren't paying attention, it is easy to let examples of insensitivity slide into print. Racial stereotypes, sexist comments, and other slights can sneak into articles with devastating effect.

Very few editors would intentionally publish such terms and comments (although there are a few magazines designed to breed ha-

> We have always been quite clear about keeping the editorial selections of the magazine completely free of advertising and commercial influences.
>
> **Roanne P. Goldfein, editor, *American Indian Art Magazine***

tred in this world). And few editors would be so asleep at the switch as to let racial slurs or derogatory words into their publications. But just beneath the surface of the obvious lies an ocean of subtle and damaging slips that can get past an unsuspecting editor's sonar. We'll go over a few of those dangers here.

• *Proper terminology.* Language changes all the time, and the terms we use for various groups of people change as well. Sometimes, this change reflects a sad tendency; people at times use a normal term as an insult, and so the group involved is forced to find a new label. The word *colored* is an example. Years ago, it was a simple—if rather crude and inaccurate—label that can still be found in a few places; for example, the NAACP is the National Association for the Advancement of Colored People. But over time, the word became a slur, and so other terms took its place: *black, African-American, people of color.* Today, referring to someone as "colored" would carry echoes of racism and segregation, and so using the term is ill-advised. Referring to someone as "a forty-three-year-old black man" probably would not offend people (as long as the other considerations, discussed later, are taken into account), but the person involved might prefer "African-American" or "person of color."

Asking for individuals' preferences is perfectly reasonable; I'd recommend asking *any* person how he or she would like to be described. But be aware that one person's preference might be another person's insult, so you can't apply one preference to an entire group.

Native American is another disputed term. To some Native Americans, the term is better than *Indian*, because Native Americans aren't from India; that word is the result of Christopher Columbus's ignorance. *American Indian*, to some, isn't any better, because the Navajo and the Mohawk were here *before* this land was America, *and* they didn't come from India. The term encompasses a double error. So *Native American* was in vogue for a while as a solution that was intended to mean something like "the people who were native to this place we now call America."

But many Cherokee, Lakota, Apaches, and others reject the term *Native American* because it implies that they were the "original Americans." They insist that they were not the original Americans—that claim is left to George Washington and his gang—and that American citizenship was forced on them at gunpoint.

So *American Indian* has returned, at least to some degree. In Washington, D.C., the National Museum of the American Indian was established fairly recently, and the museum was so named because *American Indian* offended fewer native people than did *Native American*.

To me, Canada got this one right; up there, the term *First Nations* is used. It carries good and accurate connotations—the Cree and the other groups were the first nations formed on this continent.

But the basic problem is that such labels force separate groups into one big group. Before Columbus and the rest came over from Europe, there was no term for "all the original peoples living on this continent." Instead, there were names for each group: the Comanche, the Choctaw, the Kwakiutl, and so on. A large, umbrella term is convenient, but it ignores the real differences that existed—and continue to exist—among these groups.

And then some groups have embraced terms that had become insults, turning them into sources of power and identity. Many homosexual people, for example, label themselves as *queer*—a word that used to be a slur. (Such terms can still be slurs if used by people outside the group in question.)

So it pays for editors to keep on top of terminology and not to cling tightly to the terms we learned when we were growing up. Those words might be old-fashioned at best—and insulting at worst.

• *Common phrases.* Similarly, we have to be on guard against phrases or terms that are in common currency—but that are insulting or overly narrow. Think about a phrase like *working mother*: "Maureen Reynolds is a working mother from Mystic, Connecticut." Even though there's nothing inherently inaccurate in the description—it is true that she both is a mother and works in a job outside the home—the suggestion is that the combination is somehow unusual. It hints that Maureen is somehow special in her ability to be both a parent and a productive member of the business world. The phrase is actually insulting in two directions. First, it implies that such a dual role is beyond the abilities of most women, which is, of course, false. Second, it suggests that such a dual role is not beyond the abilities of most men. If you wouldn't write "working father," don't write "working mother."

Similarly, you'll often see the phrase *inner city*: "He comes from an inner-city neighborhood." The term rarely is used as a precise geographical description referring to the very center of the city's boundaries. Instead, it is often a euphemism for a particular kind of neighborhood: poor, run-down, gang-ridden, and occupied by black or Latino families.

As such, it is both insulting (implying that black and Latino families live only in the slums) and imprecise. If you mean that he comes from a largely black neighborhood, say so—although I'd suggest describing the people, rather than the area, as black. Precision is usually fair: "Sixty-two families live on his block, and all but three of them are African-American." But such comments are fair only if they serve a legitimate role in the article. If you're writing about race, fine. If you're writing about crime, why would you mention the race?

• *Faint praise.* Another editorial trap lies in printing something that appears to be flattering—but in fact is a slap on the face: "Enrique lives at home with his wife and three kids." Good for him! But pointing out that he lives at home with his family suggests that this is somehow extraordinary; the backhanded comment is that most Latino men abandon their wives and children, but that good ol' Enrique is an unusually upstanding Latino man.

If you were writing an article about the president of your college or university, would you use such a sentence? "Dr. Marsha Phillips, president of Central State College, holds degrees in physics and philosophy, serves on the boards of five major corporations, and lives at home with her husband and three kids." Sounds a bit odd—you'd *expect* her to live at home. That's what *home* means.

Again, if you wouldn't write such a sentence about someone else, write it only if the circumstances make it highly relevant to your article.

Similar examples of faint praise to avoid include "Jerome Blake is a highly articulate black man" and "Mark Mitchell, a tough and brawny gay man from Kansas, ... " and so on.

• *Unnecessary or uneven description.* Picture this coverage of an event in Washington: "The first lady looked trim and charming in a blue satin gown, with white shoes and matching handbag."

Now flip it: "The president looked fit and dashing in a flattering gray suit with a light blue shirt and contrasting maroon tie."

We are much more likely to describe women's clothing than we are to describe men's clothing. Why?

One legitimate reason might be that women in this society have a much broader range of clothing options than men do, especially for formal events. Men pretty much dress alike: blue, black, brown, or gray suit; neutral shirt; somewhat interesting tie. Women can choose from a rainbow of colors and a world of styles, and so the choices they make tend to become the subject of conversation.

Thus for a formal social occasion in Washington, a description of the first lady's outfit might be appropriate. And skipping the description of the president's gray suit might be forgiven.

But many writers tend to make this distinction automatic. When a male senator holds a press conference on the budget crisis, his outfit is rarely described. But when a female senator holds a press conference on the budget crisis, her outfit is often described. Why? When you're talking about the federal budget, what difference does her suit make? Automatically describing women's outfits is a sexist habit; *anyone's* outfit should be described only when it's pertinent to the story.

Similarly, we tend to identify women's marital status more often than men's, we tend to indicate whether a woman has children more often than we do for men, and so on. Those habits were developed in a more conspicuously sexist age, and they have no justification today.

We do the same thing for race. We'll describe Bob Williams as "a fifty-eight-year-old man who works at Federal Bank," but we'll describe Bob Jones as "a fifty-eight-year-old black man who works at Federal Bank." The assumption behind this unfortunate habit is that people are white unless described otherwise.

• *The usual sources.* Another way that bias slithers into reporting is when only the usual sources are contacted for story after story. The "usual sources" are often people in positions of power and authority—and people in positions of power and authority are often (but not always) white men.

Good reporters, with good editors behind them, make sure they cast wide nets when looking for sources. Got a factory that's going out of business? Interview the CEO—but also interview the woman on the assembly line and the guy who drives the truck. Got a story on the boom in skateboarding parks? Interview some skateboarders and their parents—but also interview the neighbors of some of these parks; the police officers who have to patrol them; the admitting nurse at an emergency room who has seen collarbones snapping, cracking, and popping; and anyone else who is relevant to the issue.

Some of these people might represent established minority groups, and that's great. The goal is to be inclusive, rather than defaulting to the typical narrow range of standard sources.

Many people would argue that it is inappropriate to seek out the black neighbor, the Asian police officer, or the Hispanic nurse; selecting these people on the basis of their race (or religion or other such characteristic) is not much better than ignoring them for the same reason. By casting a wide net and interviewing people beyond the typical set of familiar faces, journalists increase the odds of inclusion and proper representation without deliberately skewing the picture.

Power

Magazine editing carries with it a lot of power. As an editor, you get to decide what your readers will read. You get to decide how the world will be presented. You get to decide how people will be portrayed—or even whether they will be portrayed at all.

With that power comes responsibility. You have a responsibility to your readers to deliver useful, valid, and accurate information in every issue of the magazine. You have a responsibility to your sources to present them in fair and unbiased ways. You have a responsibility to your advertisers to maintain the high standards that will attract the kind of audience those advertisers seek. You have a responsibility to your writers to help them keep bias, unintentional insult, and other gaffes from appearing under their bylines. And you have a responsibility to yourself to be the kind of person you want to be.

Understanding in advance the ethical challenges that you will face can give you the tools you need to make reasonable, fair, and defensible decisions once you're on the job. Sissela Bok urges us to work through potentially difficult situations before they actually arise, so we can develop a rational position in a calm and reflective atmosphere.

Don't mystify the thing by thinking that ethics is some kind of magic field that you have to master the way you might have to master a new language or something. Every schoolchild has an idea of what's right and wrong. Just apply that.

Victor Navasky, publisher and editorial director, *The Nation*

Then, when a crisis hits, we can rely on the experience we gained through that preparation, and we can use it to make decisions that people will understand and accept—even if you won't always make everyone happy.

It's a smart strategy.

Layer
Layer
Layer
Layer
Layer
Layer
Layer
Layer
Layer
Layer
Layer 2.

The Big Questions

I always give all writers one chance to revise. I will literally take their initial text and write in every single question that comes from me, from my top editor, and from the editor in chief in reaction to their text. I'll lay out where they need to do more of this, where they need to do less of that. I have a piece right now that has a suicide in it, and the writer said, "We had a perfect relationship." I'll say something like "Can you explain? What does that mean? Why was he perfect? I'm not sympathetic to this guy." The key to a *Cosmo Girl* article is that you show everything—and that's what most writers fail to do. When you've done it right, you know it, because there's a vibrancy to the work, like the story's coming off the page.

Leslie Heilbrunn, senior editor, *Cosmo Girl*

6. The Plan's the Thing:

Planning Issues and Working with Writers

I quickly realized that if editing was like playing speed chess—all instinct, quick reflexes, and stamina—editing a monthly like *Esquire* is more like playing three-dimensional chess. You've got to visualize your moves in several realms at once. You've got to figure out what you want to do, anticipate what others will do, and commit to your plans long before you actually know whether your hunches are right.

Edward Kosner, editor in chief, *Esquire*

Every issue of every magazine begins as Emptiness and Nothing, and it is the job of the editor to replace that blankness with scintillating articles, compelling photos, and catchy ideas that will keep the readers coming back again and again. Because of this demand—and because each issue can take as many as twelve months from "I have an idea!" to "Start the presses!"—editors must be masterful planners. That bitterly humorous review of this summer's blockbuster movie might be beautifully written, but most monthly magazines would have no use for it; the tape would be growing brittle in the back corners of the video stores long before the review was published. Editors have to look into the future and determine the topics and people who will be most engaging when the issue hits the stands, and then they must get the process moving to deliver those topics and those people on time.

But how do you do that? How do you sit in your office in the broiling heat of August and think up adorable articles for your magazine's Valentine's Day issue? How do you know what your audience will want to read during the holiday season—*next* year? How do you work with people to inspire brilliant ideas, convert them into words and photos on paper, convert them into gorgeous layouts, and convert the whole thing into a printed magazine, beginning far enough in advance to get it all done on time?

Editors are nearly always behind in our correspondence and other work that does not specifically relate to our magazine schedules. Our work time is so centered on deadlines that it is easy to fall into the bad habit of giving lower priority to everything that does not help us meet them. It might help students to know that it is to their advantage to learn to organize the paperwork and to delegate administrative tasks early on.

Bonnie Leman, editor, *Quilter's Newsletter Magazine*, *Quiltmaker*, and *Quilts and Other Comforts*

As always, the plan begins with the magazine's mission. Editors don't have the entire universe to choose from, thank goodness. Rather, their missions focus their thinking onto a particular topic area, a particular audience's needs, a particular set of information, sources, or questions.

Backed with the insight and confidence that a strong mission statement can bring, the editor then tries to anticipate what her readers will want to see several months from now. This foresight is necessary because print magazines have relatively long "lead times." Most editors, in fact, determine the "release date" of the magazine—the date the magazine should hit the newsstands and the mailboxes—and then work backward to determine the key deadlines along the way. For an issue intended to be released on July 15, for example, typical schedule might look like that in the table.

In this example, which is fairly tight as magazines go, the editors will spend January and early February brainstorming ideas for their August issue. (Issues are often released before their cover date. Doing so makes the magazine seem fresh and current.) In other words, they will brush the snow off their cars, drive down slushy roads, walk across a slippery parking lot, enter a heated building, ride the elevator upward while their overcoats and boots are dripping onto the floor, hang their outerwear on the hooks behind their doors, grab a cup of steaming coffee, and talk about the guide to the country's hottest beaches, the best and worst boogie-board styles, and the back-to-school fashion preview that will fill their August pages. Editors are always working months into the future.

Activity	Days before release date	Date
Ideas for features completed	RD-148	February 16
Features assigned to writers	RD-147	February 17
Ideas for departments completed	RD-141	February 24
Departments assigned to writers	RD-140	February 25
First draft of features due to editors	RD-133	March 4
First draft of departments due to editors	RD-105	April 1
Final draft of departments due to editors	RD-84	April 22
Final draft of features due to editors	RD-77	April 29
Departments to graphic designer	RD-63	May 13
Features to graphic designer	RD-49	May 27
Final materials to printer	RD-21	June 24
Release Date	0	July 15

This future orientation means that editors have to anticipate skill-fully, and the main way they go about this task is by keeping an eye on trends. And the way they do *that* is by talking to a lot of people (that's why the cocktail parties can come in handy) and by doing a lot of reading: of newspapers, of competitors' magazines, of government reports—anything that will give them a sense of what is happening and what is likely to happen.

Want to publish a celebrity article? Talk to some well-connected movie reviewers and find out who the newest up-and-coming stars are. Want to do a science piece? Get on the phone to an engineer at the Jet Propulsion Laboratory in Pasadena, the head of the artificial intelligence project at MIT, a marine biologist at Wood's Hole, the director of the Hurricane Tracking Center in Miami, or a geologist at

Once a year, [the editors] come up with two feature ideas an issue. Then about eight months before the publication date, we plan the issue fully. This is not to say you can't add things at a later time, but you have to be prepared ahead of time. Many people (freelancers, PR companies pitching articles) forget that magazines HAVE to work months in advance in order to meet their printing dates.

Rieva Lesonsky, vice president and editorial director, Entrepreneur Media Inc.

the Kola Hole Project in Russia. Want to do a car story? Chat with designers in Detroit, Tokyo, and Seoul. Want to do a new-makeup how-to? Get in touch with the people at Revlon, Maybelline, and Mary Kay. And all the while, read, read, read. Know what has been published recently; there's little point in rehashing something your readers have already seen somewhere else. Know what *hasn't* been published recently; constantly be on the lookout for the missed opportunity. Know which topics are gaining favor and which are fading out ("That actress is *so* 2003"). And keep an eye out for fresh and exciting ideas—quirky inventions, swelling revolutions, daring reversals, bold changes, astonishing revivals—that can become fascinating articles for future issues.

It's a fun task, but the field is thick with traps. The rising young superstar could fizzle into obscurity by next fall. The promising new breakthrough in energy development could prove to be hopelessly flawed after further scrutiny. And the latest outrage that is buzzing around the water cooler today will be ancient history by the time the presses roll—and the hot topic *then* has scarcely been dreamed of today.

So editors have to think carefully about trends and determine whether they are likely to continue. Today's hot new fashion is tomorrow's garage-sale embarrassment. But the trend that looks like it is serious, strong, and rising might be a good bet for that future cover story.

Ideal Ideas

Once you have thought ahead about the trends that are likely to indicate the sorts of things that will be interesting in the future, you have to bring your thinking down from the abstraction of the future to the reality of a solid idea.

Coming up with ideas for articles is difficult, fun, maddening, joyous, frustrating, and triumphant. (Of course, the same could be said about most editors.) Many ideas come from the trend spotting we just talked about. But most magazines also rely on several other approaches to keep fresh ideas flowing onto their pages.

• *Curiosity.* One good source of article ideas is the editor's own creativity. By nature, editors tend to be curious people, wondering why things are the way they are. Why are almost all calico cats female? Is there any truth to the rumor that there once was a female pope? Are rocket scientists really that smart? Why do we call certain fast-paced banjo music "bluegrass"? What makes beautiful people beautiful? How can salmon live in both salt water and freshwater?

This kind of curiosity resulted in a wonderfully fascinating article published many years ago in *Smithsonian*. The writer (and/or editor) asked an interesting question: If people vanished from the Earth, what would happen to our structures, our monuments, our physical legacy? The writer interviewed experts in engineering, architecture, and other fields, and the article presented the information in an engaging and easy-to-understand way. One example: the Hoover Dam, which generates an enormous amount of electricity, would continue to do so after people disappeared. It runs relatively automatically, and so lights in the surrounding towns—and on the dam itself—would continue to glow for years. The gates that control the flow of water through the turbines, however, are held up by steel chains, which eventually would give way, dropping the gates and halting the flow of water. The turbines would stop spinning, and the lights would go dark.

The dam would sit in silence for many years. But then, far into the future, the iron gates would rust through and crumble, allowing water to flow through the turbines once more. So all at once, after decades of darkness, lights would brighten once again—even though humans had long since vanished. Without the controlling influence of the gates, however, the water would flow unabated, and the turbines would spin faster and faster. At last, they would burn out—and darkness would return again.

That article remains one of the truly great examples of magazine writing. The idea began with a conundrum: What *would* happen to our stuff if we all disappeared? And, backed by solid research and buoyed by lively writing, it became a memorable magazine article. Human curiosity can lead us in fascinating directions, and magazine work gives us the license to follow our minds wherever they go.

• *Brainstorming.* In addition to relying on their own curiosity, editors use the related technique of brainstorming to come up with good article ideas. In brainstorming sessions, which always involve two or more people, ideas are tossed out without screening. No idea is too silly, too dumb, too weird, or too unusual in these meetings—everything is accepted and written down. The advantage of brainstorming is that one person's thoughts can spark interesting ideas in other people's minds, and *their* ideas can trigger still more.

Once the group's creative energy seems to be dwindling, the session ends and everyone goes about their business. But later on—the next day, the next week—the list of ideas is brought up for scrutiny. *Now* editorial judgment can kick in. Ideas can be dismissed as impractical, offensive, goofy, boring, or indicative of a serious need for therapy. Eventually, as the list is winnowed down, the strong ideas will begin to stand out, and they can be discussed in greater depth and considered for publication.

Brainstorming is a great technique for getting editors out of ruts. It is easy for magazines to carve their own channels and deliver the same kind of material year in and year out. But readers like some excitement every now and then, a bit of whimsy, a chance to delight over something different for a change. (This tendency explains the April Fools' Day editions that several magazines publish.) At one magazine where I worked years ago, the editors were presented with

Finding good writers—now there's a subject I could go on about all day. Car magazines are often in tough positions. Most people who love cars have an affinity for things mechanical; you could say they had engineering at the top of their priority list. And we all know that engineers do not have an affinity for the art of the clever, commercially written piece. We are staff written—that is, the road tests and the preview tests of new cars are written by staff writers, who have their hands full keeping up. A lot of our feature material is written by three or four writers listed under our "Contributing Editor" list on the masthead. None of them is an engineer; they're all quite good writers, and most of them are able to deal with some degree of technical/mechanical material, but their strong point is their ability to collect information, chase after it, dig up angles, pursue, and then write entertaining stories. Good writers who have an interest in cars and writing do not pop up. We have to find them, and like most magazines, that means we find them in other magazines, usually smaller ones.

Steve Spence, managing editor, *Car and Driver*

So many freelancers send in queries to us without really knowing much about the magazine. They read something in the paper about hydrogen cars and then propose a story. Our problem is that the story has no focus. We don't have a clue who the writer is or what he/she is capable of doing, and usually the story ideas are generic and somewhat dull. It's rare that we ever buy a piece that comes unsolicited over the transom. The last one I remember was a guy who went from Costa Rica to Cuba to offer a story about the old cars of Havana—but with a difference. He actually understood engines and photographed under the hoods of a couple of ancient '50s cars that were running on systems of gasoline AND kerosene. It was so well thought out, with rough photos of the systems and the people with their cars, that I couldn't refuse it. But that shows you how rare it is that we buy over-the-transom stuff. So often—no joke—we get queries like "My Pop's Crazy Old VW Bug." That sort of thing. The person proposing it doesn't know who we are.

Steve Spence, managing editor, _Car and Driver_

a challenge: we were to brainstorm ideas that were guaranteed to get us fired. We had a great time, and we came up with some truly shocking article ideas that probably would have gotten us fired _and_ locked up. But in the process, we found a few ideas that we could adapt into articles that would be not only acceptable but also fun, surprising, and offbeat.

• _Writers._ Fortunately, editors aren't limited to their own minds when searching for story ideas. For most magazines, writers provide much of the freshness and the "I never would have thought of that!" surprises that keep magazines lively.

Typically, a magazine employs a small number of staff writers, who earn set salaries and come up with a steady stream of ideas that fill a portion of the magazine's space. Adding to this flow is material sent in by freelance writers from all over the country.

If you ask an editor about unsolicited freelance submissions, get comfortable. You're about to receive a long and anguished diatribe about the fuzzy thinking, unwarranted arrogance, and sorry language skills that abound among people who like to call themselves writers. Even the language of the editorial office reflects this frustra-

I receive five to ten queries per day, almost every day, from writers with travel ideas or who are submitting manuscripts for consideration. It is a knowledge of our needs and a focus based on the mission statement that allows me to weed through these queries and reject ideas not appropriate to *EV*. Secondarily, of course, is writing ability, which wipes out about 80 percent of them. We ask for strong concepts, interesting angles, and well-researched information, and we demand a strong writing ability. Many of our ideas come from the staff. We watch travel trends, read competitive sources, and travel ourselves, and through this knowledge, we develop ideas for stories we think our readers might enjoy or find useful.

Jackson Mahaney, associate editor, *Endless Vacation*

tion: unsolicited submissions come in "over the transom" and coalesce into the "slush pile." Even outside writers who supply a reliable inventory of good material are said to make up the magazine's "stable" of freelancers.

The reason for this wailing and gnashing of teeth is that most submissions that come in from freelancers are truly awful. They often are badly written, badly conceived, and badly misplaced at maga-

Ideas for articles in the *National Geographic* are derived from the staff and from suggestions by our members and outside writers. Story suggestions are submitted in writing to our Planning Council, a group of about twelve editors who meet periodically to decide which stories should be pursued. Editors meet weekly for the purpose of deciding story length and sequence. When a subject is first suggested to the Planning Council, preliminary research begins immediately to determine the photographic and editorial possibilities. (Photographs—especially photographs—and other visual elements, such as maps, diagrams, and paintings, are crucial elements of any *Geographic* article. If an article cannot be illustrated in a dynamic way, it is of little interest to us.) When a topic is accepted for a future *National Geographic* article, a photographer and writer are assigned to thoroughly cover the subject. Upon completion of this coverage, picture and text editors edit the material.

Patrick J. McGeehan, research correspondence, *National Geographic*

zines that don't run that kind of material. Mike Curtis, a senior editor at *The Atlantic*, once lamented that his magazine—which focuses on politics, society, the economy, and the arts—receives an inordinate number of submissions about whales. The title of the magazine causes some misguided writers to think that an encyclopedia rewrite about humpbacks would be welcomed with enthusiasm.

That kind of unfortunate thinking drives editors to unhealthy habits. But deep within the mantle of the slush pile, if the editor is attentive and has led a blameless life, shining crystals of good writing and clever ideas can be found. These gems make the search worthwhile, even if it is time-consuming and life-shortening.

Pruning the Editorial Landscape

Generating article ideas is only one step on the road toward a good magazine. Once a swarm of ideas has been set loose in the room, editors have to tackle the tough work of figuring out which ideas should be pursued and which should be rejected—even though some culling has happened already. The ideas that survived the earlier winnowing range from decent to outstanding, but not all of them will materialize into articles. Before an idea results in an assignment to a writer, editors have to take several factors into account.

• *Mission.* Yes, it's the mission again. In fact, it is at this stage that the mission does its most crucial work. In thinking about the people and issues that will be interesting a year from now, we might come up with a whirling flock of ideas: some fascinating, some bizarre, some silly, some kind of boring. But we can't just grab the most interesting of these ideas and declare victory. We have to make sure that the ideas we pursue fulfill our mission.

We always keep the magazine's focus in mind while assigning articles. We view an article as a contract with our reader—what should we be providing the reader? Once we determine what an article should contain—what our contract with the reader is—we make that clear in our assignment letter to the writer.

Karan Davis Cutler, managing editor, *Harrowsmith Country Life*

The reason for this caution is probably clear by now. If we seize on any idea that captures our fancy and throw it into the pages of our magazine, our readers are going to feel somewhat bewildered. "Gee," says Hypothetical Reader, "I just traded my lunch money for this cool-looking magazine. But inside, I found articles about chinchilla farming, hairdressing, blue-chip stocks, roofing techniques, geology, and how to have killer abs in just thirty days. The chinchillas are kind of interesting, and I sure could use some killer abs—but the rest of this stuff really isn't for me."

And with that, our circulation just dropped by one. Repeat the same feeling of confusion in each reader's mind, and the magazine will close its doors within the next few issues.

So we can analyze trends and brainstorm ideas all we want, but before we actually commit an idea to a particular issue of our magazine, we had better be sure that it delivers the information and tone that our readers expect. Throughout my career as an editor, I have had to reject quite a few fascinating and well-written articles simply because they didn't fit in my magazine. I always offer the writer encouraging words, but I never let off-target pieces appear on my pages.

The best test at this stage is to ask yourself, "Precisely what part of my magazine's mission would this article fulfill?" If you can't specify the actual phrase in the mission that will be moved forward by this article, then you might be better off scrapping the idea.

• *Balance.* Imagine if you picked up the latest issue of *Sports Illustrated*—and all you found in it were articles about hockey and golf. No football. No baseball. No basketball. No Olympic games, no World Cup soccer, no competitive water-skiing or snowboard–bungee jumping. Just hockey and golf, from cover to cover.

Readers interested in hockey or golf would be happy, and readers interested in hockey *and* golf would be thrilled. But most of *SI*'s readers have broader interests than just those two sports, and so a lot of people are going to be put off by this strange issue.

The problem with the issue has to do with its balance of topics. Yes, articles about hockey and golf fulfill the *Sports Illustrated* mission, but the issue as a whole falls short. *Sports Illustrated* is a general-interest sports magazine, and so each issue has to reflect at least a good-size portion of the sports spectrum.

The editors' responsibility goes far beyond editing and assigning. Most crucial, it is their responsibility to plan the entire issue—and a year of issues—to think through its balance, its flow. To determine how topics and articles will mesh, or not mesh, and how the design of each will or won't fit together. To ensure there's plenty of variety—in subjects, in style, in presentation. A magazine, in other words, is far more than a dozen articles published between two covers.

Karan Davis Cutler, managing editor, *Harrowsmith Country Life*

Similarly, you can image the reaction if *Cosmo* ran an issue with nothing but lipstick and travel articles in it. Or if *Newsweek* filled an issue with nothing but articles about China and Finland. Each article might be fine, but the overall issue is too tightly focused to suit a wide range of readers.

So editors worry about each issue's balance. How will any given idea mesh with other ideas in the same issue? How can we cover a broad range of topics, so a lot of our readers will appreciate this issue, without coming across as random, haphazard, or scattered? If our cover story will be about global warming, should we include this great idea about fuel economy—or should we save fuel economy for a later issue? If we're offering a moving piece about world hunger, should we brighten the issue with this humorous look at Christmas shopping—or would those two articles clash?

Editors consider the relationship among article topics in an effort to find the strongest possible balance in each issue. It's a bit like planning a dinner party. You want to invite guests who will play off one another, sparking stimulating conversation, but you don't want serious conflicts that will shatter the evening.

In their consideration of each issue's balance, editors might find themselves putting good article ideas aside for months at a time—and sometimes even scuttling them altogether, if a suitable place can't be found for them.

• *Overall mix.* Just as each issue must be balanced to keep a broad range of readers happy, the "mix" of stories that a magazine runs from year to year must be watched carefully.

> Every issue of our magazine includes an article about tomatoes, because it is uncontested as the most popular garden crop. The staff has seen tomatoes every which way and is truly bored by them. But about 40 percent of our readers are new to the magazine each year, and they have signed up expecting information about their interests. Our constant creative test is to keep finding new ways to present information that fundamentally never changes, doesn't bore the long-term readers, and still meets the needs of the newer subscribers.
>
> **Scott Meyer, senior editor,** *Organic Gardening*

On the one hand, editors want to make sure that a particular topic isn't presented too often, which might bore readers. If *Working Woman* offered a profile of the first lady in every third issue, readers would become tired of the topic and suspicious that the magazine was furthering some kind of hidden agenda. Similarly, if the February issue of *Travel & Leisure* included an in-depth feature about the sights and sounds of Morocco—and so did the June, August, and November issues—readers would believe (quite rightly) that something had gone horribly wrong at the magazine's editorial offices.

So editors keep in mind the articles they have run recently, and they generally try to avoid repeating any topics too soon. *National Geographic*, for example, has a policy that prohibits the publication of an article about a subject that has appeared in the magazine within the past ten years (unless important new information turns up).

On the other hand, editors keep an eye out for topics that haven't been covered enough recently. This is often the harder task; it is easier to spot excessive repetition than to think of something that's missing. But by scanning recent tables of contents, looking over the past several years' worth of covers, rereading the mission statement, and thinking carefully about readers' needs and desires, editors attempt to ensure that no holes remain unfilled for long. The cry of "Hey, you know, we haven't done an article about X in a long time!" is relatively common in magazine offices, and it often results in an assignment designed to close the gap.

Desperately Seeking Writers

Once ideas have been chosen and agreed on, editors assign the articles to the writers who have the best tools for the job.

Often, if an idea was submitted by a freelancer, that writer gets the assignment. She has, after all, done some preliminary research, so she has something of a head start. She also obviously cares about the topic, wants to write the article, and is available to do so. Besides, unless some serious concern about the writer make the assignment unwise, it just seems like the right thing to do.

Editors are not legally obligated to assign an article to the freelancer who suggested the idea. Because article ideas cannot be copyrighted, patented, or otherwise protected in any way, editors are free under the law to grab an idea from the slush pile and give it to the staff writer down the hall. But generally, that tactic results in more anger and backlash than it's worth.

Editors get their writers in several ways. Let's look at freelancers first.

As most people know, freelancers submit ideas to magazines "out of the blue." While many of these ideas are off-target, as mentioned previously, some are solid—and some of the writers are clearly talented, dedicated, and serious. Freelancers who offer good ideas and who deliver consistent, engaging, and well-researched material often are used on a regular basis, joining the "stable" of writers an editor can call on for articles. Frequently, once a freelancer has written two or three pieces for an editor, the ideas begin to flow in the other direction: the editor will call the writer about an idea that came up in a brainstorming session or through some other avenue.

An ethical problem arises: Suppose a writer suggests something, and it is a good idea—but he's a bad writer. What do you do about that?...Those are difficult decisions. One solution to the problem is to pay him for the idea. A second solution is to ask if you can proceed with the idea without payment. But it gets very difficult—not just because ideas are not protected under the copyright law. It's that ideas are in the air, and the same ideas are had by many people from different perspectives at the same time.

Victor Navasky, publisher and editorial director, *The Nation*

Freelancers sometimes are approached by an editor from the beginning, although this happens less often. These freelancers typically fall into two categories. The first is experts who possess in-depth knowledge about a particular topic. If an editor wants an article about the likelihood that an asteroid will smash into the Earth and obliterate all life as we know it, she might contact an astrophysicist at Cal Tech or MIT. The scientist's reputation inspires the editor to call, even if no prior relationship exists.

The danger with this approach is that experts often can't write well. When the manuscript arrives in the mail, the editor tears open the envelope to find an article that is packed with so much dense information that readers aren't likely to follow it. The sentences are huge, the logic is complex, and the writing is just plain dull. Now the editor has to work with the writer as much as possible to simplify the article, and then she often must take charge of it completely and rewrite it to make it interesting. Sometimes, though, this is the only way to get the information and expertise you need, so it can be worth the effort.

The other circumstance in which a writer is approached by an editor at the outset involves lively competition and a bit of corporate intrigue. Editors are always on the lookout for good writers, and sometimes a writer who appears in another magazine's pages will become irresistible. If an editor finds a skilled and engaging writer working for the competition, a charming phone call and the offer of more money and greater editorial freedom can bring about a little treason. Under these circumstances, editors sometimes can lure excellent writers away from rivals—but then the editor knows that the writer must be treated well to prevent a second defection.

As for staff writers, editors hire them in relatively straightforward ways. They place ads in *Editor & Publisher* and other trade publications. They place ads in the *New York Times* and other major newspapers. They scan the latest crop of interns from colleges and universities, looking for the drive, personality, and talent that suggest a good fit. And, yes, they steal them from other publications.

A lot of new hires come from the freelancer pool. If you take out an ad for a writing position, you'll be swamped with hundreds of résumés—mostly from people who know how to type and therefore declare that they are Writers. You'll dig through this miasma of mush, truffling out the small handful of reasonable résumés. Then

Finding good freelancers is a chore. Reading other magazines is a start. Treating freelancers well once you find them is another way of keeping good writers.

Scott Daniels, executive editor, *Exploring* and *Scouting*

you'll narrow the list down further, choosing three candidates or so to bring in for interviews. You'll chat with each of the candidates for a while, asking pointed but pointless questions and trying to figure out if you can stand working with any of them. Then you'll make your final decision, and you'll place one pleasant phone call and two unpleasant ones. Deep down inside, you'll know that you just hired a stranger, and you'll hope that she works out.

Or, you scrap the ad and call Karen, who has written five excellent freelance pieces for you. You like working with her, and you know that she can write strong articles that your readers love. You tell her about the job and offer it to her. If she accepts, you're both happy people.

Editors would much rather hire a reliable freelancer than a promising stranger.

In general, if you look at most magazines' mastheads, you won't see a lot of "staff writer" positions. Most magazines have small writing staffs, relying heavily on freelance work. Some have no staff writers at all. Furthermore, nearly everyone at a magazine is one kind of "editor" or another, even if they do little or no editing. Contributing editors, for example, are typically staff writers or regular freelancers. Assistant or associate editors often write a great deal of copy for the magazine, while tending to small but important editing tasks. I'm sure the day will come when the janitor will be listed as the "environmental editor" and the guy who delivers pizza to the editorial meetings will be the "nutrition editor," but maybe we'll come to our senses before that.

The Care and Feeding of Writers

Once the assignments have been made, the editor and the writer work together to develop the best possible article. The relationship between writer and editor can be as complex as any marriage.

The common perception seems to be that the editor holds all the power. "Do it my way, or forget about the assignment!" he bellows. "And forget about ever working here—or anywhere else—ever again!"

In reality, the relationship is much more balanced than that. Yes, the editor can block the publication of an article. But as we just discussed, editors are hungry for talented writers, so the last thing an editor wants to do is leave a good writer feeling abused, mistreated, neglected, or otherwise stiffed. The rivals are too close, and they bear enticing gifts.

In addition, writers also have the power to block publication under most circumstances. While this might seem a bit self-defeating—"Oh, yeah, well I won't *let* you publish my article. And I won't cash your check, either. So there!"—in reality, the collapse of a promising article can be painful for an editor. Editors seldom work in isolation; they discuss their writers' projects in editorial meetings and in the hallways. They negotiate for space to be reserved for upcoming pieces, and they spend company money on photographers, artists, graphic designers, and other talent. If a writer is working on an exciting new article about how shaving cream cures acne, the editor involved with the project has to make sure that everyone at the magazine knows about it. If that article then falls through because the writer feels offended by the editor, a cascade of problems tumble onto the table: another article has to be found to fill the space, and photographers and artists have to be rallied on very short (and often expensive) notice. The "coming in the next issue" ad that appeared in the previous issue is now wrong—and you have to hope that no one will notice. If the story was going to be featured on the cover, the cover photo will have to be reshot, and the cover will have to be re-

How do I find and keep good writers? This is the bane of my existence. We don't have a big budget, so finding good writers is a challenge. As we're a national magazine, I deal with writers from all over the country, many of whom have impressive credentials. Despite their credentials, a surprising number of these writers turn in substandard work. In the worst cases, it's simply awful. As for keeping good writers, though I can't offer them much financial compensation, I try to offer them interesting assignments, and I throw in a fair amount of flattery.

Michael Bawaya, editor, *American Archaeology*

designed to accommodate the change. And now you're stuck with "before" and "after" shots of that pimply faced eighth-grader that are suddenly worthless.

So editors don't hold all the power. And they know that. So they work to keep their writers happy.

And yet, at the same time, editors must push their writers to ever-higher levels of excellence.

It is that tension between nurturing and pressuring that makes the writer–editor relationship so delicate and challenging. Good editors know how to walk that line to bring the best out of their writers *and* keep them loyal. Here are some of their techniques.

• *Choose writers carefully.* Yes, editors are hungry for good writers. But that doesn't mean that editors have to tolerate missed deadlines, sloppy writing, or adolescent behavior. As in any relationship, the choice of partners makes all the difference.

• *Make the assignments clear and thorough.* If you ask a writer for a 2,000-word article on hot dogs, you don't know what's going to get stuffed in there. (Much like hot dogs themselves...) So savvy editors spell out their needs in precise terms. They'll indicate length, tone, recommended sources, essential information—and sometimes even the structure of the article and its lead and conclusion.

Writers often chafe under this direction, but it serves a useful purpose. With a comprehensive assignment, the editor and writer can negotiate key points *before* the writer pours valuable time into the research and writing. It is always easier and more pleasant to hold such discussions before the writer has completed twelve interviews and

Energize your staff. Writing and editing are fast-paced, highly personal, and creative jobs that are richly rewarding—but they can also be exhausting. Staff meetings can help with this. But more important, you have to give your staff a clear sense of the magazine's direction, along with enough authority, responsibility, resources, and support to make them want to tap into their innate enthusiasm.

Mariette DiChristina, senior editor, *Popular Science*

written six pages of highly polished prose—only to discover that the editor would prefer a different angle or another set of information.

Once the assignment has been successfully hammered out between the writer and the editor, the writer should know exactly what he should do and when he should have it done. Armed with this information, the writer should be able to proceed with a minimum of surprises.

• *Keep in touch.* Good editors keep in close contact with their writers, making sure everything is going smoothly and eliminating any roadblocks that threaten the project.

For example, a good editor knows better than to issue an assignment and a deadline and then let the intervening time evaporate quietly, all the while assuming that the writer is dutifully conducting interviews, reading documents, and putting words on paper. Such a blissfully naïve approach might feel good at the moment—it brings with it plenty of time to sharpen pencils and think deep thoughts, you know—but more often than not, the editor is in for a rude surprise when the deadline approaches. The classic phone call goes something like this:

"Hello, Ms. Vasquez?"

"Speaking."

"Hi, Ms. Vasquez. This is Barbara Jones. I'm working on that article about the probable fate of the universe for you."

"Yes, Barbara. I'm looking forward to reading that tomorrow."

"Good, but, um, well…The thing is, I've had a little trouble reaching, well, basically all of my major sources. They've been busy and haven't had a chance to talk with me yet. I was wondering if I could maybe hand the article in late, like maybe sometime in February?"

At this moment, the editor feels that icy flash to the stomach common to all people faced with a Crisis They Should Have Avoided. Suddenly, there's a four-page hole in the features well of the magazine—and the editor has nothing to fill it with except for that lame piece about the history of cheese. Visions of an angry ad manager, a bewildered readership, and a disappointed—*fatally* disappointed—publisher flash through her head.

But of course, experienced editors don't let things fall apart that badly. And keeping things from falling apart is the core of the editor's job. Editors struggle to come up with solid ideas, assign them to talented and experienced writers, and then manage the projects until they are ready. That management means that they don't assume that their writers are progressing smoothly on their articles. A few days after an editor makes an assignment, she will pick up the phone and give the writer a peppy call: "How are things going? Running into any problems? Looking forward to reading the article!" Of course, the editor knows that the writer hasn't gotten started in any serious way, but this phone call suggests that perhaps he should get going. It's guilt through pleasant chit-chat.

Then, every week or two, depending on the length of time the writer has to work on the article, the editor will find one excuse or another to ring the writer's phone once again: "Hey, I thought of a source you might call." "Any luck reaching so-and-so?" "Just wanted to tell you how glad I am that you're working on this article for us!" With these light communications, the editor is able to keep up with the writer's progress, and any delays, snags, crises, distractions, or other diversions will become apparent.

Meanwhile, of course, the editor has several other articles in hand and ready to go into that slot if disaster strikes, and she has other writers working on additional articles that could come through soon. And the much-maligned history of cheese manuscript is turning moldy in the bottom of a rusty file drawer.

• *Be frank and clear.* Writers are grown-ups. (Well, granted, such magazines as *Stone Soup* publish writing from children, but you get the point.) When an editor reads a manuscript for the first time, he'll develop a list of concerns that have to be addressed. Maybe the tone isn't quite right for the audience. Maybe the lead is boring. Maybe the structure is sloppy. Maybe the quotes are handled awkwardly. Maybe the ending is too abrupt. Whatever the concerns, the editor will almost always ask the writer for a rewrite. Experienced writers anticipate this and don't object; it's just part of the process of making the article as good as it can be.

But some beginning editors, worried about their writers' feelings, will try to couch the feedback in careful euphemisms, gentle language, and timid phrasing:

> "Rachael, this article is really good. I mean it. It's wonderful. I think that maybe some people might like to see a more exciting beginning, but I think it's just great. I mean, if you wanted to work on the beginning some more, that would be fine. You might be able to make it zip along a little more. But it's really quite good. I love every word. It's just that some people might be more likely to stick with the article more completely if the lead were just a bit peppier. But don't get me wrong. I *love* this article."

While the intentions here are kind, the results are weak. The poor writer doesn't know whether she should rewrite the lead or not. She also doesn't know what's wrong with the lead, other than a bit of slow pacing.

Experienced editors state their views clearly, directly, and respectfully:

> "Rachael, I read the article. I think it's quite good, but I have some suggestions for ways to make it great. For one thing, I'd like you to rewrite the lead. It seems to drag a bit, but I'm sure you'll be able to liven it up once you look at it again. You might try leading with that funny story that you tell on page two.
>
> "Also, I'd like you to work more direct quotes into the article—it seems a bit distant, like there are no living people in it—and I need you to shorten it by about 500 words.
>
> "Can you do all that by the 15th? That would be terrific. Let me know if you have any questions or concerns. Thanks."

With direct communication, the editor can be confident that the writer understands what has to be done. For even greater clarity and certainty, some editors follow up the phone conversation with a short letter, reiterating the main points. That way, there is little room for confusion or disagreement about what was needed.

And contrary to the instincts of beginning editors, the direct approach is actually more respectful than the kid-glove technique. Spelling out your suggestions in clear terms suggests that the writer is a professional, that she wants the article to be excellent, that she is willing to work hard, and that she is capable of making the improvements.

• *Let the writer do the rewriting.* Writers, from beginners to bestsellers, hate it when editors rewrite their work. Writers pour a lot of sweat and time into their words, and they suffer deeply when they open a magazine to see their byline over someone else's sentences.

The best editors rewrite as little as possible. If the initial assignment was clear, and if the editor has communicated with the writer throughout the research and writing process, the manuscript should land fairly close to the target. If the article is way off base in some important way—topic, sources, tone, length—something went wrong early in the game.

But no manuscript is perfect, and it's the editor's job to make each article as good as it can be. In my years as an editor, I almost never accepted an article on the first submission. Improvements are always possible, and editors owe their readers consistently polished and excellent work every time.

So savvy editors build time into the schedule for some back-and-forth after the manuscript has arrived. This time not only makes the revisions relatively painless, but also allows the editor to give the manuscript back to the writer with clear instructions, rather than

As for helping writers do better work, I try to point out the flaws in their reporting and writing and make suggestions as to how to remedy them. I prefer that they fix the problems. I try to give them clear directions as to what I want. I don't mind answering their questions and I hope, if they're uncertain about something, they'll bring it up with me sooner rather than later. I think it's important that editors respect writers and good writing. I have no interest in getting my fingerprints all over a writer's manuscript, but I get quite a bit of bad writing. When the piece finally hits print, I want the writer to feel that it's his/her piece, but the article also has to meet our editorial standards. In situations where I think these two objectives are in conflict, our editorial standards take priority. If a piece is flat-out bad, then I'll do whatever I think is necessary to salvage it, even if it means the writer will barely recognize the printed version.

Michael Bawaya, editor, *American Archaeology*

I just edited a story about a 22-year-old woman who had breast cancer at age 20. We did it for Breast Cancer Awareness Month in October. The writer had done the piece, and it was OK, but it just wasn't alive yet. I gave her all my comments and I told her exactly what I thought it needed—where it was too jumpy and where she needed to focus and all of that. Then I sent her an article—the first article I ever wrote for *Cosmo Girl*. It was about a heroin addict.

I said, "Read this article, and I'll call you at five."

I had given her all the comments about her draft. I called her at five, and she said, "Your article was chilling!"

And I said, "That's how yours should read."

That's what people don't get. A good article jumps off the page. I owe that to my reader.

Leslie Heilbrunn, senior editor, *Cosmo Girl*

seizing control at the last minute and making desperate changes in the waning moments of the schedule.

And good writers appreciate the chance to revise their own work. They want to look good to those 1.5 million readers who will see the article next, and they want great clips that can help them land assignments in the future. Revision isn't drudgery. It's a chance at excellence.

With clear feedback and ample time, writers can rise to the occasion and turn decent articles into masterpieces. And the extra work is

Editors spend much of their time rewriting submitted articles and negotiating changes with authors.... As is true of most aspects of editing, deciding how deeply to edit requires judgment and literary tact, which can be developed only by years of heavy-duty reading. I feel I must add that the editor, although dealing aggressively with the words on the page, does so in a spirit of humility. Almost never does an editor know as much about the topic as the writer, and the interchange between the editor and the writer must reflect this. In particular, editors need to periodically ask themselves whether they could support themselves as freelance writers.

Diane Lutz, editor, *Muse*

worth the payoff: a stellar article that was written—*entirely*—by the writer.

But there are times when the editor has to take over the rewriting duties. Sometimes, the writer has moved on to other projects and no longer has the time to work on this one. Sometimes, the writer is burned out on the topic and just can't bring himself to look at the article one more time. And sometimes, the original manuscript really does represent the writer's very best work—and so any improvements have to come from someone else.

• *Uphold the bargain.* Good editors know that writers require certain things. The writers might put words to paper for the greater good of humankind, but there are necessary ulterior motives that the editor would be wise to address.

For one thing, good editors pay writers promptly. Whether you're working with a highly successful and expensive writer whose work commands thousands of dollars, or a rookie who would be happy with a byline and a free lunch, the deal should be honored quickly and completely. Just as soon as the final draft has been accepted for publication, good editors initiate the paperwork that will make a check appear in the writer's mailbox. In some companies, the check-cutting procedures can be prolonged and cumbersome, so the editor should get the process going right away.

Building Relationships with Writers

One goal of every serious editor is to build close relationships with several talented, dedicated, and hardworking writers. Such relationships represent success, and they allow the editor to focus on the things that matter—delivering solid, engaging, informative articles that readers love—rather than training a new crop of writers with each issue.

How do you find and keep good writers? Find them by trial and error. Keep them by offering them challenging, interesting assignments. Keep them motivated by developing a personal relationship with them. By being understanding, respectful, offering useful feedback and praise—and paying them promptly.

Jeff Csatari, executive editor, *Men's Health*

Q: How do you find—and keep—good writers?

A: You find good writers by reading, acquire them by asking, and keep them by treating them—and their work—with humility and respect.

Q: How do you keep them motivated?

A: You keep them motivated by reminding them that the fate of the world hangs on what they write, and by demanding that they do their very best work. You get their best by granting them freedom—mostly freedom to fall flat on their faces. If that happens, you must be prepared to rescue them but let them believe they did it themselves. They'll need all their confidence to get through the research process.

Q: How do you keep writers from driving you crazy?

A: I'm crazy already, so I'm inoculated. Behavioral excesses just bounce off my feathers like a raindrop.

Q: How do you edit a manuscript without losing the writer's voice?

A: By pretending I am the writer. I told you I was crazy!

Don Belt, senior editor and geography/world affairs editor, *National Geographic*

Like any good relationship, the bond between writer and editor has to be based on trust, respect, and support. A lot of people believe that the relationship is adversarial, but in most cases it is not. Both the writer and the editor want the same thing: an excellent article that the readers will love. They might disagree here and there about how to accomplish that goal, but negotiations—rather than threats, raised voices, ultimatums, and pointed references to the fine print in contracts—tend to produce results that please both parties. Some of my best writers have grappled with me over article ideas, sources, structures, and leads, but in the end, the articles were strong and both the writers and I were eager to do it again.

It's the balancing of the short-term goal—an outstanding article—and the long-term goal—a productive partnership that results in good articles over and over again—that presents editors with the greatest challenge and the sweetest successes.

Good editors understand that, and they work hard to accomplish both.

7. Hands Off!

First, Make Sure It Makes Sense

When I look at manuscripts the first time out, when a reporter files to his or her editor, I will give my thoughts. I'm not line editing at all. I'm the ultimate backfield editor, and then I don't see it again until that reporter's editor is finished with it. Then I take a look, and I will put in my comments—but once again, I'm not line editing.

Margot Slade, editor, *Consumer Reports*

You have a solid sense of your magazine's mission and character. You developed a drop-dead-perfect idea that is sure to grace the magazine's cover and convince scores of readers to subscribe for life. You scoured the planet for the perfect writer for the job. The writer was thrilled with the assignment and dug into the research with near-giddy abandon.

And then you waited.

The calendar sloughed off pages slowly as the deadline approached. For the writer, the deadline means pressure and productivity, but for the editor, it means patience. You chat with the writer, who assures you that everything is going well. You hang up the phone.

And you wait some more.

But then the day arrives, and the mail carrier trudges up the stairs. You grab the stack of envelopes and ferret through the unimportant, uninteresting, and unworthy, searching for the article you have been anticipating for weeks.

There it is! You tuck it under your arm and scurry into your office, closing your door and taking your phone off the hook.

And you start to read. The lead looks good, although that adjective really ought to come out. With a deft flourish of your pen, it is marked for permanent removal. And that comma splice—*tsk, tsk!* A swift dot converts the comma to a semicolon that brims with punctuational correctness. And that metaphor—what *was* this writer thinking? Replacing that clunky comparison with scintillating simile makes the sentence shine. This is great! Weak writing is dying at the tip of your pen! Improvements are leaping onto the page! This is terrific! This is editing at its best!

No, it's not.

In fact, it's awfully close to editing at its worst.

Time to rewind the tape and play it again. The mail carrier delivers the manuscript. You ensconce yourself in your office and open the envelope. Then you put all pens, pencils, markers, white-out, and sticky notes away. This is not the time to mark up pages.

This is the time to read.

Your readers will approach the article empty-handed, ready to appreciate the piece without worrying about the intricacies of punctuation or grammar or structure. And for this first read, you should do the same. Just read it. Enjoy it. Pay attention to your feelings, your thoughts, and your reactions as you take it all in. But don't make any marks at all.

Just read.

The impulse to grab a pencil and start making corrections as you dig through a manuscript is strong. After all, if you see something that should be improved, every editor gene in your body screams for the change to be made right away.

Still, there are several good reasons for approaching a manuscript in this hands-off way.

• *Changes should be made only after you understand the entire manuscript.* Writers often do things for effect. That word repetition that jumps out at you, screaming for a thesaurus and a few clever marks on the page, might have been intentional—but you won't know that until you read on. That misspelling might be part of a deliberate pun. That metaphor might be essential for the ending of the article to make sense.

Until you have read the manuscript from beginning to end, you can't possibly know how all the elements fit together. Hacking away at each sentence as you read it is a little like unveiling a sculpture one section at a time and critiquing it ("That finger is obviously too large. Now let's look at the entire hand"). Only by understanding the article as a whole can you begin to determine whether changes to any specific part of it are necessary.

Along similar lines, immediate and vigorous editing—while sometimes quite satisfying and ego-inflating ("Look! There's the lead! I'll move it up")—is insulting to your writer. You hired her to do a job, and she has done it, presumably, to the best of her ability. She has worked hard to gather information, organize it in a rational way, and write it up with clear and engaging prose. Pouncing on the dangling participle in the second sentence is hardly helpful—whether the writer is present or not. Good editors respect their writers, and respectful editors want to savor and appreciate the entire work of art before imagining ways to improve it.

• *The writer should make the changes.* As discussed previously, the best editors develop thoughtful critiques of their writers' articles—and then ask the writers to make the changes. Writers generally prefer to change their work themselves, rather than opening the magazine only to discover that altered—and sometimes erroneous, offensive, or embarrassing—prose has crept beneath their bylines.

For example, we were all taught by blue-haired fifth-grade English teachers that passive voice is wrong. Bad, bad, bad. We should sniff out all passive voice and stomp it into activity.

So an overzealous editor might shriek at a malingering passive construction on page 2 and scramble for a large and colorful marker with which to correct it. It's bad, after all—bad, bad, bad—and it feels valorous to choke the life out of passive voice and replace it with its vibrant and living cousin.

But what if the passive voice is deliberate? What if the writer built the sentence that way on purpose? Passive voice can be quite useful, for example, when writers want to conceal the active agent in a sentence. If a White House staffer offered dark secrets in a shadowy parking garage, passive voice can (and sometimes must) be used to keep that person's identity secret:

The president has been accused of...

So the overactive editor might introduce trouble by correcting each "error" as she finds it. She also might compound that blunder because she has to infer who the active agent was supposed to be—and she just might be wrong.

A respectful editor would flag such passages and ask the writer to make the changes if necessary. This procedure gives the writer a chance to point out the rationale behind the sentence, and the editor could then weigh the validity of the argument and negotiate solutions with the writer.

- *The first job is to evaluate the manuscript as a whole—not as a collection of sentences.* Diving immediately into sentence-level editing reflects a certain lack of priorities. There's little point in correcting the small things if big problems threaten the whole project. That would be like asking your mechanic to clean the fuel injectors—and then asking him to replace the engine.

If the article makes no sense, then fixing the noun–verb agreement on page 3 is a waste of time.

If the article's tone is all wrong, then moving the fourth paragraph to the lead is pointless.

If the article doesn't fit with the magazine's mission, then correcting the punctuation is silly.

That's really the point behind the "layers of editing" concept. We start with the big picture, and then we gradually work our way down to the smaller details. We begin with thoughts about a magazine's character, purpose, and function. We grapple with issues of audience and needs. Then we move down to a narrower field, exploring ways to convert our understanding of the magazine and the audience into article ideas and assignments.

And now that the manuscript is in our hands, we will continue with this large-to-small progression. We'll start with the big manuscript-level questions, working our way down to nitty-gritty grammar problems only after the larger issues are settled.

The first three manuscript-level questions have nothing to do with grammar or the order of paragraphs:

1. Does this article make any sense?
2. Does the article represent a good fit for this magazine?
3. Is the tone right for the topic, for the magazine, and for the audience?

We'll explore these questions in greater depth, in this chapter and the next.

Sense

It seems like such a simple question: Does this article make sense?

But one of the many challenges of editing is to stop and think seriously about something that otherwise might trip right off the tops of our heads. It would be quite easy to read a manuscript, ask whether it makes sense, think for half a second, shrug our shoulders, say "Sure!" and move on.

But *are* we sure? Can we say with authority, confidence, and enthusiasm that this article makes sense? that every facet, every point, every paragraph is clear, logical, and sound?

The sense of something comes to us so readily that is easy to glide right over this all-important question, especially under the heat of deadline pressures and amid the distractions of all the other demands on our lives.

And yet, of course, few problems would be as destructive to an article—and a magazine—as not making sense. An article that forces its readers to say, "Wait a minute. What? I don't get it," is destined to lose them. Readers love a good mystery; they adore suspense; they enjoy puzzles and riddles and quests. But only if it appears in an article that is well presented, strong, and clear—not if the article itself is a mystery. If the article fumbles and stumbles along, leaving readers confused and creating more questions than it answers, then readers will not have a good time. They will not devote time and energy to the task of deciphering what the writer meant to say. Or was supposed to say. Or should have said for the sake of clarity and confidence. Instead, they will mutter something unpleasant and turn the page, never to return to that article again. Or worse: they will note the writer's name and never read any of his articles again. Or even worse: they will throw the magazine down in annoyance and never buy it again, turning elsewhere for their information and entertainment.

They have lots of options. Magazines have lots of competitors.

So we had better not let that happen. We had better make sure—absolutely *certain*—that each article makes sense.

To do that, we would be wise to break apart this concept of sense and convert it into a series of questions we can ask. These questions, taken together, constitute what it means for an article to make sense.

1. *Does the article stick to one topic?* An article that jumps around from one topic to another, or that tries to encompass too much, isn't likely to make much sense. It would be like a haphazard and overstuffed suitcase—sure, everything is in there, but good luck trying to find the item you need.

A good article should have a single point that is well focused, clear, and easy to state in a single sentence. Not like this:

> This article is about a local heavy-metal band, and how hard it is to break into the music business because the record labels and the radio stations want only the typical, corporate kind of sound, which means that small but inspired bands like Iceberg Lettuce, which has a hip and really cool sound, can't get any airtime. It's also about how the band was formed, and how cool each member is, especially Mange, who plays bass. And it also talks about why the music scene in my town is really lame, except for Iceberg Lettuce.

But like this, which is dramatically better:

> This article, which focuses on one heavy-metal band called Iceberg Lettuce, is about the struggles that up-and-coming bands experience as they try to move from local popularity to national stardom.

Gone from the dramatically better version of the article is the scattering of random, tangential points that the bad example tried to cram into the article. This improved version won't tell readers why the music scene in one particular town is lame (which also reeks of personal, unsupported opinion). It also won't focus on how the band was formed, unless it dispatches that point with a flicker of a phrase and moves on to the main point. And it really won't talk about how cool each band member is. Mange is on his own.

The core of the improvement from the bad to the dramatically better example is focus. The improved version focuses on a single, clear idea: the difficulty that small bands experience when they try to break onto the national scene. As heartbreaking as it might be for the writer, the rest of the material has got to go.

2. *Is the article well organized?* Even an article with a tight focus will still offer a galaxy of interesting points. The challenge for writers—or editors, if the writers fail—is to make sure that those points are presented in some kind of logical and satisfying order. We'll

look at article structure more fully in chapter 9, but at this initial level, organization matters because it has a direct impact on sense.

So for now, as you read and think about the manuscript for the first time, you should consider whether it flows rationally from one point to another, or whether it jumps around like a nervous frog. Articles that leap from point A to point C, then point B, then a little more about A, then finish up C on our way to G, then backtrack to D, E, and F, and finally skip over G because it's been done already and get on to H—obviously, that article will be difficult to follow. It won't flow, it won't educate, it won't entertain, and it won't make sense.

There are a few good tests to determine whether an article is organized well enough to make decent sense. If the article seems awfully long, for example—even though it really isn't—it probably suffers from an organizational problem. It feels long because the reader can't tell where he is amid all that clamoring information, because the article repeatedly touches back on points that were already made, and because in the absence of a good structure it feels like it's never going to end.

Another test for organization is to insert subheads over each section. A subhead is a single word or short phrase that serves as a section break and an interesting label for the upcoming section. By putting subheads over every section, you can see whether any given section contains information that actually belongs to another one. You also can see how the sections relate to one another; your fifth section might be closely linked to your second one, so you might want to move it up.

The third test also serves as a good remedy for bad organization. I have recommended this approach to many writers who have submitted good articles that suffer from wandering or loose-jointed organization. The test feels cumbersome and old-fashioned, and my writers rarely actually did it if I stopped short of insisting on it. But it works.

For this test, print out the article and tape the pages together: bottom of page 1 to top of page 2, bottom of page 2 to top of page 3, and so on. You'll end up with one long ribbon of text, much like the printouts from older computer systems.

Now take a pair of scissors and cut up the ribbon of text, paragraph by paragraph. You should end up with a ragged stack of smallish pieces of paper, each with a single paragraph on it.

Now hold the stack of papers, stand in the middle of the room, close your eyes, and toss the paragraphs vigorously into the air.

Now enjoy the sight of dozens of overgrown snowflakes fluttering clumsily to the floor.

With luck, the paragraphs are now rather randomly scattered across the carpeting. Grab any paragraph, read it quickly, and write a topic label on it. For this example, let's say the article is a profile and the paragraph you just grabbed has to do with the person's family. You write "Family" on it and put it down.

Grab another paragraph. If it also is about the person's family, put it underneath the paragraph labeled "Family." If it is about something else, give it another label—say, "Job"—and use it to start a new stack.

Keep going.

When all the paragraphs have been sorted, you should end up with several piles of papers, each with its own theme. You also might end up with a small collection of paragraphs that don't really fit into any of the labeled stacks. Look them over. If they might work in the lead or the conclusion, give them that label and make a new pile. If not, wad them up and see if you can hit the trash can from where you're sitting. With every stray paragraph you discard, the focus of the article becomes sharper.

Now that you have all the paragraphs sorted into their thematic piles, look at the paragraphs in each pile and sort them—which should come first, which second, and so on.

Now things get easy. Just decide the proper order for the themes, gather the stacks according to that order, and sit down at the computer. If the order in the Grand Pile is roughly similar to the order of paragraphs on your screen, the article is probably well organized. Any disagreements can be considered, and you can decide which version works better.

If the order is dramatically different, you (or better yet, your writer) should reorder the paragraphs on the screen to reflect the order in the Grand Pile. Then she should go over the resultant article a few times, smoothing transitions and enhancing the flow.

3. *Does the article answer all the questions it raises?* Playwright Anton Chekhov once wrote, "If there is a gun hanging on the wall in the first act, it must fire in the last." The advice is sound for magazine articles as well. If you introduce something that raises a ques-

tion, you really ought to answer that question before ending the article and leaving the reader to spend the rest of her life wondering about it.

Articles naturally raise questions as they go along: Why did she do that? What's going to happen with that teetering boulder? Did the bomb ever go off? Did they get married? How did he get that black eye? Was the operation successful? Who won the game? And so on.

For an article to make sense, any questions that it brings up in the reader's mind should be wrapped up eventually. (Unless, of course, the writer is trying to be enigmatic for stylistic reasons.) Sometimes, it takes a discerning eye to detect and predict the questions that readers will ask, and it often is an easier task for the editor, who reads the article with fairly fresh eyes, than it is for the writer, who is trying to create order out of the jumble of information lurching around in his mind.

And so, once again, the editor will deliberately stop, think, and consider the question. I often find it easier to state the question in an emphatic form. Rather than asking, "Are there any unanswered questions here?" I'll ask, "Which questions are left unanswered?" I then scour the manuscript looking for them.

4. *Does the article leave any loose threads?* This is related to question 3, but it has an important distinction. For question 3, we were looking for specific questions that were likely to pop into readers' minds. Now we're looking for paths of discussion that were opened but never completed.

For example, if your writer submits an article about the New York subway system, and she leads the article with an anecdote about a young man scrambling to get through the system in time to make an important job interview, then before the end of the article, the success or failure of the young man's quest should be presented. Did he get there on time? How did he do? Did he get the job?

Similarly, if the article is about camping in the Adirondacks, the article really should discuss the wildlife there—particularly the bears, which can rip apart a campsite in no time as they search for easy snacks. Mentioning camping in the Adirondacks opens the "wildlife" path, and readers won't feel satisfied if they article doesn't venture in that direction.

5. *Does the article talk about what it talks about?* Seems a bit mysterious, like the philosophical difference between "being" and "be-

coming," but the question actually is valid. Some articles purport to be on a particular topic—how to avoid getting fired from your first job, for example—when in fact they really focus on something else altogether, such as why the managers of retail stores are so mean to their employees.

For an article to make sense, it should aim at the target it sets for itself. If the goal is to tell readers about the dangers of skin cancer, the article should relay that information. If it concentrates on the lunacy of tanning beds instead, then something's amiss. Either the article should be reworked to focus on its stated topic, or its stated topic should be adjusted to reflect the actual content of the article.

One of the most common ways that articles misrepresent themselves has to do with the writer's infatuation with himself. The article ostensibly is about learning how to snowboard, but in fact it's *really* about how cool I am on the slopes. The article seems to be about the Rolling Stones, but it's *really* about the fact that I got to spend time with them in their dressing room. The article says that it's about the nutritional value of hot dogs, but it's *really* about the fun I had driving the Weinermobile.

In cases like these, not only should the article be reworked to align the stated topic with the real content, but the writer's name should also be placed in a "Use with Caution" file. The writer might think that "Me, Me, Me!" is an interesting topic, but most readers will find it Boring, Boring, Boring.

6. *Will the article make sense to readers who possess ordinary vocabularies?* Unless your magazine is aimed at specialists who use certain esoteric terms regularly, you'll have to make sure that the terms used in the article can be understood by your readers. Few things cause readers to toss aside a magazine faster than a word that is unfamiliar and undecipherable.

This doesn't mean that your writers should shun precise language. If *jejune* is absolutely the right word for a particular point, then *jejune* it is. But if *immature* works just as well, and your readers aren't likely to know what *jejune* means, then *immature* is a better choice. As the editors at *International Wildlife* put it: "Avoid the lingo of biologists or wildlife managers. Remember, our readers, no matter how well educated, are 'just folks.'"

Sometimes, unfamiliar language creeps into an article because the writer is so close to the subject that the jargon seems fine. If your writer has been interviewing America's Cup racers for weeks now, references to spinnaker poles, lay lines, and jib sheets might strike her as reasonable and proper. And for the readers of *Sail Magazine*, those terms would be fine. But if you're working for *Men's Health*, you can't assume that your readers will be able to tell a boom vang from a back stay. Because the writer is too involved in the story to remember what ordinary people will understand, it becomes the editor's job to draw the line and make sure that all terminology is either appropriate to the audience or properly defined in the article.

Another reason that bewildering terms sneak into articles has to do with thesaurus abuse. Writers who want to liven up their writing, or who feel that they are using certain terms too often in a particular story, sometimes turn to a thesaurus to find suitable alternatives to basic words. It's a dangerous move. In one thesaurus, for example, the following alternatives are offered for the noun *secret*:

- Mystery
- Riddle
- Labyrinth
- Problem
- Hyrcynian wood

Mystery, of course, has connotations profoundly different from those of *riddle*. "Why did the chicken cross the road?" can hardly be called a mystery. A labyrinth is a maze, and a problem is any challenge that carries negative potential. So a writer who grabbed a thesaurus in an effort to modify her natural vocabulary might present something truly odd:

I was pregnant, and I just couldn't keep it a labyrinth any longer.

It doesn't work. The writer chose a word she clearly isn't familiar with, and the result is a sentence that is both off-putting and just plain wrong.

And, for the record, any writer who inserts *Hyrcynian wood* into a sentence when *secret* would do should be legally barred from touching keyboards ever again.

The third reason that unfamiliar terms wiggle their way into articles has to do with ego. Some writers feel that articles offer them a chance to impress people—and they probably do. Articles allow writers to showcase the thoroughness of their research, the grace and precision of their writing, and the passion and humor with which they grapple with the world's challenges.

But not their vocabulary. No one is going to be impressed that they know what *jejune* means.

No one at all.

Readers won't say, "Wow! This writer knows a lot of big words! I wish I were as smart as he is!" Instead, they'll say, "Wow! This writer is a jerk, and I can't figure out what this article is talking about. I wonder what's on Oprah." And away they go.

One writer I worked with wrote an article in which he described himself as the *penultimate* professional. He probably thought he was bragging, but in reality he was telling the world that he was next to last.

Big words aren't the only facet of vocabulary that editors have to monitor. Sometimes writers insert foreign words and phrases into their writing, *n'est-ce pas*? It's one of those lose–lose maneuvers. If the reader knows what the phrase means, she won't be dazzled that the writer knows it, too. And if the reader doesn't know what the phrase means, she won't be impressed—she'll just get annoyed and turn the page.

When unfamiliar terms are tossed into articles, editors face the responsibility of spotting them and getting writers to replace them. In the heat of deadline pressures, and in the momentum of receiving an article and hoping that it's perfect, it's easy to glide past strange words and phrases and assume that the people who understand them will probably think they are just fine. But editors can't do that. Because editors are responsible for the material they publish, they can't simply hope that everything is accurate and proper. They have to check the facts—and that means that they have to understand the facts. They have to get to people who can explain the terms, and then they have to make sound editorial decisions based on that understanding. Nothing should ever get past an editor if he doesn't understand it.

7. Is all the math correct? Yes, it's the *M* word. Math is why a lot of people become writers and editors in the first place: we don't have to do all that much of it. But if an article includes mathematical formulas or computation of any sort, we have to make sure the math is right. Otherwise, how can we be sure that the article makes sense?

I once edited a booklet for a private secondary school. The booklet mentioned that the school had a $19 million endowment, and that "5 percent of the income" was used to fund the day-to-day operations.

That sounded fine, but dutifully, I checked the math. In a good year, an endowment earns about 8 percent. So a $19 million endowment would bring in $1.52 million each year.

So far, so good. The phrase I was checking said that "5 percent of the income" paid for salaries and lightbulbs. So that means 5 percent of $1.52 million. I did the math, checked it twice—$76,000. Five percent of the income from a $19 million endowment is $76,000—enough to pay the salary of one experienced, senior teacher or a low-level administrator, but nowhere near enough to run the entire school for a year.

When I pressed for clarification, I found out what was meant by "5 percent of the income." If the income from an endowment is usually around 8 percent, *five of those 8 percents* would go toward running the school, and the other three would be rolled back into the endowment. So the endowment kicked almost $1 million into the operating budget. Oh! That's what they meant, but it's not what they said. If I hadn't checked the math, I would have published incorrect information.

8. *Does the logic hold up?* This is an especially important question when writers are dealing with politicians and businesspeople, who want publicity skewed in particular ways. They also can be quite charming in person, so writers are sometimes caught in the spell and reluctant to look too closely at the validity of the actual statements.

A situation from Indiana can illustrate the point. A challenger for governor a while ago accused the incumbent of raising taxes thirty-four times. It seems a bit difficult to cram thirty-four tax hikes into a typical political career, so the claim was checked out. It turned out that the incumbent had supported a bill that raised taxes for a certain type of inn—and there were thirty-four of them in the state. The incumbent had raised taxes once, but his opponent tried to paint him as tax-happy and irresponsible.

Some basic facts about logic can help editors make sure that the information in their articles makes sense:

• *Trends are not predictors.* Just because the population of Boomville has doubled every twenty years doesn't mean that it is going to double in the next twenty years. Trends almost always level off—or even reverse—eventually, and it can be difficult to predict when that turnaround is going to happen.

This doesn't slow down some people, though. You'll still hear arguments that say things like "at this rate, Boomville will be larger than New York in a century and a half." No, it won't. It won't double in population every twenty years for the next century and a half. Sooner or later, the big steering-wheel factory is going to move somewhere else, the waterfront will catch on fire, the railroad will stop stopping in town, or something else will happen to change the trend. New York is huge for a reason. The population of small towns go up and down over time.

• *The past is not a predictor in every case.* This fact is similar to the first one, but it doesn't necessarily involve trends. If I flip a coin and get heads, the odds that I'll get heads on the next toss are 50–50. If it comes up heads a second time, the odds that I'll get heads on the third try are still 50–50. I could flip a coin a hundred times and get a hundred heads—and the odds on the next flip would be 50–50.

• *It is extremely difficult to prove a negative.* If an article alleges that the mayor keeps his grandmother chained to an anvil in the attic, it is nearly impossible for him to prove that he doesn't. Sure, he could give a tour of his attic—but he might have shuffled Granny off to the basement just in time. Yes, he could produce Granny, happy and healthy, at a retirement home in Boca Raton—but she might be an actress taking the place of the real thing. In other words, it's basically impossible for him to prove that the allegation is false.

Writers have to be especially sensitive to this pitfall when dealing with politicians and others who stand to benefit from another person's fall. Branding someone as unpatriotic, for example, is a standard political ploy; the target of the accusation will have a hard time proving that he isn't an America-hater. But again, writers can get swept up by the charisma and generosity of the people they interview, so the real work falls to the editor, who must think rationally about every claim and make sure that all arguments are fairly and reasonably spelled out.

• *Beware of* all, every, none, *and similar generalizations.* There's an old saying: It takes but one white crow to prove that not all crows are black. In other words, if an article claims that everyone supports the president's agenda, it is almost certainly wrong. All it takes is one person to oppose the agenda, and the claim is invalid. If an article says that no motorcycle can go faster than 150 miles per hour, all you need is one big guy going down a steep hill on a Harley with a tailwind, and the article is inaccurate. If an article states that all laptop computers are priced under $3,000, all you have to do is stop by Wild Ralph's Computer Barn during double-markup day, and the point is false. There are no statements that hold up 100 percent of the time. Well, almost none, anyway.

9. Should any of the information be presented in another format? Sometimes, the best thing you can do for an article is to remove the "heavy cargo"—the statistics, facts, and other pieces of hard data—and present the information in another way. Rather than making your readers hack their way through a dense undergrowth of facts and figures, you might make them happier by presenting that material in a chart, a graph, an "infographic" (*USA Today–*

Presentation is everything. Coming from a word person, this advice is sometimes even hard for me to swallow. Usually when our art director suggests changes in a story because of a design constraint, my first reaction is "Why can't you make the design fit the copy? I need those 20 extra lines." But usually once I see his design concept, he wins out—because we really do believe that presentation is everything in making a story or even a special report accessible to the reader. Be committed to integrating pictures and words—using graphics to their best advantage.

Susan Ungaro, editor, *Family Circle*

> We have to think in terms of "Is the written word the best way to convey this information, or is a graphic more informative?" Will readers understand more quickly and more accurately if they see illustration plus text? Your information can be fabulous, but if the consumer can't access it quickly and easily, then it's useless information. I always tell editors that their responsibility is not only to make sure the stories are readable—but that they get read. If it's too dense on the page, if the information is not understandable, if it's not presented in a form that welcomes the reader, you're not doing your reader a service.
>
> **Margot Slade, editor, *Consumer Reports***

type graphic that conveys information), a sidebar, or another form of presentation.

Putting the heavy cargo in a nearby box helps in several ways. First, it relieves the main article of a hefty burden, letting readers get on with the story you are trying to tell. Second, it allows readers who are interested in the material dig their way through it, while those who aren't interested can just skip the box and move on.

If you keep these thoughts in mind, and you take the time to look over the manuscript and challenge it to make sense to you, you'll catch and correct a lot of sloppy errors that otherwise would have confused or mislead your readers.

Adspeak

Advertising lingo, phrasing, and thinking have crept into our daily communication, and the result is slippery logic and shoddy sense. For evidence on the lingo front, listen to any newscast and hear how often the anchor uses the word *plus* instead of *and*:

> Coming up, the latest developments in that Brownie-Scout crime spree. Plus, we'll have the up-to-the-nanosecond forecast from meteorologist Willie Freeze.

Would *and* have killed them? That *plus* came from advertising; someone apparently determined that *plus* sounded like a bigger deal than *and,* and the rest of the English-speaking world is beginning to follow suit.

The problem here—besides the erosion of the English language to the point of babbling incoherency, but that's another point—is that adspeak deliberately uses shifty logic to make its claims. As the approaches of advertising elbow their way into everyday language, so does the logical misdirection that goes with them.

For example, innumerable ads insist that the products being pitched do more: "Buy Skam—the *tastier* spiced kangaroo meat!" Tastier? Tastier than what? The ad doesn't say. The makers of the ad left that part out on purpose. They aren't making a logical argument; they're just trying to plant a thought in people's minds: Skam = tasty.

Such approaches are standard fare in advertising, but they can cause real problems in magazine articles. If an article states that readers should use varnish on their front doors because "it dries faster," then it's up to the editor to challenge the statement. It dries faster than what? Jello? molasses? The implication is that it dries faster than other forms of wood protection—but that's not what the article says. And editors have to ensure that articles say what they mean, rather than offering vague implications and hoping that readers will figure them out.

Similarly, ads often waltz around with numbers and statistics in ways that would be inexcusable in articles. "More people prefer Frizz—the caffeinated breakfast cereal!" Prefer Frizz to what? Even if the line provides that information, it's still goofing with logic: "More people prefer Frizz than any other caffeinated breakfast cereal!" OK, that helps—but we still don't know how many people like Frizz. For all we know, only five people in the world like caffeinated breakfast cereals, and three of them prefer Frizz to the other brand. That still leaves us with just three people on the planet who like this stuff.

For one last example, consider the "nothing is proven more effective" line: "Use Slugz! Nothing is proven more effective at keeping nasty, ugly slugs from sliming up your garden." If we think about that line for a moment, we realize that the Slugz people haven't said a thing. First of all, they say that nothing is *proven* more effective. More effective products might exist, but no rigorous experiments have been done to *prove* their superiority. Also, we have no reason to believe that any studies have been done about Slugz. For all we know, it is completely useless. But technically, nothing has been proven more effective.

In ads, that's pretty much the way the game is played. But in magazine articles, we have to be more careful. We have to state numbers when we have them, and we must establish clear relationships even when the numbers are absent. We have to avoid sweeping claims that no one can validate. We have to make sure that the arguments hold water.

Symbolic Logic

All magazine editors should take a course in symbolic logic. (That's an unsupported, personal opinion—a weak technique in magazine articles, but sometimes tolerable in textbooks.)

Symbolic logic uses symbols to spell out the core argument in any given claim, and it offers rules for determining the validity of that logic.

For example:

If you own a Maserati or a Lamborghini, then you own a
    sports car.
You own a Maserati.
Therefore, you own a sports car.

Is that argument reasonable? Yes. The symbolic-logic folks would put it this way: assign the letter A to the fact of owning a Maserati. Assign B to owning a Lamborghini. Assign C to owning a sports car. So:

If A or B, then C.
A.
Therefore, C.

According to the rules of symbolic logic, that's a good argument. But now we can play with variations: you own a sports car. Therefore, you own a Maserati or a Lamborghini.

Valid? No. You might own a Porsche, which would be considered a sports car but is not a Maserati or a Lamborghini. The symbolic part would look like this:

If A or B, then C. (Same as before.)

C.

Therefore—nothing. (*C* doesn't necessarily get us *A* or *B*.)

Understanding symbolic logic can help editors detect logical traps. A publication in my former town once ran an article that talked about the recent hiring of a women's basketball coach at the local university. The writer noted that the person hired had less experience than did the other two candidates for the job. The writer also noted that people with more experience tend to command higher salaries than do relative beginners. "It can only be assumed, then," the article read, "that the university administrators were more interested in saving money than they were in having a strong women's basketball program."

Bad logic for several reasons. First, just because experienced coaches tend to require higher salaries than do the rookies, that doesn't necessarily mean that the less-experienced coach who was hired cost less than her rivals would have. In this case, the successful candidate might have racked up a dazzling track record in a short amount of time, and she might have been confident and aggressive enough to demand a whopping salary. So:

Most *A*s (experienced coaches) require *B* (lots of loot).

Not-*A* (we have a relatively inexperienced coach).

Therefore, not-*B* (low salary).

Wrong, wrong, wrong. The key to this problem is the word *most*. Obviously, there are exceptions—otherwise, the word would be *all*.

The logic problems continued. The writer assumed that only two things matter when hiring a coach: experience and salary. But, of course, you might choose a less-experienced coach for several reasons that have nothing to do with money: she is smarter, she is better at motivating student athletes, she offers expertise in a particular area that the university wants (conditioning, teamwork, on-court strategy, and the like), she is an alumna of the university, and so on.

A course in logic can help editors spot these problems and arrest them before they end up in print. Such phrases as *it can only be assumed, it stands to reason, it seems clear that,* and *common sense suggests that* should serve as red flags, alerting editors to areas in which the logic might be a bit shifty. And, again, it might not be the case that the writer is trying to fudge the information. Writers can get so close to their material, to their stories, and to their sources that cold-blooded logic gives way to enthusiastic sentiment. Working at a distance from the on-the-ground research, editors can challenge articles and make sure that only the most valid arguments are placed before readers.

Sense and Sensibility

It would take a somewhat neurotic editor to pore over a manuscript with a condensed version of this chapter as a checklist: Does the article stick to one topic? Check! Is it well organized? Check!

Nevertheless, these are the kinds of things that good editors consider when they read a manuscript for the first time. They read the article carefully, and then they put it aside and stare out a window for a while, thinking over the piece as a whole. They know that the challenge facing them has little to do with the rules of grammar, the organization of paragraphs, or the spelling of proper nouns. All of that is important—but not right now. If an article makes no sense and has to be dramatically rewritten—or scrapped altogether—it doesn't matter a whole lot that the twelfth paragraph refers to Vincent Van Goo.

So the thing to do when the much-awaited manuscript finally arrives is to read it all the way through without allowing a pencil to touch your hands. Your goal at this stage is not to decorate the manuscript with colorful and witty comments about punctuation and dangling modifiers. Your goal is to decide, on a grand scale, whether the article makes sense. If it doesn't, nothing else is important. You must get in touch with the writer, explain the shortcomings, negotiate a deadline for the rewrite, and work closely with the writer to make sure that the new draft makes sense in every way. Editors can't inject sense into a manuscript; the only one who can fix it is the writer.

If the article passes the "sense" test, then you can move on to the next stages of editing confident that the article has held up under your careful and logical scrutiny.

8. Editorial Muscle:
Checking an Article's Fit and Tone

If the writer knows exactly what you want—and delivers that—you won't have to mess with his voice. But that voice should be consistent with the voice of your magazine or what you expect when you first make the assignment. But you should also not be afraid to lose the writer's voice if he can't make the piece work through revision. That's when you have to think only of the reader. Deliver the best piece for the reader.

Jeff Csatari, executive editor, *Men's Health*

So far, so good. The idea was brilliant, the writer delivered the article on time, and the whole piece seems to make sense. You have considered it carefully from several different angles, and the article holds up.

Now it's time to check the next two important aspects of the article:

1. Does this article "fit"?
2. Is the tone appropriate?

First, however, a reminder—we're still in "hands off" mode. You have read the article through and checked it carefully to be sure it makes sense, and still the manuscript doesn't have a single mark on it. You might have a dozen questions for the writer, all scribbled on a sheet of notebook paper on your desk. But the manuscript is pristine—and for now, it should stay that way.

Questions about fit and tone occupy the same layer of editing as sense. We're still thinking about the article as a whole, making broad decisions about its appropriateness for the magazine. We're still at that stage in which problems or concerns could—and probably would—result in large-scale rewrites, so any little sentence-level problems should be ignored. There's no point in fixing a sentence if the rewrite is going to result in its demise.

Facets of Fit

When talking about newly submitted magazine articles, the term *fit* takes on several different meanings. All of them focus on specific questions that the editor should ask during and after the first read of the manuscript.

Some of these questions harken back to the time when the assignment was first made, but they have added significance now. At the assignment stage, ideas are general and visions are blurry. Now that the article is in hand, you can judge more precisely how well it fits. You can assess the original idea more clearly, and you can weigh the article itself against the demands that you place on it.

• *Does the article fit the magazine's mission?* When the article idea was proposed by the writer or cooked up by the editor, it was scrutinized by the editor to make sure it meshed with the magazine's mission. Presumably, the fit seemed good; otherwise, the assignment would not have been made.

Now that the wispy idea has morphed into black letters on white paper, you have another chance to evaluate it. Does the idea serve your mission? Which part of the mission does it serve? Can you name that part of the mission, or is it just a vague feeling of support? *How* does this idea mesh with the mission? *Why* does this idea reinforce that particular part of the mission?

In addition to reevaluating the original idea, you now can gauge the fit of the article itself. Does the article fulfill the assignment so precisely that it upholds the same part of the mission? Or did the article drift a bit between the assignment and the submission? If it drifted, does it still fulfill some part of your mission? If so, it might still be acceptable. If it no longer helps the magazine meet its mission, though, the entire operation is in trouble.

If at this stage an editor detects a problem in the fit between the article idea and the magazine's mission—or between the actual article and the mission—the article will have to be rewritten, postponed, or killed altogether. If you kill it, you'll have to rearrange other assignments and articles to fill the space that was reserved for it.

And somewhere in here, you'll have to decide what to do about the writer. If the idea was fine but the writer delivered an article that misses the mark, you can simply reject the article and clean up the damage. But if the calamity happened because you and the other editors did a bad job of understanding the fit between the original idea and the mission—and the writer hit the target you set out for her—you might have to pay the writer a "kill fee." Either way, everyone ends up with a bad taste in their mouths, and professional relationships can suffer.

• *Does the article fit the magazine's audience?* Again, this question first came up at the idea stage. But now that the article is in hand, it has to be asked again. What will your readers think of this article? Will they be glad they read it? *Why* will they be glad they read it? What does it tell them that they don't already know—or can't find out easily on their own? (If most of the research for the article was conducted on the Web, you might have a problem. Anything your writer can find on the Web can also be found by your readers. So why would they want to buy a magazine that gives them information they can grab for free through a search engine?) Will the information in the article be interesting to your readers? What about it will they find interesting? What sorts of responses—letters, e-mails, comments at gatherings, and so on—can you anticipate receiving from your readers? horror? delight? amusement? confusion? anger? Which of the likely responses do you want, and which would you rather avoid?

• *Does the article fit the requirements spelled out in the assignment?* As mentioned before, a bit of wandering between the assignment and the submission is easy to do, so editors have to be careful. You crafted the assignment carefully, and the requirements in it were put there for good reasons. If the manuscript fails to meet those requirements, you have some serious decisions to make.

The kinds of things that editors check for at this stage include

• *Length.* If you asked for 2,000 words on submarines, but the writer submitted 8,000 words, then the fit between the assignment and the article isn't very good. Your next move should be to reach for the phone; you and the writer must discuss those extra 6,000 words.

• *Sources.* If you insisted that the writer include quotes and information from a marine biologist, a submarine captain, and the guy who scrapes the barnacles off the hull, then that's what the article should include. If additional sources are consulted, that's fine. But the assignment should be taken as a serious minimum. If the writer failed to talk to the captain or the barnacle guy, it's time for a rewrite or an explanation.

• *Structure.* We'll discuss structure more later, but for now the fit should be checked. If the assignment calls for a top-ten list, the article should be structured as a top-ten list—or the writer should explain to you why the change was made. If the assignment calls for a narrative but the writer delivered a step-by-step procedure instead, the phone should be ringing.

• *Tone.* More on tone later.

Even if you like the result, it is important to note if the article as submitted strays from the article as assigned. The editor should be aware of the differences and understand the reasons for them. For example, the assignment might have asked for an article about organically grown vegetables. The writer leaped into the research, talked to a lot of people, got really excited about the topic, and met an organic farmer who raved about the nutritional value of papayas. Blinded by enthusiasm, the writer produced an article that was really about the glories of organic papayas—a nice piece, but not exactly what the assignment called for.

Editors, of course, are not mindlessly bound to the assignment. If the new article misses the mark but still offers interesting information that readers would love, no sane editor would turn it down. But serious questions will have to be asked about the appropriateness of the submitted article and the reasons for the shift in focus. And

Each issue must be carefully balanced, with articles ranging from projects to personality profiles. Achieving balance requires subjectivity, but if you are open-minded when you evaluate this, if you know your subject, and if you have a defined audience, you can develop a strong sense of balance. This balancing stage cannot be done on a deadline. It requires more reflection than the magazine-production process allows.

John McDonald, editor, *Woodwork*

> We strive to present a varied but balanced selection of articles. Although there is no hard-and-fast rule, we attempt to include in every issue a United States subject; a story about some faraway, exotic area; an up-to-date, detailed view of a foreign nation; and an article on science, natural history, or adventure. Although we often present coverage concerning newsworthy places, we also strive to make the coverage timeless, so that an accumulated collection of *National Geographic* magazines can be used as an encyclopedia of sorts.
>
> **Patrick J. McGeehan, research correspondence, *National Geographic***

often, a "drifted" article is unsuitable precisely because the focus has shifted, and the writer will be asked to seize the reins and steer the article toward its proper course.

• *Does the article fit in with others intended for the same issue?* Articles rarely turn out exactly as expected, so even if the assignment looked good for that special June issue on great summer getaways, the article itself might not fit in so well. An article on the spirit of the Florida Keys might end up focusing heavily on Key West—and run into conflicts with the profile of Jimmy Buffett planned for the same issue. An article on the beautiful beaches of southern California might talk a lot about the great tan you can get there—and clash with the neighboring article: "Skin Cancer: Get Out of the Sun or Die."

So at this stage, editors have to look not only at the article in hand but also at the issue as a whole. Even slight adjustments in focus among a few of the articles can result in redundancies ("The Joy of Sailing" versus "The Pleasures of Boating"), conflicting information ("Exercise and Eat What You Want" versus "The Dangers of Processed Foods"), or the sense that the editors at the magazine never talk to one another ("Karen Jones, a Dynamic Young Democrat" versus "Bobby Smith, a Democrat to Watch"). Editors have to keep the issue as a whole in mind as they consider the articles they receive.

• *Does the article fit in with pieces we have published recently?* Along similar lines, you want to make sure that this great new article doesn't clash with an article you ran in the last issue, or in the issue before that. (Keeping in mind, of course, that editors plan issues far in advance.) This fantastic travel article about things to do and places to eat in London might work well in the June issue, as planned, but that article in the July issue about hot tourist spots in England might cause problems. Do the articles complement each other? That's great. Or do they detract from each other, offering similar or conflicting information that ends up confusing your readers? That's not so great.

One factor that editors consider when making these decisions is the turnover in the readership. Some magazines' audiences turn over faster than others. Subscribers to *Smithsonian* or *National Geographic* are often subscribers for life. But the bridal magazines know that their readership is constantly in flux; women start their subscriptions when they are beginning to plan their wedding, and they cancel the subscriptions once the rice has been thrown and the suggestive comments have been washed off the car windows. So editors at the bridal magazines don't mind repeating a topic every year or two. As mentioned previously, however, *National Geographic* has a much more stable readership and won't publish an article if a similar topic has been covered in the magazine within the past ten years.

Depending on the article and the readership, the solution to a clash with articles in previous issues could be simply to move an article to a later issue. With a bit of checking to make sure that the restaurants are still in business and that Buckingham Palace hasn't fallen into the Thames, you could hold the London article until, say, March, by which point your readers will have forgotten much of the related (but not identical) material you published last June.

All these considerations boil down to meeting your readers' expectations—expectations that the magazine itself created. They expect to receive material that is at least generally consistent from issue to issue; that's why *Cosmopolitan* doesn't publish articles about the Mars mission, no matter how well researched and written they are. Readers also expect to receive material that doesn't shock or offend them, at least in unexpected ways. Subscribers to *Rolling Stone* expect to be shocked, in certain ways, by the magazine; that's part of its allure. But they would be shocked in unpleasant ways by an article that seriously addressed the dangers of marijuana or that rallied readers to support and trust whatever administration controls Washington. Editors have to understand their readers and the promise that the

> We try to forecast a good mix for each issue, assigning the pieces well ahead according to the schedule we envision when we assemble the proposed issue. We try for a balance between aviation and space; past, present, and future; hardware and people; and there are other categories, of course. We like to teach something in every issue.
>
> **George C. Larson, editor, *Air & Space***

magazine makes to them, and then deliver articles that uphold that promise.

Similarly, readers expect the material to show some variety; readers of *Field & Stream* might appreciate an article about how to hunt pheasant successfully—but not if that topic were covered in three issues in a row. Readers understand the parameters of most magazines, and they want to read about a variety of topics within those parameters.

As always, success means offering readers an enticing promise and then delivering on it. Thinking carefully about an article's "fit" can help editors achieve this goal.

Editors often do this thinking intuitively, relying on their innate understanding of the magazine to alert them to problems. It is smart, however, for editors to make this consideration conscious—especially if they're new to the job. If the boss challenges you later, asking why you decided to include a particular article in the magazine, you'll be prepared with mission-based answers that are solidly anchored to the core of the magazine.

Tone

Fit—in all its facets—is important, but tone is critical as well. When a manuscript arrives on the editor's desk, she has to consider whether the tone is appropriate. A laugh-a-minute article about last year's train wreck might not be the best way to commemorate the event. A dead-somber story about the upsurge of children's theater might fall a bit flat, too. A scientist develops a new fat-free cheesecake. Do you want a hard-hitting Q&A with the scientist? a straightforward blow-by-blow account of how the cheesecake was invented? a warm profile of the inventor? an upbeat story about a taste test of this new dessert? a detailed retrospective about Americans' battle to rid their food—and their bodies—of excess fat?

We did a story about a Palestinian suicide bomber, which we've definitely gotten mail about. The idea was not to say that what this girl did was right—because obviously, how can you justify murder?—but to show how someone who was apparently so promising could end up doing something so sick. It was very interesting because capturing the right tone was an issue.

Leslie Heilbrunn, senior editor, *Cosmo Girl*

Before we can think about the right tone for a story, it would help if we knew what tone is. Generally, it's the voice, the personality, the perspective, the approach, the *feeling* of the article—all rolled up into one term. Tones come in nearly infinite flavors. The same set of information can produce a rainbow of different tones:

Nancy Greenfeather was born in Smalltown, Oklahoma, during the summer of 1937.

In Smalltown, Oklahoma, the summer sun bakes the ground until it cracks. Dogs lie panting under creaking front porches, and the air smells of tar and lethargy. Nothing breaks the taut stillness of an August afternoon. But on August 13, 1937, the cries of a new baby echoed among the sticky tarpaper houses. Nancy Greenfeather had come into the world, and she wasn't happy about it.

Florida babies love the sun. Oregon babies love the rain. But Oklahoma babies love the dirt, and Nancy Greenfeather was no exception.

Nancy Greenfeather learned to crawl at a very early age, undoubtedly eager to get the hell out of Smalltown, Oklahoma.

Smalltown, Oklahoma, might be a fine place to live, but it's a lousy place to be born. Hot in the summer, freezing in the winter, flat as a griddle, and not exactly known for its enriching cultural milieu. What was Nancy Greenfeather thinking?

And so on. Whether straightforward, somber, playful, funny, sassy, or any of the other shades, the tone of an article plays a potent role in the way the article will be perceived—and in its entertainment value.

Describing the desired tone with precision is challenging, but harder yet is figuring out—and explaining—how tone is achieved. If your writer asks you *how* she should make the article funny, goofy, or whatever, what can you say? The answer is that tone is the result of several factors:

- *Nouns.* Is it an umbrella or a bumbershoot? a cloud or a thunderhead? underwear or skivvies, unmentionables, undies, boxers, Fruit of the Looms, and so on? By changing the choice of nouns, writers can alter the tone of a story dramatically.
- *Verbs.* Similarly, verb choice plays a large role in the development of tone. Did he *walk* out of the room, or did he *storm* out of the room? Did he flee, or did he skulk? Did he dash? or dance? or prance? or amble? or vanish, two-step, wander, or ramble? Verbs are always powerful, and the tone of a story depends heavily on them.
- *Sentence structure.* Long, complicated, flowery sentences tend to suggest formality, seriousness, and high-brow affectation. Short sentences are punchy. The combination of the two can create a range of effects.
- *Paragraph structure.* Like sentences, long paragraphs come across as flowing acts of literature, while short paragraphs come across as hard-hitting jabs of journalism.
- *Exaggeration and minimization.* Exaggeration and minimization can lend humor, sarcasm, irreverence, and other tones to a story. The neutral

He's eighty-five years old.

can be exaggerated:

He's ancient.

or minimized:

He's a wee bit past his prime.

- *Metaphors and similes.* Metaphors and similes can be effective, especially when combined with exaggeration or minimization: a super-size cheeseburger could be as big as a mailbox. Or large enough to sink a tugboat. Or enough food to feed West Virginia for a year. Enough for Goldilocks *and* the Three Bears. Half the size of an average iceberg. And so on.

• *Parody.* Mimicking a well-known quote or style can make writing lively, playful, or silly:

Listen, my children, and you shall hear of how Freddie Williams lost his ear.

Four score and seven years ago, Nancy Greenfeather was brought forth upon this continent.

What light in yonder window breaks? It is the east, and Mrs. Abernathy obviously is having trouble sleeping again.

These and a host of other techniques allow writers to adjust the tone of their stories until just the right shade of irony or seriousness or humor or agony is achieved. Tone is built into the very fabric of the writing; it can't be tacked on easily. The best advice to give writers is to put themselves into the proper mood when they sit down to do the writing, and the appropriate tone is likely to emerge. When you're in a goofy mood, it's tough to write anything grim or flat. The writer's mood will ooze through the keyboard and color the article itself.

Essential to the smooth creation of an article is an assignment that describes the desired tone. With a clear description, the writer knows what to do, and the editor avoids lurching surprises later:

"This is funny?"
"Funny? I didn't know you wanted funny!"
"Of course I wanted funny. How could I not want funny? This is a funny topic."
"Not to me it isn't."
"I can tell."

Because the tone is so inherent to the fabric of the story, it is very difficult for the editor to alter it once the manuscript is in hand. Perhaps you wanted something pretty funny, but you got something serious and straightforward. Or you wanted sarcastic, and you got reverential. In those cases, the editor's best bet is to talk with the writer, explain or describe the proper tone thoroughly, and let the writer take another stab at it. The writer probably will have to rework the writing from the beginning—you *don't* want him inserting a few jokes here and there to "liven up" the piece. Better yet, of course, is an assignment letter that spelled out the tone clearly from the outset. If the tone is explained clearly and the writer misses the mark, the rewrite is her responsibility. If the tone were left unspoken, the writer might resent having to retool a perfectly good, funny article into a serious one just because you didn't make the desired tone clear.

When evaluating the tone of a manuscript, the savvy editor will make a decision based on several factors.

• *Does the tone meet the needs of the audience?* Editors think a lot about why people read their magazines. Do they like a magazine because it makes them laugh—or because it provides them with information they can use? Do they like it because it lures and absorbs them into an exotic world of mystery, intrigue, and suspense—or because it helps them solve their problems? Do they like it because it moves them to tears over tragic stories of disaster and heroism—or because it allows them to pursue their hobbies with greater professionalism?

The answers to these questions drive the tone of the magazine. If readers need hard information to help them with their careers, finances, and related aspects of their lives, a straightforward, direct approach might be best. If readers expect high entertainment value from the articles themselves, a straightforward approach might be too boring or flat; a livelier storytelling approach might work better.

• *Does the tone meet the tastes of the audience?* Just who are these people, anyway? What do they like? And what offends, insults, irritates, annoys, exasperates, frustrates, riles, rankles, ruffles, and generally ticks them off?

At the core of this concern lies money. Put less crassly, this concern is essential to the financial health and longevity of the publication. Magazines, as we have discussed, carve out narrowly defined niches from the overall pool of potential readers. But within those niches, editors want to attract and keep the largest percentage possible. In an ideal world, *Model Railroader* would attract 100 percent of all model-railroad enthusiasts in the United States. Every music buff in America would subscribe to *Rolling Stone*, *Spin*, and the bevy of other music magazines published today. All owners of bassets and beagles would read *Dog Fancy,* and all owners of sophisticated Siamese and colorful calicos would look forward to *Cat Fancy* every month.

This desire for the largest possible audience within the parameters of any given niche means that editors are careful to avoid upsetting or disappointing large chunks of their readership. Your tongue-in-cheek praise for the glory of botulism might alienate your readers—if you're the editor of *Canned Food Digest.* Your straightforward review of the latest boot-lace technology might put your readers to sleep—if you're the editor of *Adventure Hiking.* With each misstep comes a flurry of letters from people who believe that they can find what they want elsewhere. They cancel their subscriptions and sign up with other publications, and so your readership base dwindles. With a dwindling readership comes evaporating income from subscriptions and a perilous plummet in advertising revenue. The downward spiral has begun, and the end result can be the death of the magazine.

• *Is the tone appropriate for the topic?* Regardless of the readers' tastes, some topics are better suited to certain tones than others. Probably the worst move is to use a humorous tone when discussing a sad or distressing topic. Cancer, AIDS, famine, war, poverty—subjects like these are difficult to pull off with humor. It's been done, but to succeed, the use of humor generally has to meet two requirements. First, the humor will be appreciated more fully if the writer is involved with the issue. Mark Price writes a powerful and engaging column about AIDS, and he often uses humor to make his point. But he's not laughing at *people* who are HIV-positive. He's laughing at some of the *situations* that being HIV-positive can bring about—and he's HIV-positive himself.

Second, the humor should point to some hope, some good news, some bright side to the situation. Humor can be inspirational, or it can be mean-spirited. Readers will turn away in disgust over inappropriate humor, and they'll take their subscriptions with them.

Similarly, humor can be touchy when you're dealing with delicate or sensitive issues. Even if the topic avoids the gloom of cancer and famine, it might call for a respectful, serious tone. Issues of public safety, some aspects of sexuality, certain health problems even if they fall short of dire threats, and other subjects might be better handled with sobriety than hilarity.

And humor isn't the only approach that can backfire. A funny article about a wedding might work, but a bitterly sarcastic piece might come off as pathetic or grim. A wildly sarcastic article about politics could be great, but an inspirational article about the same topic might be regarded as naïve.

So editors think carefully about their topics and the right tone for them. Obviously, the goal is to entertain and inform, and the right tone can hit that target with flair.

• *Does the tone work well with the other articles that will run in the same issue?* Just as you don't want to run two articles about the joys of kayaking in the same issue, you don't want to overload any given issue of your magazine with articles that reflect the same tone over and over again. Unless you're editing *Mad Magazine*, your readers probably don't want hysterically funny articles from cover to cover; they might also want helpful information, powerful profiles, searing exposés, and other approaches as well. Similarly, unless you're editing *Guideposts*, your readers probably don't want a steady diet of purely uplifting inspiration.

When editors plan issues of their magazines, they think about not only the topics but also the tones that will appear each time. Is a third funny piece all right, or is it a bad idea? Are two tearjerkers in the same issue tolerable, or should one be held to the following month? How much variety is essential? How much is too much?

• *Does the tone mesh well with articles that have run in recent issues?* Again, just as editors think about topics that they have run recently, they think about tone over time. If July was a pretty hilarious issue, it might be a good idea to make August a bit more somber. If you've published a couple of basic, straightforward issues in a row, it might be a good idea to cut loose for the April Fool's Day issue.

The concern here is that readers are pretty quick to spot trends. If you publish three lighthearted issues in a row, readers will begin to suspect that the magazine has gone through some kind of editorial shift and that they should expect greater levity from now on. Some readers might find this delightful—but then be disappointed when the next issue reverts to the magazine's usual mix of tones. Other readers might find the perceived shift distasteful—and cancel their subscriptions before they see the return to normalcy.

Hands-off Editing

The mail carrier who delivered the manuscript is long gone. You tidied up your desk, cleared your calendar, took the phone off the hook, and settled down for some good, solid editing. The shadows are getting long, the evening sun is cooling into beautiful shades of purple and orange on the horizon, and you're still hard at work, editing the article. You've taken several laps through it by now, asking a lot of questions and challenging the article to meet your standards.

And still, you haven't made a single mark on the manuscript. It is as fresh and pristine as it was when you opened the envelope.

Have you actually been editing? Absolutely. You just haven't been *copy editing*—that comes later.

Editing is the asking of questions, not the rewriting of material. So far, you've asked a lot of questions, making sure the article makes sense in many different ways; making sure it fits the assignment, the audience, and the magazine; and making sure the tone passes muster from a range of perspectives.

If the manuscript is still looking right for your magazine, then congratulations! Through your insightful thinking early on, your reflection about the nature and character of your magazine, your creativity in choosing just the right topic, your wisdom in choosing just the right writer, your clarity in assigning the article to that writer so that he understood exactly what you wanted, and your steady and cheerful communication with that writer throughout the writing process, you now have an article that clicks. The sense, fit, and tone are just right. Pat yourself on the back.

If the manuscript is starting to look a bit off-target, however, this layer of editing is not yet done. At this stage, the editor's role is to ask the questions and be bold and honest about the answers. It's the writer's role to rework the article to meet the expectations.

So talented editors don't try to fix anything at this level. Instead, they communicate with the writers, clearly and completely, and ask for rewrites. In my years as an editor, I almost never accepted a manuscript on the first try. It was routine for me to ask these questions, find a few "no" answers, and get back to the writer for another round. A rewrite isn't a sign of failure. It's a sign of high standards.

Some beginning editors are sheepish about asking for rewrites. They think that the writer already did his job, researching the topic and writing the article. They worry that the writer will resent being asked to do more work. And they fear that rewrites will "burn out" the writer by forcing him to backtrack through old articles rather than surging ahead to new ones.

Mercifully, it doesn't work that way—at least, not for good writers. The best writers I know, including a few with Pulitzers on their résumés, are not only content but actually eager to rewrite their articles. Good writers want their very best work to appear in print, because it enhances their reputations. If editors catch problems, that's great! It beats letting those problems stay in the article and sending them out to 150,000 readers. Good writers don't want lazy or timid editors. They want editors who will challenge them, demand excellent work, and keep them from making fools of themselves. As long as the requested improvements are reasonable, significant, and respectfully presented, talented writers are happy to jump in.

Which brings us to another point. Respectful requests don't dictate changes—they point out concerns. Writers will bristle under this kind of instruction:

> "Walt, I'd like you to change 'between' to 'among' on page 1, fix the dangling participle on page 2, clarify the source's title on page 3, and cut the final paragraph."

The problem, of course, is that you could have done those things yourself, in less time than it took to explain them to Walt. Instead, because this layer of editing calls for broad thinking and big questions, the instruction should simply explain what doesn't work and why it doesn't work. Then leave it to Walt to fix. This approach is respectful because it assumes that Walt is a talented professional who is perfectly capable of understanding the problems and finding creative and brilliant solutions for them:

> "Walt, this article is good, but I'd like to suggest some improvements. The lead seems a bit confusing to me—can you help readers understand the situation more clearly? Also, the article drags around the middle; some restructuring might help. And the ending is rather abrupt. What would you think about ending with the last part of the story you introduce in the lead?"

With this kind of feedback and a reasonable amount of time to make the changes, Walt is likely to get to work and produce an improved manuscript. Many writers actually come back with a rewrite that not only addresses the concerns mentioned in the feedback but includes additional improvements as well.

And all this counts as editing. In fact, it is the very best kind of editing, in which the editor asks hard questions and inspires the writer to make the article as good as it can be. The time will come when the editor has to take the manuscript into her own hands, making final corrections and getting it ready for publication, but for now, the editor is functioning as editors should—as the First Reader.

I once was asked to edit a series of short biographies. I glanced at them and mentioned that I would need about two hours to edit each one. "Why? Are they that bad?" came the astonished reply. I explained that the amount of time had nothing to do with the quality of the writing; it had everything to do with the quality of my questions. I had to ask all these questions of each manuscript, whether or not any changes turned out to be necessary. If the answers to all my questions were "yes," then that's fine. But I would not be doing my job as an editor if I failed to ask them for every single biography.

Once the questions have been asked, the feedback given, and the rewrite handed in, this layer of editing begins all over again. On occasion, a second rewrite might be necessary. Maybe even a third. (Usually not a fourth—if the writer can't get it right in three tries, it's time to move on.)

My wife is a quilter, and she once told me that the proper procedure for washing a quilt is to soak it in a bathtub, drain and replace the water, soak it again, replace the water again, and continue repeating this process "until the water is so clean you're willing to drink it." This layer of editing is similar; you work with the writer until the article fully satisfies your standards.

9. Beginnings, Endings, and All that Comes Between:
Structure, Leads, and Conclusions

An article is well organized if I understand it with one quick read. I want logic and simplicity. If I have to work while reading, then the article doesn't.

Jeff Csatari, executive editor, *Men's Health*

You've survived the Big Picture, thinking through audience, mission, and other Deep and Philosophical Things. You've gotten through the assignment phase, choosing the very best article ideas and assigning them to the very best writers for the job. And you've worked diligently through the other Big Questions, making sure that the manuscript you have received makes sense from all perspectives, fits the assignment and the audience, and carries the proper tone.

Just one more set of questions, and you will be done with layer 2.

This set has to do with what I call the "chiropractic" work of editing. For this approach, you scrutinize the skeleton of the article, making sure it hangs together properly. We'll look at structure, leads, and conclusions—all the while, as before, keeping our hands off the manuscript. We're still in the area in which the best bet is to let the writer make the changes.

We'll start with the article's structure. A lot of editors want to attack the lead first, mainly because it's important and it's the first thing the editor sees. But while leads are important, they aren't as important as the overall structure of the article. To test this theory, just work through the possibilities: Would you rather edit an article that had a bland lead but a clear and compelling structure, or an article that had a riveting lead but wandered and twisted in random and baffling ways?

To look at it another way: changing the lead doesn't typically mean reworking the entire structure of the article, but changing the structure often results in a new lead. To keep your writer from fixing the lead only to have it disappear when the structure is examined, we'll look at structure first.

Bones

Most beginning writers don't think much about the structure of their articles. They put down the information in the order that seems to make the most sense or that seems to just "feel right." But that approach can lead to some deeply embedded problems.

The first problem is that in the absence of a deliberate structure, writers tend to present information in the order in which they received it. So if they conduct an interview with the vice president of the United States, and he talks first about his impending bunion surgery and then about the administration's decision to declare war against Canada, these beginning writers often fall into the trap of writing the bunion stuff first and the war stuff second. But readers, of course, don't care much about the veep's foot problems, and they probably care a lot about our decision to go to war—especially against Canada, which seems to be rather peaceful and friendly. So the structure of this article is likely to be irritating and distracting, and most readers will turn the page halfway through the bunion description and long before they discover that the United States is hatching secret plans to take over Saskatchewan.

The other problem that beginning writers can run into involves putting down the information in the order that it occurs to them. These writers don't think much about the structure of the article, the order that would suit readers best, or anything other than getting the words down on the page. The information comes out in a haphazard, confusing way that readers find frustrating.

The antidote, of course, is for writers to think a little bit about the structure of the article before they start wiggling their fingers on the keyboard. What order would make the information flow better? What would enhance clarity? What would build in some suspense, some humor, some impetus to turn the page and keep reading?

How can you tell whether an article is well organized? If it flows nicely from point to point and covers all of the main points of interest. I make sure it flows from point to point—a lot of writers, in my opinion, have trouble with this—and that the important information is given the proper emphasis.

Michael Bawaya, editor, *American Archaeology*

A good structure accomplishes several important goals.

• *It offers information to readers as they need it.* Readers strongly prefer a clear, rational order to their information. If the article ignores this preference, two possible problems loom on the horizon.

The first is that the article is forever filling in necessary information in awkward ways. One symptom of this problem is an overuse of parentheses, dashes, flashbacks, and other asides:

> So they decided to hold a race to see whose car was faster.
>
> The race began at ten o'clock on a chilly Saturday in March. Bob, who was driving a 2001 VW Beetle, which had a 150-horsepower turbocharged engine, revved enthusiastically at the starting line. Karen, who sat behind the wheel of a 2002 jet-black Hummer, which sported a 316-horsepower V8 under the hood, was quietly whistling a jaunty tune. Mandy (who was Bob's cousin, although Karen didn't know that) waved a flag, and the race was off. The two cars squealed off the starting line, which was at the end of Main Street where no one ever went. The Hummer, which had the right lane, soon ran into a bunch of potholes—Bob and Mandy knew they were there, but Karen had never driven this stretch of road before—and Bob's Beetle buzzed into the lead. The potholes, which were caused by some hard frosts the previous week, were no match for the Hummer's four-wheel drive, and Karen churned her way to victory, which earned her a free dinner at Denny's later that night.

That passage is clogged with clauses, fraught with phrases, and tangled with turns and twists. The poor reader needs a road map just to figure out the information and sort out the story.

The problem isn't too little or even too much information. The problem is that the information is presented without much thought to what needs to be known and how the presentation of information can shape and color a story. A minor bit of chiropractic work—by the writer, not the editor—can bring about staggering improvements:

> So they decided to hold a race to see whose car was faster: Bob's 150-horsepower, turbocharged Beetle, or Karen's 316-horsepower Hummer. The loser would buy the winner a meal at Denny's that night.
>
> The race began at ten o'clock on a chilly Saturday in March. Bob had suggested the location, the sparsely traveled end of Main Street, and the racers took their positions at the starting line. Bob revved his engine enthusiastically, but Karen quietly whistled a jaunty tune.
>
> Assisting in the race was Bob's cousin Mandy, although Karen was unaware of their relationship. Mandy waved a flag, and the two cars squealed off the starting line.
>
> Karen soon discovered why Bob had suggested this course—and why he had given her the right lane. The Hummer had to churn and growl over a long series of potholes caused by a hard frost the previous week. Bob, however, sailed along on a smooth surface and buzzed into the lead. But the potholes were no match for the Hummer's four-wheel drive, and Karen churned her way to victory.

This version, while still in need of some improvements, is much easier to read and understand than the first rendition because the structure works better. Information is presented in the order that the reader probably wants to receive it:

1. Set the stage. Describe the contest, complete with information about the contestants and the prize.
2. Get to the start of the race. Include the location and the day and time.
3. Introduce the first twist: Mandy is Bob's cousin.
4. Begin the race!
5. Introduce the second twist: the right lane has potholes. Bob takes the lead.
6. Present the outcome. The Hummer overcomes the potholes and wins the race anyway.

With this order, readers can follow the story easily, without jumping through time and space to fill in important details.

In this book, we've talked about how good writing presents a kind of continuous dream; you want your readers to mentally depart from their living rooms and subway seats and join you at the end of Main Street, watching a race between Bob's Beetle and Karen's Hummer. You can't create this kind of dream if the information comes in a bad order. You want the story to unfold logically for the readers, without making them stop repeatedly to fill in key details.

• *It offers information in a natural way.* The goal is graceful, fluid storytelling—not herky-jerky, start-and-stop mayhem. We've all suffered through the guy at a party who loves to tell jokes but doesn't do a very good job of it:

> There was this chicken, see—Or maybe it was a turkey. No. A chicken. It was a chicken. So this chicken goes into a bar and says— No, wait. It was a turkey. A big, fat turkey. So the turkey goes into a bar and says to the bartender, "Could I have a glass of water?" And the bartender—I think his name was Hank—the bartender says— That's right. Hank. I'm pretty sure it was Hank. Anyway, the turkey asks for a glass of water, and the bartender Hank says, "Do you have any ID?" And the turkey says—Oh, wait. Did I mention that this was the day before Thanksgiving? Well, this was the day before Thanksgiving. That's why it's a turkey. See? A turkey on the day before Thanksgiving. So the turkey says to Hank—

At this point, you just want to stomp on his foot and join some other conversation. The problem is that the information isn't flowing. It's coming, in its own haphazard way, but it isn't being offered in a smooth, well-orchestrated manner.

Every piece must have a structural backbone, just as every piece should have a topic paragraph, a "billboard" that points the way for the reader, telling him exactly what the story is and where it is going to take him. This orientation paragraph should generally appear high up in the story, preferably immediately after the lead.

International Wildlife Guide for Writers

A good structure lets the information flow without interrupting the continuous dream. Readers learn what they need to learn, but they don't have to stop the dream to learn it.

• *It gives the article a sense of cohesion and control.* As discussed previously, readers want a calm and competent guide to lead them through the material. They are like big-game hunters in this way. They become uneasy when it appears that their guide is lost, uncertain, nervous, or unable to find the ammunition. Readers, like hunters, get a bit distressed when their guide begins to mutter to himself, sweat more than is strictly necessary, or dig through his pockets trying to find a map.

A weak structure brings about those concerns for readers. As they find themselves backtracking over tired ground, jumping from one topic to another like seal hunters on shrinking ice floes, or leaping wildly around a topic like a little kid walking a Great Dane—they begin to worry that their guide is a disaster, and they begin to think about abandoning the article to save themselves.

A strong, clear structure, on the contrary, lets readers relax and enjoy the trip. They understand where they are, they have a pretty good idea of where they are going, and they know why the guide is taking them to the various stops along the way. With this confidence, they can immerse themselves into the continuous dream, confident that their guide knows what he's doing.

• *It can show relationships among facts, characters, and actions.* A good structure makes connections clear; readers are introduced to a character, for example, and then they get to meet that person's best friend. The message is easily understood: the friend is important to this character and to the point of the story.

A structure that jumps around runs the risk of shattering such links. If we meet Clara, then we meet her mother, then we watch Clara go through crisis number1 with her sister, then we meet her best friend, then we listen in on a conversation between Clara and her mother—at this point, we have no idea what is important, what is related, and what is filler. Everything is presented with equal, confusing weight, and evaluating the information and connecting the dots is nearly impossible. The readers would be better off with something more straightforward—like a Dostoyevsky novel.

• *It can build suspense or add surprise.* A fractured structure can't present anything surprising—because *everything* is surprising. Why did you tell me *that*? Who *is* this person? What's going on here? Why did she do *that*? Am I supposed to care about this guy? Everything is bizarre because nothing fits together well, and any attempt at surprise is lost in the chaos of information.

A rational structure, however, can build suspense and add surprise easily. The article introduces the main character, her mother, her sisters, and her great-aunt Edna—and then it goes on with the story. The readers, of course, have followed the introductions well and are wondering why the father wasn't mentioned. Is he dead? divorced? living in some faraway land? What's up with Dad?

The writer can keep readers in suspense—for a while—before introducing Dad, who is doing hard time at Attica for having attempted to overthrow the government. The suspense sharpens the delivery, giving it emphasis and attention that would be lost if Dad were simply thrown into the introductory mix.

Through the manipulation of information in a clear structure, writers can exercise some degree of control over what the readers are wondering, delivering the key information at a prime moment later on.

• *It can give the article a logical, natural ending.* We'll talk about conclusions later in this chapter, but the important point here is that without a strong structure, a strong conclusion is almost impossible.

When information is presented haphazardly, how are the readers supposed to know when the article is finished? First, they get one bit of information, then another, then another, then another, all without any obvious logic. The article has no choice but to simply run out of steam, ending when the last bit of information has been delivered.

With a solid structure, however, articles can end with strength and satisfaction. Readers will sense that the article is over because the path was clear and its endpoint is obvious. They will feel the ending coming, and they will greet it with a calm embrace.

So a good structure is critically important. In fact, the structure of an article often marks the difference between a professional writer and an amateur. For editors, then, two skills become important: knowing how to detect a weak structure, and knowing how to suggest improvements to the writer.

Detecting weak structure can be difficult for editors. Especially if a writer is skilled at graceful wording or clever turns of phrase, an article can seem to be interesting even if the structure is flawed. Good editors take the time to ask themselves about the structure: Is it clear? confident? strong? Does it move the story along? Does it make me want to read more? Is anything about it irritating, confusing, wearying, or just plain difficult? Does anything seem out of place? Do I find myself needing information I don't yet have? Only by taking a moment to consider the structure of the article, independent of the quality of the clever sentences and artful paragraphs, can the editor be sure that the article is structurally sound.

Some specific questions can help editors figure out whether the structure of an article is strong.

• *Does the article feel too long, even if it isn't?* The feeling that the article is too long—despite the actual word count—is often a tip-off that the structure is shoddy. Articles that jump around from one topic to another and back again feel long because the reader gets lost easily, recognizes rehashed topics that keep recurring, and isn't sure where she is going or when the journey will ever end.

• *Is the article confusing?* Some topics are more difficult to understand than others; the story of a grandma who rescued six kids from a burning building will be easy to follow, while a rundown of the changes built into the new tax laws can be a navigational nightmare. But good writers can present any information in such a way that readers grasp the key points and stick with the article to the final sentence.

Once again, structure is the key. Even with the tax codes, a clear and logical structure can make any topic relatively simple to comprehend.

• *Does the article feel like it ends several times—or never?* Bring to mind a lecture you've attended in which the speaker said, "And so, in conclusion..." five or six times before she actually meant it. Or the person on the phone who says, "Well, I should let you go..." and then talks for another twenty minutes. Articles with scattered structures do the same thing; they seem to end, but then they go on, and then they appear to end again, but they're not quite finished, and then they seem to end at last, but then a new topic is introduced, and so on until the *reader* declares that the article is over and turns the page in midsentence.

The converse problem is an article that doesn't seem to end at all. It just fizzles out and sputters to a graceless stop. Often, writers will lament that "I just don't know how to end this article," or they'll paste on some cheesy, cornball ending just to bring the article to a halt. In both cases, the problem is most likely related to the structure. The article can't reach the end of its journey because it never started one—it just wandered around the parking lot until it got tired.

Assembly Assistance

When you, as an editor, run across an article with a messed-up structure, what should you do? (A related problem: What can you do when your writer calls and confesses that he's having trouble turning his research into something that makes sense?) Mercifully, you can take any of several helpful steps to guide your writer toward a more cohesive article.

Probably the most helpful thing you can do is explain your concern and suggest a structure that might work for the story. Most writers, when they are presented with a suggested structure that makes sense, are relieved; it's as though they can suddenly see the whole article in their minds, and writing it becomes dramatically easier.

But of course, you will have trouble suggesting structures if you haven't thought through some possibilities. In truth, the options are probably infinite, but a small set of basic structures can handle most situations.

• *Chronology.* Chronology is the most common—and probably easiest—structure available. Just start with the beginning of the story and describe the events in order until it's over.

The chronological structure works well for narratives—articles that tell actual stories: the time that Nancy tricked her teacher into thinking that the exam had already been given, the time that Dad tried to fix the roof by himself, the time that someone slipped vodka into the punch at the nursing home's Christmas party. It works well for almost any historical story also.

It doesn't work as well for articles about concepts or situations. A chronological presentation of the nature of superconductors wouldn't be likely to triumph.

Writers can, however, turn nonnarrative stories into narratives—and hence use a chronological structure—with certain shifts in perspective. You can, for example, tell the story of how you found out about something:

> I was told to write a five-page article about superconductors, and I was in a panic. I knew nothing about them; for all I knew, they were railroad workers who could fly faster than their trains.
>
> So I tromped over to the physics department at Central State University, where Professor Juanita Jimenez was working with these superconductor things.
>
> Boy, did I learn a lot! It seems that superconductors...

You also can tell the story about how someone else learned about the topic, how the thing was invented, how it was used in a new and innovative way, and the like. Any of these approaches could use a chronological structure well.

• *Step-by-step*. The step-by-step structure is similar to the chronological structure, except that a step-by-step approach *prescribes* action, rather than *describing* it. In other words, it talks about something that will be done, instead of talking about something that has been done.

This structure is a classic for how-to articles. The most straightforward way to present it simply follows the steps one at a time:

> Here's how to build a submarine.
> 1. Find a really strong can, big enough for you to sit in.
> 2. Cut out an opening for a window.
> 3. Put thick glass in the window and glue it well enough to withstand 3,500 pounds per square inch of pressure....

You also can weave the steps into a more flowing paragraph form, but the structure is still the same:

While the glue is drying, take a trip to the local junkyard. Dig through the rubble carefully; what you're looking for is a discarded Pratt & Whitney XJ7 Submarine Engine. Not every junkyard will have one, so you might have to shop around.

Once you have the engine, fit it into the end of the can that does not have the window. Be sure to point the propeller shaft toward the back....

- *Inverted pyramid*. The inverted pyramid is the classic newspaper approach, in which the most important information is given first, followed by the next most important, and so on down to irrelevant trivia. In magazines, this approach is best suited for articles about important and current events.
- *General to specific*. Think of a video camera. The general-to-specific approach involves starting all the way zoomed out, and then gradually zooming in to greater levels of detail.
- *Specific to general*. Same idea, the other way around. Start with a small detail and work your way out to the big picture.
- *Geography*. If you were writing an article about New York City, you might use geography to structure the piece. You could begin at the southern tip of Manhattan and work your way north. Or you could start at the center of Broadway and sweep clockwise around the city.
- *Frame*. In the frame approach, the article typically begins with an anecdote—something compelling that will make the reader want to learn more. Then, in the middle of that story, you freeze the action and cut away to the background, context, and other information necessary for the reader to fully understand what is going on. Then, at the end of the article, you return to the anecdote and finish the story.
- *Spine*. Using the spine approach, you follow one action or process from beginning to end, stopping as needed to fill in the background. The action forms the spine that holds the article together, with ribs of information hanging off it.

Dan Okrent wrote an entire book that used this structure. Called *Nine Innings*, it uses one baseball game as its spine. After some introduction, the action begins and the pitcher winds up for the first pitch of the game. Freeze! Okrent then fills in information about the pitcher, converting him from a two-dimensional baseball player into a three-dimensional, interesting, complex human being.

Then the pitch flies across home plate. Freeze! Now we learn about the catcher, and another character comes to life.

The book continues in this vein, following the action of the baseball game but stopping it often to flesh out the players and their lives.

• *e.* The *e* structure is the classic John McPhee approach. McPhee, one of the greatest nonfiction writers in America today, begins many of his works with the most engaging story he can find. He tells that story well—this is the horizontal line of the lower-case letter *e*—and then he concludes it. He then backs up (the top of the *e*) and fills in the context and background necessary to understand the significance of that engaging story. Then he continues on with the information that readers want to know about the topic.

There are myriad other structures for magazine articles, of course. All are useful in their own ways, as long as writers choose one and stick with it throughout the article. Jumping from one structure to another could be dangerous; the whiplash will deeply annoy readers.

The important task for editors is to know the common article structures and to understand the kinds of articles for which each is best suited. When you are reading a manuscript, you should consider the structure of the article and make sure it is both sound and appropriate. If you have trouble describing the article's structure, it might not have one—and then it's time to worry.

As always, the best plan if you detect a structure problem is to discuss the problem with the writer and allow him to fix it. Editors who jump in and start rearranging an article's vertebrae almost always court disaster; your writer might have valid reasons for presenting information in a certain way. By asking your writer to think about

How do you organize a messy or disorganized manuscript? Well, you do it once, but not twice. And you kiss off the writer if it's truly terrible. But there are a few guys who work so hard and go anywhere and to any lengths, that you don't mind cleaning them up.

Steve Spence, managing editor, *Car and Driver*

structure and rework the article to strengthen its skeleton, you run a better chance of success—and you send a clear message to the writer that you respect his talents and are confident that he can rise to the occasion.

If your writer struggles with the reworking of an article's structure, you might suggest the cut-and-paste technique described in chapter 7.

Several times in this discussion of structure, we have touched on the two key elements in a strong article: the lead and the conclusion. These elements are so critical that they deserve special attention.

And So We Begin

Some highly invasive studies that involved electrodes and eyeballs provided valuable information about how people look at a magazine page when they first turn their attention to it. Our eyes, it seems, are attracted to contrast, and so we first tend to look at the pictures. Then we look at the captions, to figure out what's going on in the pictures. Then we look at the title or headline for the article.

Assuming that we're still interested in the article—that nothing in the photos, captions, or headlines made us shrug our shoulders and turn the page—we then look at the lead, the beginning of the article. Because the lead is the first piece of actual sentence-length prose that readers see, it plays a critical role. It can engage them, drawing them into the article and persuading them to devote twenty minutes of their lives to it, or it can turn them off, convincing them to grapple with one of the other challenges in their lives.

On the surface, then, the lead has one major job: to inspire the reader to read the article. If the lead fails to do this, none of the witty, brilliant, informative, life-altering material that follows will matter at all. The reader will never see it.

That is the Prime Directive, but leads have several other jobs as well.

• *Introduce the topic.* By the time readers reach the lead, they are at least a little bit curious about the article. They want to know the article's topic, and the photos and headlines can only do so much. The lead should indicate, in at least a general way, what the article will focus on.

• *Set the tone.* Just as the topic can inspire or repulse potential readers, the tone is important as well. Is this going to be a funny article? Good! I could use a few laughs. Is this going to rip my heart out and make me cry? Good! I'm tired of all that funny stuff. Before readers are willing to commit to an article, they want to know what to expect, and the tone plays a big role in that decision.

• *Provide a transition.* We all know about the transitions between paragraphs and sections of articles; they provide a smooth segue from one point to another and keep a reader from feeling like a fast-running dog on a short leash. Thinking about the goal of every good article—to escort the reader into a continuous dream, guided by the writer—the lead also serves as a transition. The lead brings the reader gracefully from her own world into the world of the article. You want the reader to forget that she's sitting in her kitchen, that the microwave is beeping, that the kids are trying to light the stove, that her favorite television show is about to start. If the article is about the Australian Outback, you want her to *be* in the Outback, to see the evening shadows on the red hills, to hear the thump of the kangaroos leaping through the mulga brush, to smell the eucalyptus trees and the drying mud. If the article is about robotic welders, you want your reader to hear the clanging of metal and see the showers of sparks. If the article is about quantum physics, you want her to duck as electrons buzz overhead and protons rumble underfoot. Good leads make the transition—from the real world to the article's world—smooth and seductive, letting the reader slide right on in.

This is why leads that are too abrupt, too jarring, or too sudden often fail. The reader wants to glide into the story, and an introduction that crashes like a ton of manhole covers makes the transition too harsh.

Articles can begin any way that the writer sees fit, of course, but there are several classic types of leads. Editors know these types and can recommend them—or even assign them in advance—as necessary.

• *Anecdote.* Anecdotal leads tell little stories, and they use strong storytelling techniques to envelop the reader with an engaging tale. If the article is about the Red Cross, the lead might tell the story of the family whose mobile home was smashed by a tree:

"If it weren't for the Red Cross, I don't know what we would have done," said Biff Jones. The Red Cross gave them shelter, food, and help with the insurance forms, and now the Joneses are moving into their brand-new double-wide.

Anecdotal leads are often quite powerful; everyone loves a good story. They are commonly used, but they don't seem to wear thin.

• *Rich description*. This approach relies on the writer's skill with words and images, weaving a tapestry of description that is inviting and intriguing. This lead doesn't have a plot line—it's not a little story—but it sets a scene so beautifully (or strangely or horrifically) that the reader presses ahead to find out more.

•*Mystery or suspense*. Leads that rely on mystery or suspense raise compelling questions, and readers stick with the articles because they're dying to know the answers. Just think about the cliffhangers that many television shows use at the end of their seasons, to keep viewers excited about the series until it resumes in the fall. Who got shot? What happened to the baby? Why is this woman crying? Who is that stranger in the shadows? How will they get out of that trap?

Mystery leads often work well, but they also can backfire. They succeed when they pique readers' curiosity and make them want to know more. They fail when they attempt to capture readers' interest but offer a mystery so shallow, so inconsequential, or so bizarre that readers just can't be bothered to care.

• *Humor*. The best of leads, and the worst of leads. When it works, humor can be terrific; it's engaging, it's fun, it's clever. But when it backfires, it explodes horrifically. At best, failed humor is modestly disappointing. At worst, it is insulting, offensive, and distasteful.

One tip for writers of humorous leads: if you're going to make fun of anyone, make fun of yourself. No one will be appalled.

• *Interesting character*. Introducing an interesting character often works well. People like to read about people, and if an article leads with a colorful, odd, amazing, wonderful character, readers are likely to be enchanted and read on.

• *Then–now*. In the then–now approach, the writer sets up an interesting contrast between the past and the present:

In 1971, Hal Beeblefritzer became the forty-ninth person to set foot on the moon. Achieving that goal took dedication, determination, and a lot of hard work. Today, Hal applies those same principles in a different way: helping people invest wisely for their retirement.

• *Surprise!* Surprise is a risky technique, but it can succeed. For this lead, the writer uses a kind of misdirection, a sleight of hand that will allow reality to appear one way and then suddenly turn out to be something different altogether:

Monique Blake gets up at 6:30 every morning to make breakfast for her family. She scrambles some eggs, fries some ham, and pops a few pieces of bread into the toaster. When everything is ready, she announces that breakfast is served—and puts the plates of food on the floor.

Blake is one of a growing number of people who feed their pets the same food that people eat....

This kind of lead is risky because readers don't like to feel conned or tricked. The surprise must be natural to the story and not forced or tacked on by the writer.

• *Quote.* Another risky technique, but also successful when done well, is to lead with a quote. For an article to begin with a quote and not turn the reader off, the quote must be extraordinarily strong and highly relevant to the story. A flat, boring quote will suggest to the reader that a flat, boring article will follow. And a quote that seems spicy and interesting—but that bears little connection to the rest of the article—will leave the reader feeling burned.

• *List.* The lead in the form of a list offers several examples of something, and then ties them all together quickly:

Hank Schlobatnik serves up dishes of chocolate and cones of vanilla at the Dairy Puff on Route 47.

Margaret Carney delivers newspapers each morning from 4:30 to 6:00.

Takela Washington mops floors at Central Junior High.

Each of them is happy to have a job, but that happiness doesn't make the future any brighter. Last month, they all had high-paying positions at the Williamson Television Plant in western Indianapolis.

When the Williamson CEO announced that the company would move the plant to Mexico, few of the workers...

These leads represent just a few of the many ways that good writers get their articles under way, and if done well, they all share a number of traits: they are engaging, they set the tone, and they give the reader some sense of the article's topic.

They also steer clear of gimmicks and tricks that tend to turn readers off. Readers don't pick up magazines intending to be offended, annoyed, frustrated, disgusted, or otherwise repulsed; on the contrary, they pick up magazines because they want to be enchanted, educated, and entertained. But some kinds of leads are so irritating that the reader has little choice but to roll his eyes and turn the page—or put the magazine down altogether. Here are a few common traps. Note that many of them are similar to the successful techniques; the difference is often a matter of degree or tone.

• *Blown suspense.* Suspense can be blown in two ways. The first has to do with actual events that have already occurred:

As President Clinton ran for reelection, everyone wondered, "Can he make it?"

Well, shoot—every reader already knows that Clinton won reelection, so attempts at suspense come across as rather sad.

The other way that suspense can be blown has more to do with the editor than the writer. If the writer builds suspense into the lead, the suspense can be slaughtered by the headline, the photos, and the captions:

McGillicuddy Announces Presidential Bid

As the field of potential candidates for the presidency becomes increasingly crowded, one name remains strangely absent. Will Betty McGillicuddy run, or not?

Any suspense that the writer was trying to build was destroyed by the headline, which gave away the answer.

• *Deception.* Readers love to be puzzled, but they hate to be conned. Leads that build legitimate intrigue are great, but leads that deceive the reader are annoying. I once read an article about the president's daughter—only to discover (much) later that the president in question was not the leader of the free world but the president of a small corporation in western Pennsylvania. The writer obviously felt that he couldn't gain people's attention without jazzing up the topic, but he went so far with his little ploy that I daresay few readers stuck with the article after the truth was revealed.

• *Gratuitous sex or violence.* Grabby, maybe. But unless it's intrinsic to the story, sex or violence that is tacked onto the beginning of an article just to get readers' attention is sure to backfire. Once the sizzle is gone, so are the readers.

• *Overpromising*

There's a riveting, breathtaking new sport sweeping the nation. Move over, bungee jumping. Move over, jet skiing. The hot sport for the in crowd today is—checkers!

Nice try. But all the spicy PR-language in the world won't make an article about checkers interesting to people who don't care about the game. The way to make an article about checkers engaging is to present fascinating characters, offer interesting information, or position the game in a relevant context.

• *Worn-out techniques*

What do President Bush, Madonna, and Tiger Woods have in common?

The answer: Who cares?

When archaeologists 500 years from now dig up our homes, they're sure to puzzle over the (microwave/toilet/remote control).

Yeah, we know—those foolish archaeologists always think that the item in question had some kind of religious purpose. That lead was probably cute the first twenty times it was used, but now it should be retired.

What do you get when you mix a quart of sunshine, a pound of warm sand, a heaping spoonful of fun, and a sprinkle of sexual intrigue?

The answer: a bad lead.

Webster's Dictionary defines chewing gum as a sweetened, fla-vored...

Oh, great. Now I'm reading the dictionary.

As Henry Wadsworth Longfellow wrote...

I slept through that lecture once already.

The bottom line: leads are critically important, and good writers spend a lot of their time thinking about them. The corollary to that statement is that good editors spend a lot of their time thinking about leads as well, and every manuscript that lands on an editor's desk is scrutinized like a horse at a country fair. Because a weak lead means that the rest of the article goes unread, editors owe it to their writers and their readers to make sure that every article's lead is strong and captivating.

The Heart of the Matter

Whatever approach is taken for the lead, sooner or later an article must deliver the basics. The core. The kernel. The who, what, when, where, why, how.

In short, it has to sum up the topic and the significance of the article in a nutshell.

Editors call it the nut graf, which is short for nutshell paragraph. Good articles have good nut grafs. Bad articles have weak nut grafs—or no nut grafs at all.

Typically, the nut graf comes right after the lead. If you make the reader wait too long before handing over the explanation of the topic and the reasons the reader should care, you run the risk of making her wonder why she's reading the article at all.

While important, nut grafs are relatively simple. They cut to the chase and spell out the topic and why readers should care about it. Here's an example:

The anecdotal lead

Aarni Paul wriggles into a tight space between a rusting bulkhead and some corroded pipes. He drags a large acetylene tank behind him, its hoses and tools dangling and clanking against the decrepit hull.

Once he has braced himself tightly—one foot pressed against a red valve wheel and the other wedged between two jagged ducts—he dons his welder's mask and sparks his torch.

The blue-white flame sends eerie shadows scurrying throughout the hold of this rotting oil tanker, and the sounds echoing through the air suggest that other things are scurrying, too. Paul doesn't care. All he wants to do is cut through the steel flooring overhead without letting it fall down on top of him.

The nut graf

Paul, who lives just across the water on Barbuda Island, is one of the few remaining professionals devoted to dismantling freighters and tankers once their life spans have been exhausted. He works with a crew of twenty, expert welders all, and a handful of consultants who offer advice about such tangential topics as explosive gases.

Nut grafs are essential to the overall organization of an article. With a clear and strong nut graf, readers understand the point of the article and why it is valuable. Content that the point is worthwhile, they will turn their attention to the journey with a pleasant sense of anticipation. If they don't understand the central point, they'll spend the whole time wondering whether they've gotten on the wrong bus.

So Long, Farewell...

The other key vertebra in this skeleton is the conclusion. The conclusion is as important as the lead and the nut graf, and it serves several useful functions.

• *Closure*. A good conclusion makes the article feel like it has ended, firmly and gracefully. Many magazines these days put little icons or dingbats at the ends of their articles, to send a clear signal to readers: the article is over now, and if you turn the page you'll find something completely different coming up.

Articles with strong conclusions, however, don't require dingbats; readers will both *know* and *feel* that the article has ended just by reading the last few paragraphs.

• *Summary*. Sometimes, especially with complicated or technical articles, the conclusion can help summarize the overall set of points and their relationships to one another. If the article is long, readers might not remember everything that came early on, especially if they read it in more than one sitting. A good conclusion reminds them of the general gist of the article.

• *Significance.* It's been a long time since the readers have looked over the nut graf, so the conclusion also can be used to remind them of the significance of the article. It can be used to say, "You just spent twenty minutes reading this article, and don't forget why you bothered with it—this stuff is important."

• *Memory aids.* The conclusion can offer ways to help readers remember key points or essential facts. This is the "if you hold on to just one point here, this is it" approach. Most writers want their articles to be remembered and discussed later; we want to have an impact in this world. Giving readers something small and easy to remember can help them at work the next day, when someone asks, "Read anything interesting lately?"

• *Tone, character, style.* The conclusion also can reinforce the tone of the article. If it's a funny piece, the ending should produce a chuckle. If it's a sad piece, the ending should bring about a final round of tears. Often, the tone of the piece *is* the main point, and the conclusion should reinforce it.

Good conclusions add strength and power to articles, and they shouldn't be overlooked in the haste of getting something done by deadline. Think of popular songs that just repeat the last few lines and fade out:

Oooh, baby,
Yeah, yeah.
Oooh, baby,
Yeah, yeah.
oooh, baby,
yeah, yeah.
ooohbaby,
yeahyeah.

Not exactly a compelling ending. Talented writers give their articles endings that impress the mind and stir the soul.

Two other small points about conclusions:

1. The conclusion should wrap up the entire article, not just the last point. Each point should have its own mini-conclusion, but the last mini-conclusion doesn't serve as the ending for the whole article. The conclusion should bring everything to a close.

2. The conclusion is the "power" position. Numerous psychological studies have shown that in any series of things—numbers, words, sentences, paragraphs—we tend to remember the last one best. Articles shouldn't waste that power on something limp and ineffective.

All of this means that editors should pay attention to endings. Ask yourself whether the article ends powerfully, forcefully, memorably. Ask yourself whether another paragraph in the article would make a better ending. Ask yourself whether, three days from now, you'll remember anything about this article. Ask yourself whether, without a dingbat, your readers will be likely to turn the page and look for the rest of the article.

And still, if changes need to be made to the conclusion, give the article back to the writer with clear instructions and a new deadline.

Drink Milk

Just as a strong skeleton gives support, shape, and power to a body, a good structure is essential to an article. The best articles published today provide irresistible leads that entice readers into the story, a logical progression of information blocks throughout the piece, and a strong and satisfying conclusion.

With these parts solid and in place, articles will deliver on their promise to readers. Readers expect articles to attract their attention, guide them confidently through interesting material, and leave them deeply glad that they took the time to enter the world that the articles created. Haphazard, flighty articles cannot do this.

But well-built articles do.

Layer
Layer
Layer
Layer
Layer
Layer
Layer
Layer
Layer
Layer 3.

The Small (but Important) Stuff

A devastating blunder is one that significantly affects someone's life or livelihood; everything else is merely embarrassing. Our errors are of the embarrassing kind: a jump rope in space that turns out to be toothpaste being squeezed in zero g, a billion that should have been a million, a misidentified French village on the beaches of Normandy. Even the misidentification of Mount Everest in an article about that mountain is merely embarrassing. No one has been injured; life goes on. Of course, at the time of discovery, most errors are devastating to the person responsible, but eventually perspective is gained.

Lesley Rogers, senior editor and head of National Geographic Magazine Research, *National Geographic*

10. How's That, Again?

The Facts of Fact Checking

We fact check every story. We have an intern system where we train interns in fact checking. They are overseen by a copy chief. If someone has a story where the facts aren't critical to the story—he's wearing a red cap or an orange cap, and you can't pin it down—you might take the reporter's word for it. If the facts are critical to the story and they don't check out, you reconsider acceptance of the story.

Victor Navasky, publisher and editorial director, *The Nation*

What's wrong with this sentence: Frankenstein is a hideous monster in a book by Mary Shelley?

Grammatically, the sentence is just fine. The problem lies with the content of the sentence—Frankenstein was the name of the guy who made the hideous monster, not the monster himself. (The monster was never named in the novel.) So while the sentence meets all the rules of grammar, spelling, and punctuation, it violates a cardinal rule of journalism: it's wrong.

Publishing a grammatically perfect sentence that misstates the truth is far more damaging than messing up the occasional noun–verb agreement. The reason for that is simple.

Credibility is all we sell.

If a magazine gets its facts wrong, its readership will plummet. It's not that readers feel morally outraged if a magazine fumbles the facts—it's just that readers rely on publications for accurate information. If they can't get it from your magazine, they'll get it from somebody else's. So unless you work for the *National Enquirer*, the tabloid *Sun*, the *Weekly World News*, or any of the other publications that consider

Elvis Is Alive and Serving as the U.S. Vice President!

a reasonable headline, you've got to be careful about the information that appears in the pages of your magazine.

This is true for nearly every publication. It should be obvious that if *Newsweek* refers to Tony Blair as the prime minister of Greece, the editors there have a huge problem on their hands. But it's also true that if *Cosmopolitan* tells redheads that Maybelline's Passion Plum Pink is the perfect shade of lipstick for them—and then shoppers at the makeup counter discover that Maybelline doesn't make a shade called Passion Plum Pink—readers are going to be less likely to take *Cosmo's* advice seriously. Similarly, if *Maxim* says that Jennifer Love Hewitt is really sexy in *I Know What You Did Eight Summers Ago*—but it turns out that the movie features Jennifer Lopez—readers are going to wonder whether anyone at *Maxim* actually saw the movie.

Most editors have a pretty good idea that accuracy is important, and so they're on guard against colossal missteps. If a writer notes that it's perfectly safe to carry nitroglycerin around in a zip-lock baggie, most editors have the brains to check that out before printing it.

So mercifully, the Big Things tend to get the scrutiny they deserve. But often it's the smaller things that trip us up. These smaller things tend to fall into two categories.

• *Assumptions*. Imagine that an article says that the average American woman stands 5 feet, 6 inches tall. "Sounds right to me," the editor replies. "In it goes. I'm still trying to check on that nitroglycerin thing."

Wrong. The average American woman stands just under 5 feet, 4 inches tall. The writer took a stab at it and guessed 5 feet, 6 inches, and the editor didn't bother to check the facts. There goes another chip out of the magazine's credibility—and no publication can lose very many of those little chips before the whole thing crashes to the ground.

Assumptions are easy to rely on precisely because they feel right—that's why they're assumptions. We assume that our world is relatively normal, and we project that world outward, making assumptions as we go. Writers do the same thing. And if their world and our world overlap, then their assumptions are going to seem on target to us.

But our readers, of course, see things in many different ways. Some of them are married to starters in the WNBA. Some of them are married to jockeys. Just because our writer guessed that the average height for women is 5 feet, 6 inches—and just because that seemed about right to us—doesn't mean that it is indeed accurate. And our readers, in their myriad worlds, will catch the incorrect assumptions that we let into our magazine.

• *Terms.* A home remedy for that listless, drab, burned-out feeling says to take 18 grams of iron every day.

Oops. Nothing reduces your readership faster than killing off your subscribers.

Eighteen *milligrams* of iron per day is beneficial. Eighteen *grams* can be fatal.

It's easy to gloss over the little words and pay attention to things like numbers and dates. But those little terms can be crucial. If your bank account earns 2 percent interest per year, that's not all that great. If it brings in 2 percent per day, that's terrific! (Actually, it's beyond terrific. You'd double your money in a little more than a month. It's not going to happen.)

Good editors deliberately note each word in the sentences that they check. It does you no good to confirm the number if the words around it are wrong.

Reality Strikes

For the large magazines, staffers known as fact checkers are responsible for making sure that all the information in the publication's articles is accurate. In fact, fact checking is a pretty typical entry-level job at these magazines. But whether a fact checker checked the facts or not, it's ultimately the responsibility of the editors to make sure that the information is correct.

But of course, you have a limited amount of time each day—so which facts should be checked?

Most people who give advice to editors stick to the safe answer: check everything. Well, good. That's great advice. Check everything. Check everything fifteen times, using five different reliable sources, and cross-list all the responses.

If you do that, you'll never make a mistake.

You'll also never publish a magazine.

More helpful than the "check everything" advice is some kind of guide about the sort of information that is critically important or that frequently is mispresented. That's what this chapter is all about.

So here is a rundown of the most important things to check (and recheck). If you have time, do more. If you have enough time, check everything. Meanwhile, be sure to check at least the following.

• *Names.* Names are perhaps the most important thing to check, with the possible exception of those home remedies that will kill off your readers. Names are important because you can bet that the people you mention in articles will check their names right away. They want to make sure that you spelled their names right, and they want to make sure that they look good in the article. If you let errors slip in, they'll catch them right away. And they'll be angry, embarrassed, and absolutely convinced that you have no choice but to reprint the article with the proper spelling.

Checking names is essential not only to ensure accuracy and credibility, but also to avoid lawsuits. If you print that James R. Whetstone is an ax murderer, you'd better be right. If it turns out that James R. Whetstone is actually a respected brain surgeon—and that James L. Whetstone is the ax murderer—you can bet that the good doctor is going to hire a good lawyer and have a little talk with you.

And again, assumptions can be dangerous. Is Al Franken's first name Alan, Allan, Allen, Albert, Alfred, or just plain Al? What about Ed McMahon—Edward, Edmund, Edgar? If you need the full name, you had better confirm the full name. Assumptions can be costly.

• *Statistics and technical information.* Almost any time you see a number, you should check it. Not only are numbers complicated at times, but they are easy to transpose when typing; no spell checker will complain when you type 5,208 even though you meant 5,280.

And numbers have a nasty habit of creeping into our brains, changing into incorrect information, and then calcifying there, leaving us certain that we have them right. We carry around such a huge amount of useless information in our heads that it's difficult to keep it straight. For example, always check statistics such as

• Speeds

What is the speed of sound?	1,129 feet per second
Light?	186,282 miles per second
How fast can a cheetah run?	60 miles per hour, in short bursts

• Populations

What is the population of Denver?	About 500,000
The United States?	About 280 million
The world?	Just over 6 billion

• Averages

What is the average life span of an American man?	Seventy-four years
An American woman?	Eighty years
What is the average income of people in Nevada?	$30,529 per year
What is the average rainfall in Texas?	Just over 46 inches

Note that it's also important to make sure that you understand what *average* means.

• Records

What is the fastest speed a car has ever reached?	For a mile run, 763 miles per hour, by Andy Green on October 15, 1997 (in a "car" that looks nothing like your father's Oldsmobile)
What is the deepest that a person has ever dived without scuba gear?	594 feet, by Herbert Nitsch of Austria on February 2, 2002
What is the highest number of touchdowns thrown by a quarterback in a single NFL season?	Forty-eight, by Dan Marino in 1984

And again, pay attention to the little words. Is that miles per hour, or miles per second? or feet per second? Is it millions or billions? A difference of one word or letter can change the meaning dramatically.

Also, keep in mind that things like records change frequently. Undoubtedly, some of the records just noted have been broken by the time you read this.

• *Citations.* In a decent-size readership, it's amazing how many people will prove to be better read than you are. And every one of them, with great triumph and flourish, will write to you to point out mistakes that you make in literature, music, and other fields of study. The only way to keep them at bay is to check the information and make sure you've got it right.

Who wrote *Chitty Chitty Bang Bang*?	Ian Fleming, of James Bond fame
Who composed the *William Tell* Overture?	Gioacchino Rossini
Which U.S. surgeon general was the first to issue a report on the health hazards of cigarettes?	Luther L. Terry, in 1964

Getting some information wrong results in embarrassment, but getting a citation wrong can result in some very angry confrontations. Rossini won't complain if you say that the *William Tell* Overture was written by Bach—Rossini died more than a century ago—but living authors, composers, and other artists want proper credit for the work they do.

• *Titles.* Titles come in two types, both of which should be checked carefully.

Literary. You should check the title of every book, article, play, poem, and other work of fiction and nonfiction as well as the name of every character, fictitious land, and anything else that appear in print. Because your readers can check this information—and because half of them will remember it from their high-school English classes—you need to be sure you've got it right.

And as always, little mistakes can embarrass you. Be sure that every part of every title is correct.

What was the title of Charles Darwin's major work?	*The Origin of Species* (not *The Origin of the Species*)
In what book did Captain Nemo appear?	*Twenty Thousand Leagues Under the Sea* (which refers to the distance that the *Nautilus* traveled under the sea, not the

	depth it reached. No ocean is that deep)
For what work did Susan Sheehan win the Pulitzer Prize?	*Is There No Place on Earth for Me?* in 1983

Professional. Professional titles—*Dr.* Tekela Black, *Rev.* Hoon Yao, *Senator* Charlotte Fisher—are important for the same reasons that names and citations are important. The people you mention will read the articles, and they won't be amused if you demote them. People work hard to earn their professional titles, and they deserve to have them noted properly.

And avoiding assumptions remains an important consideration.

What should you put after a person's name if she has a law degree?	Depends on the degree. Most are LL.D. or J.D., but you have to ask.
If a person sells real estate, is he a realtor?	Not necessarily. Realtors® represent a subset of all real-estate agents, and membership requires that certain standards be met. And note that the term is capitalized and carries the registered trademark symbol.
Is a chiropractor a doctor?	Depends on who you ask. Chiropractors insist that they are doctors, and some of them serve as the primary-care physicians for their patients. But the Associated Press and other organizations insist that the term *doctor* be reserved for people with M.D. or Ph.D. degrees, which most chiropractors don't have.

• *Famous quotes.* Another big area for fractured memories is quotes from films, books, and other works.

In *Casablanca*, how many times did Rick say "Play it again, Sam"?	None. The closest he gets is "Play it, Sam."

How does that "fool some of the people all of the time" saying really go, and who said it?	According to Abraham Lincoln, "You can fool some of the people all of the time, and all of the people some of the time, but you cannot fool all of the people all of the time."

The problem with quotes is twofold. Some of the errors that afflict us stem from our own faulty memories. We're just *sure* that a quote is worded a certain way, and only through a painful consultation with the original source can we be convinced otherwise. And some of the problems stem from the variability of transmission. Maybe we heard that line from the movie itself. Maybe we read the book itself. Or maybe we first heard that quote from Uncle George, who didn't get it quite right. We tend to believe that the quote as we first learned it is the proper and official version, and that all others must be mistaken. But every now and then, we discover that Uncle George is not the paragon of accuracy that he thinks he is. In those cases, we have to hit the books again.

• *Hard facts*. We also have to be careful with simple, straightforward, factual information. Here, our own arrogance can get in the way. If we're positively certain that the capital of Australia is Sydney—and that's what the writer said in the article—then we aren't likely to stop and look it up. If we let it slide past us, however, we'll get six dozen letters from diligent (and frequently smug) readers who will point out that it's Canberra.

We don't check the accuracy of quotes, because it is our experience that [the source] may deny that he said it because he doesn't like the way it sounds. We do trust our writers on that. But if it is someone we haven't dealt with before, we may ask to see his notes or listen to his tape recording. Wherever a quote is from an existing publication, we will check it. So the line between re-reporting a story and fact checking is an important one. We try not to re-report, but we try to be as accurate as we can.

Victor Navasky, publisher and editorial director, *The Nation*

So we really should stop and check each hard fact that crosses our desks.

What is the capital of Canada?	Ottawa
What is the capital of Alaska?	Trick question. The working capital is Juneau, but in 1976 the legislature voted to make Willow the state capital. No money was earmarked for the move, though, so it hasn't happened.
How many continents exist on Earth?	Most people agree on seven: North America, South America, Europe, Asia, Africa, Australia, and Antarctica. But note that the Europe/Asia distinction is political, not physical.

• *Historical references.* As before, references to historical events can trick us with our own certainty. Even though it's been years since we took that history course with Mrs. Longview, we're confident that we have all the facts and figures solidly ensconced in our memories.

That's dangerous, of course. Because historical information can be checked by our readers, it should be checked by us first.

When did the Revolutionary War end?	1783 (not 1776)
Who was the thirty-first president?	Herbert Hoover
When did Newfoundland join Canada?	1949
Who succeeded King Henry VIII?	His son, Edward VI

We can't possibly remember all these data, so we should just get into the habit of looking them up.

• *Math.* If an article refers to or relies on any math whatsoever, you have to check it. Most of the math offered in magazine articles is pretty straightforward; average readers can't do tricky math, either. But all formulas, equations, and examples that use math must be confirmed. Hit the reference books to make sure that the equations are correct—that it's $e = mc^2$ and not $e = m^2c$—and then do the math to make sure that it all works.

• *Last but not least—anything that seems odd to you.* You have a perfectly decent set of instincts and intuitions. If you snag on anything, check it out.

If you check these pieces of information—or if you hire someone you trust to check them for you—you should do a good job of earning the loyalty of your readers while still getting the magazine out on time.

But of course, you really should check everything.

Sources, Resources, and More Sources

Most editors aren't able to set up shop at the Library of Congress, so they have to know the essentials for a good fact-checking toolkit. Smart editors keep these resources nearby at all times in order to check information without wasting too much time. And we all know that if you have to work too hard to check a fact, sooner or later you'll just shrug and assume that it's close enough. By keeping these books handy, you'll resist the temptation to let things slide.

• *Dictionary.* How many feet are in a mile? A dictionary will tell you that in no time. In addition to helping you with proper spelling, the dictionary can provide you with a wealth of basic facts quickly and easily.

Remember the "three-foot rule." Always make sure that you have a dictionary within 3 feet of you while you work. Otherwise, you won't bother to look things up.

• *Encyclopedia.* Most good encyclopedias are available online or on CD-ROMs, and they're pretty easy to work with. You'll get a wealth of information quickly, without having to dig through long, in-depth, specialized books on the topic.

I'm a big fan of encyclopedias intended for children. For very simple information, like the dates of William Henry Harrison's presidency or the capital of Australia, they get right to the point. The *Encyclopaedia Britannica* and other adult encyclopedias are great, but you'll have to wade through more details just to get the little fact you want.

• *Bartlett's Familiar Quotations.* Other good books of quotations exist, but *Bartlett's Familiar Quotations* is the granddaddy of them all. If you check a quotation in *Bartlett's*, you'll win any disputes about its authenticity or accuracy.

• *Almanac.* There are several, including *The New York Times Almanac* and the *Information Please Almanac.* These books contain millions of useful facts, arranged in easy-to-locate formats.

Just be sure to get a reputable one. Some of the fly-by-night almanacs are worthless and can get you in serious trouble.

• *Who's Who.* If you need basic information about a prominent person, *Who's Who* will have it. But beware of the many *Who's Who* knockoffs. These sucker publications make their money by listing people's information and then getting them to buy copies of the book. They'll list anyone; the bigger the pool, the more potential buyers they have. All the information is self-reported and unverified.

But the real *Who's Who* is a great resource. Use the one at a good library—it'll be legitimate.

Other Tools

In addition to books, several other resources can be very helpful.

• *Calculator.* Keep a calculator handy—in a desk drawer or on your computer's hard drive. Because you always have to check the math in the articles you edit, you should have a great calculator that will make the task easier. I prefer calculators that let me print out the math, so I can refer to it later if I wish.

• *Reference librarian.* Reference librarians are incredible. They get paid to help people find information, and they are universally gung-ho, determined, and unstoppable. And because their jobs depend on people using their services, they do not consider requests a nuisance. In fact, every request for information is one more piece of ammunition they can use at budget time.

Most community libraries have reference librarians. Just call and ask for one. In most cases, either you'll get the information you want right away, or the librarian will take your phone number and call you back.

To get the information, they'll dig through books that most people don't have at home, and they'll often find far more material than you can possibly use.

And be sure to treat these people like the golden resource that they are. You'll be glad you did.

- *The source herself.* If you can't find corroboration any other way, it is perfectly legitimate for you to call your writer's source directly. The source probably can tell you how to verify the information she gave your writer. Just be sure to make it clear that you are doing a routine fact check, not questioning your writer's professionalism, integrity, or accuracy.

- *An expert in the field.* You also can contact some other person who has expertise in the same area. If your writer interviewed a chemistry professor at Stanford, you can check the information by calling a chemistry professor at Harvard.

Most universities maintain lists of professors who have expressed a willingness to talk with writers and editors. Just call the university's public-relations office, and you'll be directed to someone who can help you.

- *The Internet.* We all know by now that anyone with a keyboard and an evil streak can toss garbage onto the Internet, so of course you have to be very careful here. Still, some Web sites are bona fide and extremely useful. Here are a few that are worth remembering.

- General

Journalists' Toolbox   http://www.journaliststoolbox.com

Journalists' Toolbox maintains links to helpful Web sites that reporters and editors might need, and it is kept relatively up-to-date.

Library of Congress   http://loc.gov
Polling Report   http://www.pollingreport.com

Polling Report samples attitudes about a variety of topics.

Poynter Institute   http://www.poynter.org

Poynter Institute provides information and Web links useful to journalists.

Search Systems   http://www.searchsystems.net

Search Systems offers searchable databases of public records in the United States and Canada, the rest of the world, and outer space (really!).

University of Michigan Documents Center	http://www.lib.umich.edu/ govdocs/govweb.html

University of Michigan Documents Center has links to Web-based resources for many governments throughout the world.

- Newspapers

Boston Globe	http://www.boston.com/globe
Native Times	http://www.okit.com
New York Times	http://nytimes.com
Washington Post	http://www.washingtonpost.com

- Political parties and elections

Democratic Party	http://www.democrats.org
Green Party	http://www.greenpartyus.org
Libertarian Party	http://www.lp.org
Reform Party	http://www.reformparty.org
Republican Party	http://www.gop.org
Federal Election Commission	http://www.fec.gov
Project Vote Smart	http://www.vote-smart.org

Project Vote Smart offers information about candidates and proposals.

- United States government

American Fact Finder	http://factfinder.census.gov/ servlet/BasicFactsServlet

American Fact Finder, a service of the Census Bureau, has tons of information about the population, communities, and businesses in the United States.

Census Bureau	http://www.census.gov
Centers for Disease Control and Prevention	http://www.cdc.gov
Department of the Interior	http://www.doi.gov

| Department of State | http://www.state.gov |
| FedStats | http://www.fedstats.gov |

FedStats provides statistics from scores of federal agencies.

| FedWorld | http://www.fedworld.gov |

FedWorld offers information about the federal government and its policies, agencies, and such.

| FirstGov | http://www.firstgov.gov |

FirstGov consolidates millions of government documents.

| National Aeronautics and Space Administration | www.nasa.gov |
| Security and Exchange Commission | http://www.sec.gov |

Security and Exchange Commission has data on publicly traded corporations.

| Supreme Court | http://www.supremecourtus.gov |
| Thomas | http://thomas.loc.gov |

Thomas (as in Jefferson) provides extensive information about the U.S. Congress, including bills and their sponsors and supporters.

| White House | http://www.whitehouse.gov |

White House covers the White House, the president, the administration, and policies.

• State governments

| Stateline | http://www.stateline.org |

Stateline covers the states, with links to individual state home pages.

• Foreign governments

| Canada | http://canada.gc.ca |
| Great Britain (10 Downing Street) | http://www.number-10.gov.uk/ output/Page1.asp |

Ah, but What Is Truth?

Sometimes, journalists are faced with a difficult but terrific problem: not too little information, but too much. What do you do when you check facts and find a disagreement? when your writer's source says that the universe will expand forever, but *your* source says that it will contract?

First, be sure the sources are talking about the same thing. The largest city in the United States is New York—if you measure by population. The largest city in the United States is Juneau, Alaska—if you measure by square miles (3,081 square miles, larger than Delaware!). So if your sources disagree, they might be using terms in different ways.

You also might have to go to additional experts, checking with several sources until a consensus appears.

And, of course, the article doesn't have to state information more emphatically than necessary. There's nothing wrong with telling readers that experts disagree about something.

Oops, We Did It Again

When publications make mistakes, their credibility suffers. One way that editors try to restore the credibility of their magazines is by maintaining an open, honest relationship with their readers.

Sometimes, that means admitting that you made a mistake. It will happen. No one can publish a magazine every week or every month, for year after year, without flubbing something.

The best response when your magazine makes an error is to inform readers of it in the next issue. If you said that the Earth is the fourth planet from the sun, that the chemical symbol for plutonium is Pu, or that whales are fish—you need to set the record straight to retain credibility. If you told readers something erroneous and unflattering about a particular person, you need to set the record straight to retain credibility and avoid a lawsuit.

Generally, corrections are run with some dignity, simply pointing out that a mistake was made and printing the correct information. In most cases, a correction will calm anyone who was upset over the blunder.

And never reprint the original error. If you do, then you've printed the wrong information twice and the correct information once—a bad overall score. Just acknowledge the error and state what should have been said in the first place:

> In our previous issue, we printed incorrect information about the population of the world. The population continues to increase despite a downturn in birthrates worldwide.

Whether you add something like "We regret the error" is up to you.

Just the Facts, Ma'am

Fact checking can be boring, slow, annoying, and tedious—but it beats apologizing for errors later on. If you keep the necessary tools nearby, and if you train your fact-checking interns well, you should be able to get into the "look it up" habit fairly easily.

If you lack a fact-checking squad, you'll have to do it yourself. When I was editing without the benefit of a bevy of fact checkers, I simply devoted an editing "lap" to fact checking. After I made sure that the article made sense, fit the assignment, and had the right tone, I worked through it, looking for nothing but information that I could check out.

The advantage of a dedicated fact-checking lap is that you can set aside your assumptions, your knowledge, and your logic—and simply challenge everything that you see. It's easier to do that for one concentrated lap through a manuscript than to keep it up all the time.

But however you do it, just do it. As we said before, credibility is all we have to sell. If your readers learn that they can't count on you for reliable information, they'll soon become someone else's readers.

11. Word World:

The Joy, Beauty, and Sheer, Staggering Unimaginable Grace of Grammar

Q: How do you make sure that every fact, every comma, every participle is proper—without going absolutely mad? A: Who says we're not mad!

Lesley Rogers, senior editor and head of National Geographic Magazine Research, *National Geographic*

A weak understanding of grammar will not kill you.

Even as a magazine editor, you won't be fired, shot, or otherwise disgraced if the occasional dangling participle creeps into your pages. Children won't call you rude names; dogs won't chase you down the street; housewives won't dump chamber pots on you from second-story windows. Even the best magazines in the country offer split infinitives or nonparallel construction from time to time. None of the editors of these magazines, so far, has been tarred and feathered for their crimes against language.

But, failing to understand the important facets of good grammar can cause you some problems. If you're a writer, for example, a barrage of grammatical errors can make your editor worry. "If she is this sloppy with grammar," says the voice in the editor's head, "maybe she's equally sloppy with facts." Now the editor is worried that your article will contain mistakes that could bring embarrassment, declining revenue, and even lawsuits to the magazine.

If you're an editor, and grammatical mistakes too often slither past you and into the printing press, your readers will harbor similar concerns. They'll worry that the grammatical blunders are close friends with shoddy research, weak reporting, and bad information. And if they worry for too long, they'll find some other magazine that will make them feel more secure.

Besides, as a communication professional, you want to wield your weapons with finesse. Annie Oakley would die of embarrassment if she tripped while getting her gun. D'Artagnan would be mortified if he dropped his rapier. Ahab would sink to his knee if he fumbled his harpoon on deck. And we, too, should feel shame and remorse if we let clumsy writing appear in print.

So it pays to know about the language you use. While the complete list of rules could fill a community library, a small core of helpful ideas can keep you out of trouble in most circumstances. This chapter will go over that small core and offer suggestions for putting the rules into action.

But first, a word about simplicity. In writing, simplicity is beautiful. A lot of people who call themselves writers like to carve out elaborate sentence constructions, pile on enormous words unnecessarily, and twist (and mangle) the flow of their logic—all in the secret belief that doing so will make readers gasp in awe over the writer's intellect.

Wrong. Sentences that are hard to follow don't make readers admire the writer; they make readers turn on the television. Fifty-dollar words don't fill readers' minds with envy; they fill the readers with impatience and disgust. Convoluted logic doesn't make readers certain of the writer's mental acuity; it makes readers believe that the writer is an idiot.

A case in point: one writer who worked for me many years ago used the word *fenestration* in an article. I had to look it up—and if *I* had to look it up, you can bet that most of my readers didn't know what it meant, either. Turns out, it means "windows." Why the writer chose to use *fenestration* instead of *windows*, I'll never know. And my readers will never know that he used that ridiculous word. The article that appeared in print had *windows* instead.

This is not to say that anything beyond "See Spot run" is bad writing. Many excellent writers—John McPhee, Henry Glassie, Richard Todd, Tracy Kidder, Mark Kramer, and scores of others—demonstrate that sophisticated writing can be spectacular. They use graceful and original turns of phrase and, at times, esoteric words that aren't in the working lexicons of most readers. The difference between the kind of elegance that they employ and the kind of arrogant clumsiness that *fenestration* indicates is that the good writers use such terms and phrases for precision—when nothing else will do the trick. If *windows* gets the point across, they'll use *windows*. But if the sound, pacing, nuance, connotation, or surprise value of the fancy word or phrase is essential to the point, they'll use it properly and with confidence. And readers can sense that precision. They trust good writers, and they trust that good writers are delivering material that is essential to the meaning and quality of the prose. Words like *fenestration*, forced into a sentence in a sad attempt to impress readers with the writer's vocabulary, make readers shake their heads and move on.

Here's a final example. Read this phrase:

To the noisy, clanging ringing that so musically wells
From the bells, bells, bells, bells,
Bells, bells, bells—

Now compare it with the phrase that Edgar Allan Poe actually chose to write in his poem "The Bells":

To the tintinnabulation that so musically wells
From the bells, bells, bells, bells,
Bells, bells, bells—

The phrase that I inserted in the first example, to replace the word *tintinnabulation*, fits the rhythm of the lines of the poem. But it doesn't have anything like the sound quality and the echoing nuance of *tintinnabulation*. Poe could have written the first one, but he didn't. He chose to use a big, fancy word instead of an equally rhythmic phrase. And his choice was sound (pardon the pun). *Tintinnabulation* has an effect on the ear that the phrase lacks. As a reader, I trust that Poe was not merely showing off the size of his thesaurus. He used the enormous word *tintinnabulation* because it works.

The rules that I will offer later in this chapter say that we should pour our sweat into choosing just the right concrete nouns and action verbs, rather than grabbing an off-the-shelf word and modifying it with a bunch of adverbs and adjectives to make it convey the right impression. Poe clearly understood that rule. Another rule I'll mention urges us to use small, easily understood words whenever possible. Poe understood that rule, too, but he also understood one of the overarching principles of good writing: Once you know the rules thoroughly, you should break them whenever necessary in service of a higher goal. Poe broke the "use small words" rule because he opted in favor of a more important quest: to give readers the richest experience possible. This overarching principle is worth knowing. No one ever got an editing job because she understood all the rules of grammar and clung to them feverishly. You get an editing job because you know good writing when you see it—and good writing sometimes violates basic grammatical rules for clear effect. So it pays to know what you're doing; don't take anything too seriously.

One other point. This chapter uses a lot of grammar terminology. The terminology is useful because it lets us refer to things without much cumbersome description. But it's important to remember that the terminology is not what matters. With the possible exception of some pedestrian little entry exam that some publishers inflict on applicants for editing jobs, you'll never really have to know the precise definitions of *participle*, *gerund*, *infinitive*, and a lot of the other words that blue-haired English teachers hurl at us in fifth grade. But it's hard to talk about—or even think about—good writing without being able to wield some useful terms. If an article is clumsy, and you're on the phone with the writer trying to get it straightened out, your life will simply be easier if you can say, "Hey, Susan, you've got a lot of gerunds in this piece, and they weaken your main point." If you don't know about the word *gerunds*, you'll end up having to say something like this: "Hey, Susan, you've got a lot of sentences in this article that use '–ing' verbs as though they are nouns, which is all right in small doses but fuzzy and annoying when done too often." At which point, Susan will say, "Did you say 'ing'? What the heck's an 'ing'?" And your conversation goes downhill from there.

So don't strain yourself over the lingo of grammar. If you can understand the point behind the terms and how things should be done correctly, you'll be all right. And if you can grasp the terms themselves, you'll be even better off.

Conviction and Good Sentences

Our fifth-grade grammar lessons evaporated a long time ago, but we can still remember what a basic sentence looks like:

A Noun,
followed by a Verb,
followed by Other Stuff.

It is this basic structure that makes up a lot of our communication:

He hit me.
Juanita is my friend.
It was a dark and stormy night.
I see an iceberg, Captain!
I love you.

This is our basic structure because it works. It tells us who is doing something. It tells us what is happening. And it tells us other things relevant to the point.

It's a good structure.

In honor of its goodness, we'll break it down and attach some of the dreaded terminology to it. We're still on familiar ground here, so the terms won't throw anyone.

The person or thing doing the action, in most cases, is the *subject*. You knew that; we're on the same page so far.

The thing that is being done is the *verb*. Still good.

Together, the verb and the other stuff make up the *predicate*. All right—we hate that word. We don't entirely know what it means. But basically, it's not too bad. The subject tells us who is doing something. The predicate simply tells us about the subject:

The girl punched her brother.

In that sentence, the subject is obviously "The girl." Now we want to know something about her. What's she up to? Turns out, she's swinging a fist. Really? Tell me more. Fine—she's swinging her fist, and it's making contact with some part of her brother. Everything after "The girl" is the predicate. It tells us what the subject is doing, and it adds information that fleshes out the situation a little.

We'll break apart the predicate more later on, but for now, we have to grapple with one big question: Who cares about the subject and the predicate? Well, editors do. Knowing something about sub-

214 **The Small (but Important) Stuff**

jects and predicates can help us understand sentences—and it can help us avoid two of the big grammatical mistakes that people make.

• *The sentence.* Because a sentence is a basic building block of the English language, it pays to get it right. A good sentence conveys a single idea,

> The clown scared the boy.

or a set of closely related ideas,

> The clown scared the boy, who notified federal authorities.

Sentences, with their tight sets of ideas, are woven into paragraphs, which cluster related ideas together into general points or arguments.

Sentences come in three basic flavors: the simple sentence, the compound sentence, and the complex sentence.

The simple sentence has the basic parts already described: subject and predicate, with a verb lurking in the predicate somewhere. It usually runs in the standard order:

> Bob juggled the torches.

A simple sentence is a kind of independent clause, because it can stand alone.

The compound sentence is two simple sentences joined in some acceptable way. (The simple sentences should be closely related in meaning; otherwise, they should be kept separate.) The most common way to join two simple sentences is with a comma and a conjunction:

> Bob juggled the torches, and he whistled a Scottish jig.

Each of the two independent clauses, "Bob juggled the torches" and "he whistled a Scottish jig," could stand alone, but if the clauses are logically related, you could link them with a comma and a conjunction (in this case, *and*). Assuming that Bob is juggling while he whistles, this kind of linkage makes sense.

Independent clauses can be linked to form compound sentences in another way: with a comma and a conjunctive adverb. Common conjunctive adverbs are *also, besides, furthermore, however, neverthe-*

less, otherwise, so, still, then, therefore, and *thus.* Conjunctive adverbs do more than link; they also show some kind of relationship:

Bob juggled the torches awkwardly, so he is now known as "Shishka" Bob.

And independent clauses can be linked with punctuation alone. For closely related ideas, semicolons do the job nicely:

Karen was beautiful, talented, smart, and ambitious; everyone at school hated her.

A colon is useful if you are introducing an independent clause that amplifies or explains the first:

Everyone at school hated Karen: she was beautiful, talented, smart, and ambitious.

The complex sentence—not to be confused with the compound sentence—contains both an independent and a dependent clause. Dependent clauses can't stand alone. "Juanita thrilled the audience" is an independent clause. "Portraying a sensitive and seductive Juliet" is a dependent clause; it makes no sense by itself. Put them together, and you have a complex sentence:

Juanita, portraying a sensitive and seductive Juliet, thrilled the audience.

And just to make matters even more complicated, you can combine compound and complex sentences to form (perhaps not surprisingly) a compound–complex sentence:

Juanita, portraying a sensitive and seductive Juliet, thrilled the audience, and she received a four-minute standing ovation.

• *Big grammatical mistake number 1.* Sentences that lack any of the necessary parts—generally, the subject or the predicate—are called *fragments.* Fragments can lack the predicate; "the clown" is a fragment because it has nothing but the subject. They also can lack the subject; "crawled through the sewer" is a fragment because we don't know who is doing the crawling.

Fragments can even lack some essential part of the predicate. "The clown, fleeing federal authorities" is a fragment. It has part of the predicate, but it lacks the main verb.

And some fragments have the subject and the predicate, but they fail to convey a coherent idea. "Because the boy turned him in" is a fragment; it has a subject, "the boy," and it has a predicate, "turned him in," but the "because" at the beginning suggests that something else is needed to make this a complete sentence. Only when all parts are present and a coherent idea is expressed do we have a complete sentence:

> The clown, fleeing federal authorities, crawled through the sewer because the boy turned him in.

Remember, however, that fragments aren't entirely evil. Despite the warnings of our blue-haired English teachers, fragments can be useful at times. Very useful. Even if they lack a key element. Really. The point is that you should know a fragment when you see one. And if a writer submits a manuscript that contains some fragments, you should ask yourself whether you can detect the rationale behind them—or whether they're just sloppy. Fragments used for impact can be effective, especially at the end of a long paragraph. Fragments that splat onto the page because the writer didn't know any better are almost always embarrassing and shoddy.

• *Big grammatical mistake number 2.* The other big grammatical mistake involves the opposite of a fragment. A *run-on* is a sentence that violates the rules of good sentences by offering more than one main subject, more than one main verb, or more than one coherent thought. This violation can happen through bad thinking or bad punctuation:

> Kim won the lottery.

This is a perfectly good sentence. One subject: "Kim." One main verb: "won." Some other predicate stuff: "the lottery."

> Kim won the lottery, and she is going to quit her job.

So far, so good. This is a perfectly reasonable compound sentence.

> Kim, a student at Central College, won the lottery, and she is going to quit her job.

Even this sentence is fine; it's a compound–complex sentence, which is acceptable.

> Kim, a student at Central College, won the lottery, and she is going to quit her job waitressing at Slab o' Beef.

Now we're inching our way toward a run-on sentence. The lottery bonanza and its immediate aftermath—the quitting of the job—can hold together as a single idea. But the details of the job really constitute another idea, and hence should be reserved for another sentence. Some editors might allow this sentence, but I think most would break it into two sentences.

> Kim, a student at Central College, won the lottery, and she is going to quit her job waitressing at Slab o' Beef, where she has been working for the past three years.

Now we're clearly over the line; this sentence is a bona fide run-on. It has too much hanging onto it, and it must be broken apart.

> Kim, a student at Central College, won the lottery, and she is going to quit her job waitressing at Slab o' Beef, where she has been working for the past three years even though the tips are lousy, the food could clog your arteries from fifty paces away, and the manager smells bad and smokes big, fat cigars in the walk-in freezer when he thinks no one is watching.

Oh, stop it.

Don't Try These at Home

Armed with a sense of what good sentences are supposed to look like, we can now turn our attention to the myriad pitfalls that can trap us within sentences. This section will address some of the more common rules and discuss how to fix—or prevent—any mistakes.

- *Pronoun antecedents.* The antecedent is the noun that a pronoun refers back to and replaces:

Fred is a nice guy. He buys me ice cream.

The antecedent for "He" is "Fred."

The antecedent for each pronoun must be glaringly obvious. Without clear antecedents, pronouns become fuzzy in their meaning. I heard a great example of this from Mick Mallon, who teaches Inuktitut, the Inuit language, at Arctic College in Iqaluit, on Canada's north coast. The example he uses refers to two male friends, Ralph and Joe:

He is happy because he loves his wife.

In English, this sentence is a disaster of confusion. There are eight possible interpretations:

1. Ralph is happy because Ralph loves Ralph's wife.
2. Ralph is happy because Ralph loves Joe's wife.
3. Ralph is happy because Joe loves Ralph's wife.
4. Ralph is happy because Joe loves Joe's wife.
5. Joe is happy because Joe loves Joe's wife.
6. Joe is happy because Joe loves Ralph's wife.
7. Joe is happy because Ralph loves Joe's wife.
8. Joe is happy because Ralph loves Ralph's wife.

It's actually much clearer in Inuktitut, whose vocabulary would make the relationships obvious. But in English, we have a serious problem. We don't know who is who. As Mick puts it, we don't know if we're talking about a seething soap opera or a vision of domestic felicity.

The core problem is that the pronouns don't have clear antecedents. Which person is represented by "he"? Which by "his"? We can't tell.

A similar problem emerges when a pronoun is supposed to stand in for an entire, general concept, rather than a specific term. For example, if the antecedent for "her" is "Susan," we're fine. But we run into trouble in examples like this:

To ferry your canoe, back-paddle rapidly across the current while keeping the canoe pointed at an angle toward the bank. This will cause your canoe to move sideways across the stream.

In this example, "This" functions as a pronoun. But what does it refer to? paddling across the current? keeping the canoe pointed at an angle? both? That little, four-letter word seems to be standing in for "back-paddle rapidly across the current while keeping the canoe pointed at an angle toward the bank," which is both unclear and a big burden for a single pronoun.

Good writers avoid this problem by taking two important steps. First, they make sure that every pronoun has an actual antecedent somewhere in the text just a short distance upstream. Then, they make sure that the structure of the sentences makes the connection clear. In general, readers will assume that a pronoun refers back to the nearest preceding word that makes sense for it. So in the sentence

> My father and Aunt Matilda went skydiving yesterday, and he landed in the lake.

the pronoun "he" clearly refers to "My father," because, of course, a masculine pronoun can't refer to a woman. However, in the sentence

> Uncle Frederick and the king of Gondwanaland had lunch yesterday, and he picked up the check.

the pronoun "he" could refer to either Fred or the king. The assumption would be that it refers to the king, because he is closer to the pronoun than Fred is, but that's not terribly clear. That sentence would be guilty of fuzziness through a less-than-solid antecedent relationship.

The easiest way to eliminate such problems can usually be found through rewriting:

> To ferry your canoe, back-paddle rapidly across the current while keeping the canoe pointed at an angle toward the bank. Taking these actions will cause your canoe to move sideways across the stream.

> Uncle Frederick and the king of Gondwanaland had lunch yesterday, and the king picked up the check.

> Joe is delighted that Ralph is happily married.

And here's another good rule: for every pronoun you write, you should be able to touch the antecedent with your index finger. If you can't poke the exact word that the pronoun stands for, you need to make sure the meaning is thoroughly clear some other way.

• *Noun–pronoun agreement.* Beginning writers commonly have trouble with noun–pronoun agreement. Good editors can sense agreement problems in the dark and can fix them almost unconsciously, but writers in the early stages of their careers need to think about them deliberately.

The Blue-Hairs drilled the mantra into our fifth-grade heads: pronouns must agree with their nouns in gender and number. So if Fred is doing something, the pronoun we use is *he* or *him*. If Suzette is doing it, then we use *she* or *her*. If forty of our closest friends are doing something, we use *they* or *them*, or *we* or *us* (depending on the point of view). If I'm doing the action, I'll use *I* or *me*.

I would add one more consideration to the mantra: pronouns should agree with their nouns in humanity. If we're talking about people, we use *he, she, him, her, we, us, they,* and *them.* If we're talking about a mailbox, a large rock, the universe, or Bowso the Basset Hound, we use *it.* (Strangely, the plural form still is *they.*) The point is that we don't refer to people as *its.*

Simple. Obvious. We know this stuff. So why is it such a common problem?

One reason it is a problem is that the noun in question can be hard to identify. Consider this sentence:

The scuba diver bumped the swimmer.

Now make it a bit more complex:

The scuba diver bumped the swimmer, and she hit him.

Wait. Who hit whom? Did the female diver hit the male swimmer? Or did the female swimmer hit the male diver? This is the same problem we had previously, with Ralph and Joe. Without a clear antecedent, we run the risk of getting the agreement wrong.

Another reason that this problem surfaces often is that intervening words can confuse us:

Bob is one of those really great guys.

That's fine. But writers who write too quickly—and who fail to rewrite carefully—can be thrown by the plural "guys" and plunk down the wrong pronoun:

Bob is one of those really great guys, aren't they?

The key here is knowing what the noun is and not letting any of the intervening words throw us off track. Obviously, what we want is

Bob is one of those really great guys, isn't he?

And here's another set of puzzles. What do we do with multiple nouns? Some of them are easy:

Karen and Sally like their cars.

No sweat. We have two people, Karen and Sally, so we have a plural situation. The "and" makes that clear. Hence a plural pronoun. Piece of cake.

Fine. Try this:

Neither Carol nor Suzette likes (her/their) shoes.

Her or *their*? You have two people, so *their* seems to make sense. But the "Neither...nor" makes it seem as though we are taking these people one at a time. So what do we do?

The answer is that *her* is correct. With the word *nor*, we take the nouns one at a time.

Now for the really tough stuff. How about this one:

Neither the firefighters nor the mayor will like (his/their) portrayal in the magazine.

This is twisted. We have a plural noun, "firefighters," and a singular noun, "mayor." They aren't linked with an *and*—that would be too easy. It's a *nor*. And we know from the "Carol and Suzette" saga that with *nor* we consider each noun separately. But which one do we go with?

The rule is that you go with the noun that is closest to the pronoun. So in the "firefighters and mayor" example, we'd use *his*. But if the phrase were flopped—"neither the mayor nor the firefighters"—we'd use *their*. The rule seems to be based on the option that simply sounds best to our ears.

And then things get even trickier. Consider this challenge:

The Four Tops released (its/their) new retro album yesterday.

Which do you choose? On the one hand, you have Four Tops. Plural. So the answer is *their*. But on the other, you have only one musical group. Singular. So the answer is *its*. But it can't be

The Four Tops released its album yesterday.

No way. Sounds awful. But rewording suggests that "its" is correct:

The group called the Four Tops released its album yesterday.

So what do we do?

This is a classic case where ears override rules. Technically, we are supposed to determine the actual number represented by the subject. In the case of the Four Tops, the number is one. Each Top didn't release an album independently; the group (singular) released one album as a unit. But we just *can't* say

The Four Tops released its album yesterday.

So we don't. We cheat. We treat the singular as though it were the plural that it sounds like.

Which makes this a good opportunity to remind ourselves of a fundamental grammar mantra. The goal of good writing is the clear and graceful transmission of a message—information, a mood, a scene, a character, and so on—from the writer to the reader. Grammar is a highly useful tool for making that transmission successful. But grammar is not the big brass ring. Treating grammar as the ultimate goal is like a woodworker who treats his hammer and saw as the focal point of his hobby. They are important, but they are just the means by which the woodworker can make chairs and cabinets. For the writer, the goal is clear, effective, and powerful communication. For the editor, the goal is to note those areas in which the communication is less than clear, effective, or powerful, and to ask the writer to work on those areas some more.

Back to the grammar.

• *Noun–verb agreement.* Noun–verb agreement presents the same basic set of problems as noun–pronoun agreement, except that it has only one consideration: the noun and the verb must agree in number. If you've got your basic singular noun, you need a good, strong, exciting, active verb that also is singular. If the noun is plural, the verb should be plural, too.

You know the drill:

> Bob throws the harpoon.

The noun "Bob" is singular, so the verb "throws" is singular. (Note how I used "is" here, even though the subject is "throws." The word *is* is correct because the word *throws* isn't plural—and because I'm referring to it as a word, not as an action or even a noun.)

Get a whole bunch of people in the bow of the ship:

> Benjamin, Franklin, Thomas, Jefferson, John, Paul, George, and Ringo throw the harpoons.

We use "throw" because we have a mob of people (plural) hurling iron rods into the water.

Switch the *and* to *or*, and we're still fine:

> Either Eleanor or Rosalyn is riding the Harley.

The "or" means we're talking about one or the other—so we're singular once again.

> Neither the cheerleaders nor the senators are talking about the party.

Both plural, so take your pick; we have a plural verb either way.

So far, so good. But then—as always—things get tricky. *And* is simple. But what if the *or* separates things of different number?

> Either the cheerleaders or the senator (is/are) throwing the harpoon.

This is the same problem we had with noun–pronoun agreement, and we solve it the same way: go with the form of the closest noun:

> Either the cheerleaders or the senator is throwing the harpoon.

or

> Either the senator or the cheerleaders are throwing the harpoon.

• *Passive voice.* Back to the Blue-Hairs. These kindly, stern, well-intentioned drill sergeants flogged the rule into our heads. Passive voice is bad. Really bad. Bad, bad, bad. It's so bad I could just spit.

So we're going to avoid passive voice. But that's hard to do if we can't tell what it looks like.

Spotting passive voice is easy if you know what to look for. First, put your finger on the verb. Then ask yourself who (or what) is doing it. If the answer is the subject of the sentence, you've got a beautifully active sentence and a personally thrilled fifth-grade grammar teacher. But if the person or thing doing the action is in some other part of the sentence—or is absent altogether—then you've got passive voice. Bad, bad, bad.

Consider this sentence:

The submarine fired the torpedo.

The verb: "fired." What did the firing? The submarine. Where was the submarine in the sentence? In the subject position. Active voice.

How about this example:

The torpedo was fired by the submarine.

The verb: "was fired." What did the firing? Still the submarine. Where is the submarine in the sentence? *Not* in the subject slot. It's lurking just below the surface in the predicate. This is passive voice.

Finally,

The torpedo was fired.

The verb: "was fired." What did the firing? Haven't a clue. The actor isn't present in the sentence at all. Definitely passive.

So that's the drill. Touch the main verb. Who or what is doing it? If it's the subject, you're active. If it's anything else—or if it's missing altogether—then you're passive.

There's a common misperception that you should banish from your brain forever. Some people *wrongly* think that spotting the *was* form of a verb—*was driven, was taken, was smashed, was tickled*—means that the sentence is passive. That can be right:

The car was driven by the old man.

But it isn't necessarily the case:

The apple was rotten.

In this sentence, "rotten" really isn't part of the verb, but it looks exactly like the other examples. The better approach is the "touch the verb" technique described earlier.

There are, by the way, times when good writers deliberately choose to use passive voice. Passive is tolerable in certain circumstances:

1. When you don't know who did the action:

The vase was broken.

2. When you know who did the action, but you don't want to say:

The information was leaked to the press.

3. When the action and the recipient of the action are far more important than the person or thing that did it:

The president was shot today (not, Byron P. Rabblerouser, 34, of 1267 Applewood Drive, Milwaukee, Wisconsin, shot the president today).

Sometimes, though, the person doing the action is essential:

The vice president shot the president today.

4. When you *occasionally* want to add some variety to your sentence structure.

• *Split infinitives.* We English speakers seem to believe that we must never split an infinitive. That's great, but first we have to know what an infinitive is.

An infinitive is the *to* form of a verb: *to run, to eat, to crush, to wink, to giggle.* The rule is that nothing should come between the *to* and the other word in the verb.

But who says we can't do that? The answer lies in Latin. Long considered the perfect language, Latin uses one-word infinitives; there is no *to* added onto the beginning. So in an effort to "perfect" English, some early crafters of the language figured that if you couldn't split an infinitive in Latin, you shouldn't split it in English. We can't say,

I want to quickly run to the store.

We have to say,

> I want to run quickly to the store.

Some people carry the rule even further, maintaining that we shouldn't split any two-word verbs at all. We should not say,

> He was happily playing.

We should say,

> He was playing happily.

In general, the rule does make the language sound better. We can understand sentences more easily if related parts are all kept close to one another. But as is the case with most grammatical rules, this one can be pushed too far. "To go boldly where no one has gone before" just doesn't cut it.

• *Clichés and trite expressions.* Every cliché started out as a brilliant, innovative, colorful phrase that added depth and richness to comparisons and observations. Then it was flogged to death. It was painted on the walls of caves, shouted from the steeples of churches, written in smoke behind stunt planes, and generally overused until it became thin, tired, and useless.

Clichés carry two levels of meaning: the literal and the metaphorical. What makes them so anemic is that the literal meaning has vanished, leaving only the metaphorical to carry on. It's like speaking in code:

> He held on until the bitter end.

What does that mean? The metaphorical meaning—the code—is that he held on just as long as he could. So when we use this cliché, that's what we want to convey and that's what the reader generally understands. (Clichés, however, are culturally specific, so people from other cultures might not understand the metaphorical meaning—and they *might* understand the literal.)

So when I write

> He held on until the bitter end.

I'm sending out code for

> He held on just as long as he could.

But if that's the metaphorical meaning, what is the literal meaning?

Most people don't know.

But sailors know.

A loop at the end of a rope is called a bit. So the end of a length of rope with a loop in it is called the bit end, or the bitter end. Now picture the free end of a piece of rope tied onto a cleat on a dock. Holding the other end of the rope is a cheerful young sailor, standing on the deck of a ship. A breeze pushes the boat away from the dock. The young sailor, not strong enough to hold the boat against the dock by himself, begins to let out some rope, calling for help all the while.

No help comes.

He lets out more and more rope, until at last all he is holding is the loop end of the rope. He leans farther and farther over the rail, stretching and yelling and hanging on, until at last he can hold on no longer. He plunges into the ocean, and the ship drifts off to Iceland without him.

He did his best.

He held on until the bitter end.

The first writer who described someone in a different situation—fading on his deathbed, perhaps—as "holding on to the bitter end" should be applauded for choosing such a colorful and vivid phrase. Back when ships were the main means of travel, most people would know what the bitter end of a rope is, and they would be impressed with the richness of the metaphor.

The second writer to use the phrase, who probably read something written by the first, gets credit for recognizing a great image when he saw it. The third, fourth, and fifth writers to use it are worthy of respect for spreading the cleverness of the comparison. Numbers 6 through 10,000 get decreasing amounts of respect and increasing suspicion of ripping off one another.

And that brings us to us. If we were to write that someone held on to the bitter end, we would be guilty of using a tired, worn-out, hollow cliché. All the life has been squeezed, strained, and extruded out of the image, and few readers would recall the maritime echoes that the phrase once had. It has devolved to code: "held on to the bitter end" = "held on as long as possible."

That's why clichés are bad. Their literal meanings have evaporated with time and use, leaving only their metaphorical husks intact, like bleached crab shells on the beach. They are substitutions for plain language, made all the worse by their feeble attempt at literature.

The antidote, of course, is original wording—and the trick to original wording is precision. If your writer notes that a night was "pitch black"—referring to the color of pine sap when it is burned, as it often was on old-fashioned torches, not that anyone remembers that these days—you should reject the cliché and instead ask the writer to describe the very dark night in such a way that it won't be confused with the previous very dark night or the following very dark night. Was it the kind of dark that makes you feel invisible and giddily omnipotent? Was it the kind of dark that makes you feel sad and alone? that makes you vulnerable and exposed? Did the stars seem close enough to swirl with your breath or so far away that the Earth seemed shunned by the rest of the universe? Did the darkness make the air warm or chilly? sexual or conspiratorial? cozy or mocking? When the darkness grew intense, what happened to sounds? Did they seem distant and hollow? or close and threatening? What sounds flickered through the shadows? rustling? the howl of forlorn dogs? whispers? the sharp crack of a banging door or a dry twig? What happened to the writer's eyes in this darkness? Did they shut down or become hypersensitive? Did they reach for every dot of light or dance with colors that no one else could see?

By describing the darkness precisely, the way that only *that* darkness ever was, your writer will have to abandon clichés and rely instead on fresh description that conveys exactly what that particular night looked and felt like. Clichés, by definition, cannot be fresh, and they have had their liveliness so completely smothered out of them that they cannot be vivid or evocative either.

Confusion Rains!

Ah, the mess we call the English language! The pound puppy of prose! The mongrel of mother tongues! The jalopy of jargon!

We mentioned *precision* previously, and nowhere is precision more important than in the realm of word choice. Select just the right word, and you'll express not only the right meaning but also the right connotations, shades, colors, tones. Choose the wrong one, and you'll look like a fool.

A television sportscaster (who shall remain nameless) once commented during an ice-skating competition that "histrionics do not favor this skater." He was trying to make the point that throughout the history of ice-skating, no skater who was that far behind had ever recovered to win the gold.

Granted—live broadcast. The heat of the moment. Anyone can slip up.

But then he said it again. And a third time.

I figured that his colleagues would point out the error once the cameras were turned off, but he said it again the following night—and throughout the competition. I suspect that his colleagues caught the error right away but let their buddy continue to make an idiot of himself, just for fun.

Histrionics, of course, means "overly dramatic or emotional." It has nothing whatsoever to do with history, and is in fact related to an Etruscan word for "actor."

In the sportscaster's defense, though, it is easy to confuse words in this language. But even though writers might make word-choice mistakes from time to time, editors are paid to know the language well and to catch—and correct—mistakes before they creep into print.

To aid in this effort, here is a rundown of several frequently confused words, along with information that might help you keep them straight:

accede   to give way or agree, with some reluctance: *He acceded the point.*

exceed   to surpass or go beyond: *She exceeded the speed limit.*

accept   to receive or agree to: *She accepted the job offer.*

except   to remove from a group: *We're all brilliant, except for Waldo.*

access   to enter: *She accessed the secret computer files.*

assess   to review or evaluate: *She assessed their value.*

excess   too much of something, a surplus: *The excess material was burned.*

adventuresome   willing to take risks: *A group of adventuresome people parachuted into the game preserve.*

adventurous   fond of adventure: *Hiking, camping, and kayaking appeal to the adventurous.*

advice   opinion or suggestion (noun): *Talented copy editors offer great advice.*

advise   to counsel or offer guidance (verb): *She advised him to prepare carefully.*

affect   to bring about change (verb): *How will the spray paint affect the new car?* (One tiny exception: "to put on airs" is to affect an attitude.)

effect   result or outcome (noun): *The effect will be awful.* (One tiny exception: "to effect change" is to bring it about.)

allude   to refer to something without mentioning it directly: *He alluded to her ambition.*

elude   to get away from or escape: *He eluded the police.*

almost   nearly all of something: *Almost everyone agrees.*

most   more than half of something: *Most people agree;* highly: *She is a most friendly cat.* (Despite what you read everywhere these days, never use *most* in place of *almost*: *Most everyone agrees.*)

among   in the midst of many things: *He ran among the trees.*

between   in the middle of two (and only two) things: *She stood between her mother and her father.* (The –*tween* refers to two things.)

amount   how much of something (an amount of money, an amount of salt): *The rescue took a large amount of courage.*

number   how many of something (a number of coins, a number of grains): *He stole a large number of cars.*

anxious   looking forward to something with anticipation and dread: *He was anxious about the test.*

eager   looking forward to something enthusiastically: *She was eager to begin her new job.*

assure   to relieve worry: *I assured them that she was fine.*

ensure   to make something certain: *I ensured that he would win.*

insure   to protect against risk: *I insured my car.*

bad   indicates emotional state: *Because I fell in the dumpster, I smell bad. I feel bad about the loss.*

badly   indicates ability to feel or sense: *Because I broke my nose, I smell badly. I feel badly because my hand is numb.*

because indicates a cause–effect situation: *I did it because I needed the money.*
since indicates time: *You've grown taller since we last met.*

bi every two: *A biannual magazine comes out every two years.*
semi every half: *A semiannual magazine comes out every six months.*

bring to carry toward you: *Will you bring me some coffee?*
take to carry away from you: *Will you take this to the cleaners?*

can implies ability: *He can open the jar.*
may implies permission: *You may take another candy.*
might implies possibility: *She might apply for that new job.*

capital governmental city: *The capital of Indiana is Indianapolis;* money: *The struggling business needed capital.*
capitol governmental building: *The capitol was evacuated and locked.*

childish to act inappropriately, like a child: *Selfish squabbling is very childish.*
childlike to retain the joy, wonder, and other characteristics of childhood: *She maintained a childlike trust in people.*

cite to quote or refer to: *He cited the source.*
sight ability to see; something to see: *I enjoyed the sights of London.*
site location or place: *The site of the Normandy invasion.*

complement to complete or fill in the missing parts: *My wife and I complement each other.* (We complete each other; we don't necessarily say nice things about each other's looks all the time.)
compliment to flatter or praise: *He complimented me on my thorough report.*

compose to make or put together: *The band is composed of a drummer, a singer, and two guitarists.*
comprise to contain; to embrace: *The band comprises a drummer, a singer, and two guitarists.* (Never use "is comprised of.")

continual repeated, but not necessarily without ever stopping: *The clock chimed continually.*
continuous repeated without ever stopping: *The waterfall flowed continuously.*

council   group of advisers: *The school is governed by a council.*
counsel   legal adviser: *I checked with my counsel before signing that paper;* advice: *He gave me good counsel;* to give advice: *He counseled me well.*

differ from   is different from: *NFL rules differ from NCAA rules.*
differ with   disagrees with: *He differed with her over the new budget plan.*

disinterested   neutral or impartial: *The judge paid close attention but remained disinterested.*
uninterested   does not care: *The young man was uninterested in politics.*

egoistic   self-centered: *The egoistic boss insisted that all memos receive her approval.*
egotistic   boastful of one's (supposed) accomplishments: *The egotistic man drove people away with his constant bragging.*

elicit   to draw out: *He elicited a response from the witness.*
illicit   illegal: *She engaged in illicit behavior.*

emigrate   to leave a country: *She emigrated from Venus.*
immigrate   to enter a country: *He immigrated to Mars.*

eminent   distinguished; prominent: *The eminent king entered the room.*
imminent   soon to happen: *The storm is imminent.*

especially   particularly: *This is an especially beautiful day.*
specially   for a specific purpose: *He made it specially for me.*

every one   every single one: *He took twelve pancakes and ate every one.*
everyone   everybody: *She gave everyone a gift.*

farther   indicates distance: *We have to hike two miles farther.*
further   indicates degree: *Let's consider this idea further.*

faze   to disrupt or upset: *She didn't let the noise faze her.*
phase   stage or period: *He's in an awkward phase right now.*

fewer   indicates number: *This beer contains fewer calories than regular beer.* (If you can count it, use *fewer.*)
less   indicates amount: *This dessert has less fat than regular cheesecake.* (If you can't count it, use *less.* And pay no attention to advertisements, which get this distinction wrong most of the time.)

gender   indicates social constructions: *Gender negotiations influence much of modern society.*

sex   indicates biology: *The trait shows up in only one sex.*

historic   something important in history: *December 7, 1941, was a historic day.*

historical   referring to history: *He offered a historical reference.*

imply   to suggest: *He implied that she chewed her food too loudly.*

infer   to deduce: *After she slammed the door, he inferred that the date was off.*

ingenious   clever or inventive: *He is an ingenious writer.*

ingenuous   honest, without pretense, or naïve: *He gave her an ingenuous smile.*

it's   contraction for *it is*: *It's a beautiful day.*

its   possessive form of *it*: *Its leash was tangled around the tree.* (To keep these straight, just think of *hers*. No apostrophe, and it indicates possession.)

less than   lower amount: *He lost by less than an inch.*

under   lower position: *The footstool was under the table.* (This distinction also holds true for *more than* and *over*.)

lightening   making lighter: *They are lightening the boat.*

lightning   flashing bolts during thunderstorms: *The lightning struck the tree.*

moot   unprovable: *It is a moot point.*

mute   unable to speak: *The man was struck mute by the amazing sight.*

nauseated   feeling sick to your stomach: *The passengers felt nauseated.*

nauseous   ability to make people feel sick to their stomachs: *The smell was nauseous.* (This word frequently is misused. Don't say that you feel nauseous unless you mean that you make people barf.)

oral   pertains to the mouth: *He had oral surgery right after delivering his oral report.*

verbal   pertains to words: *A verbal report could be written.*

principal   chief or most important: *The principal reason we're here is to get at the truth. The school principal declared a holiday.*

principle   fundamental value or rule: *My principles prevent me from committing a crime.*

rain   wet stuff falling from the sky: *Look's like it will rain today.*

reign   rule of a king or another leader: *Looks like King Henry VIII will reign today.*

real   authentic: *This is made with real leather.*

really   actually or truly: *She is a really great person.* (Never use *real* for *really*: *She is a real great person.*)

sensual   licentious: *She performed a sensual dance.*

sensuous   detectable by or appealing to the senses: *The coat was made of a sensuous velvet.*

tenant   someone who lives in rented property: *The tenant repainted the apartment.*

tenet   principle or doctrine: *The tenets of democracy call for fair elections.*

that   specifies the one being discussed: *That car ran over my foot. The car that ran over my foot is red.*

which   adds information in a "by the way" fashion: *The car, which was red, ran over my foot.* (In this use, the *which* phrase is set off with commas.)

their   possessive form of *they*: *That is their car.*

there   refers to a place: *Put the chair over there.*

they're   contraction for *they are*: *They're going to the show tonight.*

tortuous   twisting, sharply curved, or complex: *A tortuous driveway led to his house.*

torturous   having to do with torture: *The torturous exam was very stressful.*

troop   group of soldiers, police officers, or Boy Scouts: *The troops stormed the capital.*

troupe   group of actors or singers: *The troupe performed* My Fair Lady.

We hire only the best and the brightest to be researchers, people who are detail oriented, intellectually curious, and resourceful—and who take pride in contributing to the high-quality magazine we produce.

A sense of humor also helps.

Lesley Rogers, senior editor and head of National Geographic Magazine Research, *National Geographic*

vice corruption: *The vice squad arrested several bookies;* assistant: *The vice principal was promoted.*

vise press that grips something on a workbench: *He put the board in a vise.*

who subject
whom object

Here is the Michael Robert Evans Patented Simple Method for Getting This Straight. Substitute the singular male pronoun. (Sorry about the sexism, but it doesn't work with *her*.) If you would use *he*, use *who*. If you would use *him*, use *whom*. (It's the same *m!*)

He is at the door.
Who is at the door?
He is calling.
May I ask *who* is calling?
The voters elected *him*.
The woman *whom* the voters elected has a Ph.D. (Again, sorry...)

Nevers
Never qualify absolutes. There's no such thing as partially dead, rather pregnant, or somewhat unique. In addition, there are few hard rules for language. For example,

Never use *allright*. Use *all right*.
Never use *alot*. Use *a lot*.
Never use *amongst*. Drop the *st*.
Never use *irregardless*. Use *regardless*.
Never use *towards*. Drop the *s*.
Never use *underway*. Use *under way*.
Never use *utilize*. Use *use*.

who's contraction for *who is*: *Who's at the door?*
whose possessive form of *who*: *Whose lunch is this?*

your possessive form of *you*: *Your mother won the contest!*
you're contraction for you are: *You're a very lucky person.*

Underway

This chapter covers several of the Big Main Points of Grammar, but it doesn't come close to covering them all. This *book* doesn't come close to covering them all. But if you understand the points made in this chapter, you're well on your way to exercising the command of grammar that will make you a strong editor—and a sought-after copy editor.

12. Word World II:

The Cutting Edge of Tricky Grammar

National Geographic Society style is defined by our Style Manual, first printed in 1962 and since 1995 available on our intranet. A style committee with representatives from throughout the organizations (magazines, books, TV, Web, marketing, school publishing) meets once a month to discuss style issues and to add, amend, or delete entries from the manual. When questions arise between meetings, they are resolved by discussion among key editors, often with advice from the chair of the style committee and style maven of the magazine.

Lesley Rogers, senior editor and head of National Geographic Magazine Research, _National Geographic_

Now we're really getting out there. We're wading into the tricky stuff, the rarified levels, the grammar that separates the amateurs from the prose.

In this chapter, we'll look at a few of the tougher, more sophisticated rules of grammar. Good editors know all these rules, but an awful lot of the people walking around the streets out there forgot them long ago.

Don't Dangle

Some sentences begin with a phrase that modifies something:

Jumping off the speedboat, Freddie neglected to notice the crocodile.

The introductory phrase is "Jumping off the speedboat." It's a phrase because it is a string of words that lacks a subject and a predicate; in other words, it can't stand alone as a sentence. It's introductory because, well, it introduces the sentence. It modifies something—that is to say, it tells us a little bit extra about something—because it is telling us that something is jumping.

When a sentence is introduced with a phrase that modifies something, that phrase—by law, fiat, and decree, necessarily and absolutely and without exception—refers to the _subject_ of the main sentence.

So that sentence about the croc is correct, because it is telling us that something is jumping, and that "something" is Freddie. Sure enough, Freddie is the subject of the sentence. So we're in great shape.

But this sentence would not be correct:

Jumping off the speedboat, the crocodile caught up with Freddie.

The sentence could be correct only if you were talking about a particularly gruesome Disney movie in which crocodiles drive boats. Like it or not, this sentence suggests that the crocodile jumped off the speedboat.

Note that words like *law* and *fiat* appear very rarely in this book. That's because nearly every grammatical rule has exceptions, and nearly every one of them can be broken by good writers who want to achieve a certain effect. One rule, for example, says that we should never tolerate a fragment sentence. Too bad. Another rule says that we should never begin a sentence with a conjunction. But it's wrong, too.

This rule about introductory phrases, however, is one of the few that have no exceptions. The reason it is exception-free is that readers will assume it to be true, and we're not usually around to tell them otherwise. Let's say that we publish a sentence like this:

Startled by the sight of the scaly monster, Freddie swam with great urgency toward the shore.

When readers encounter that sentence, they will assume that it was Freddie who was startled. Fair enough. The introductory phrase said that something was startled, Freddie is the subject of the sentence, and indeed Freddie was the one who was startled. No problem.

But if the writer turns the sentence around inappropriately, that assumption will cause trouble:

Startled by the sight of the scaly monster, the crocodile chased Freddie.

This sentence literally means that the croc was startled by Freddie, and that Freddie has a nasty skin condition. The introductory phrase—"Startled by the sight of the scaly monster"—is required by law to refer to the subject of the sentence, which in this case is the croc.

This rule holds true for any kind of introductory phrase that refers to something in the main sentence, but there is a category of phrases that warrants special mention. Regular old phrases like this one follow the rule we've been discussing:

> Although he said he wasn't scared, Freddie managed to get to shore without actually touching the water.

The special kind of phrase follows the same rule but looks like this:

> Gasping for air, Freddie insisted that he was just out for an afternoon stroll.

In the example, "Gasping" is a participle; it normally is a verb—"He was gasping for air"—but in this case it is used as an adjective (telling us about Freddie). That's what participles are—verbs used as adjectives.

So *dangling participle* refers specifically to sentences that lead with a participial phrase that is supposed to refer to the subject but doesn't:

> Splashing his tail in disgust, Freddie was dismissed by the crocodile.

Whether referring to a generic modifier or the more specific participle, the rule still holds: if the introductory phrase refers to something in the main sentence, it *has* to refer to the subject.

This is not to say that all introductory passages refer to the subject of the sentence; some don't refer to anything at all:

> Although the croc wasn't hungry, Freddie looked pretty darn tasty.

(One of the differences is that this sentence begins with a clause, not a phrase.) But if the introduction refers to something in the sentence, that something is the subject. No exceptions.

As editors, we have to watch for these to make sure that the meaning of our writers' work is clear. If we're not careful, Freddie ends up with green scales and a long tail.

In Sync

Human beings crave logic, balance, and symmetry. Just look at any building from ancient Greece, and you'll see that perfection has often been associated with these ideals.

This holds for sentences as well. In proper writing, then, any parts of a sentence that have the same function should have the same structure:

Susan is young, popular, and happy.

That's great—both for Susan and for the paragons of grammar. After the "is," we get three things, and they're all alike: "young" (adjective), "popular" (adjective), and "happy" (adjective).

But consider this example:

Susan likes fishing for marlin, climbing the Alps, and José.

Problem. Susan likes three things. Two of them are activities—fishing and climbing—and are presented as verbs. The third is a person, a noun. Not the same thing. Not parallel.

And we do like our sentences to be parallel in their construction. In fact, we call this consideration *parallel construction*—and we like it.

To make the previous example fit the symmetry called for in parallel construction, we have to make the three things the same:

Susan likes fishing for marlin, climbing the Alps, and skiing with José.

Now Susan likes three verbs: "fishing," "climbing," and "skiing." Much better—although still not perfect. (More on that later.)

Parallel construction makes sentences graceful and easy to follow. And in extreme circumstances, a lack of parallel construction can actually change a sentence's meaning. For example:

Susan likes fishing for marlin, tuna, and José.

What the writer probably intends is that Susan likes three things:

- Fishing for marlin
- Fishing for tuna
- José

It's possible that Susan likes fishing for marlin, *eating* tuna, and José, but that's not clear. The problem with the sentence, of course, is that it could be completely misunderstood to mean that Susan likes fishing for marlin, fishing for tuna, and fishing for José. The idea of "fishing for José" could make sense—it could refer to pursuing José in a flirtatious manner, or it could refer to interrupting José's scuba-diving trip—but it's probably not what the writer meant.

So making the related parts of a sentence similar to one another in structure improves the grace, strength, and logic of sentences. This sentence is not parallel:

I got the job through hard work, strong connections, and getting a good education.

The problem is that after "through" we get

- Hard work (an adjective and a noun),
- Strong connections (an adjective and a noun), and
- Getting a good education (a gerund, an article, an adjective, and a noun).

Because the related parts of the sentence are not built in the same way, the sentence is not parallel in its construction. Correcting the sentence isn't difficult:

I got the job through hard work, strong connections, and disciplined study.

This version is nicely parallel: "hard work" (adjective, noun), "strong connections" (adjective, noun), and "disciplined study" (adjective, noun).

Here's another way of looking at the problem. Any time you build a sentence like this, you should be able to break it into its component streams without causing problems. Let's take another example:

We make our salad dressing with wholesome herbs, pure vinegar, and grinding fresh spices by hand.

We should be able to unbraid it to look something like this:

We make our salad dressing with → wholesome herbs,
pure vinegar,
grinding fresh spices by hand.

Now the problem becomes quite clear. Continuing the unbraiding, we can create three sentences by following the three different paths:

We make our salad dressing with wholesome herbs.

Great.

> We make our salad dressing with pure vinegar.

Terrific.

> We make our salad dressings with grinding fresh spices by hand.

Hold it. It's easy to see that the last unbraided sentence is a mess. We have to make the sentence parts parallel to make the three paths work properly.

So let's change "grinding fresh spices by hand" to something more parallel to the others: "hand-ground spices." Now we're cooking:

> We make our salad dressings with wholesome herbs, fresh vinegar, and hand-ground spices.

That sentence is parallel. After the "with," we have nice symmetry: an adjective–noun phrase in each slot. Beautiful.

You can even finesse this further. This sentence is somewhat parallel:

> I got the job through hard work, serious networking, and disciplined study.

But it isn't perfectly parallel; after "through," it uses an adjective–noun phrase, an adjective–gerund phrase, and then another adjective–noun phrase. A gerund is a verb acting like a noun, but it's not exactly the same thing as a noun.

Fretting over perfect parallelism can result in awkward sentences, not to mention a severely shortened life span. But the closer to perfect parallelism you can get, without sacrificing grace and clarity, the better.

Your Finest Crystal

Speaking of clarity, several problems can weaken clarity without directly violating any grammatical rules. We generally know when something is clear or not, but concerns about clarity can be difficult to put into specific terms that make sense to writers. Here are some things for you to check—and for your writer to fix if needed.

• *Keep subjects and verbs close together if you can.* When you put too many words between the subject and the verb, the reader can lose track of who is doing what. For example, this sentence makes perfect sense:

Betty roped the steer.

Who did the roping? Betty did. No problem.

But when you add too much stuff between the subject and the verb, you present a maze of twisty passages that can bewilder even the most patient reader:

Betty, who was the best in her class at the Hank McCallister Steer-Roping School in McAllen, Texas, which is where her best friends, Juan and Kim, also learned how to bring down a steer with a quick toss of the lasso—a harder task than it sounds, given that the steer weighs hundreds of pounds and is running like mad to keep from having a loop of rope thrown around its legs, sending it thundering to the ground with a thud that has got to leave a nasty bruise—roped the steer.

In this version, by the time we get around to the roping, we've completely lost track of who's holding the rope. Too many words intervene between the subject and the verb, leaving poor Betty lost in the verbiage.

The solution, of course, is to break this monster into several separate sentences. That way, you'll have an easier time keeping the subjects close to their verbs.

• *Keep the parts of verbs together if possible.* We all know the rule about not splitting infinitives (the *to* form of the verb). That rule isn't nearly as ironclad as the blue-haired English teachers would like us to believe; Captains Kirk and Picard did just fine when they announced that their mission was "to boldly go where no one has gone before."

Nevertheless, it is generally a good idea to keep the parts of a verb close together for clarity's sake. If you split them apart too far, you get sentences like this:

He likes to sometimes—well, pretty often, actually, although not all the time, of course, because that would be way overdoing it—eat squid.

Or like this:

> She would if the tingling in her nerves that began shortly after she fell out of that tree house weren't bothering her so much walk into town every day.

The gap between "He likes to" and "eat squid" in the first example is big enough to drive a cephalopod through, and the same problem holds in a more intricate way in the second example. These sentences are hard to follow because the verbs have been exploded to make room for a whole lot of other commentary. Awareness of the problem makes the corrections simple:

> Without overdoing it, he likes to eat squid as often as he can.

> A fall from a tree house still caused tingling in her nerves; otherwise, she would walk into town every day.

Getting "likes to eat squid" and "would walk into town" together, in discrete units, makes the sentences easier to read and easier to comprehend.

• *Make sure every pronoun has a clear and obvious antecedent.* We talked about antecedents in chapter 11. Every pronoun should have an antecedent (the word it's taking the place of) that you can literally put your finger on. If your sentence has a *he* in it, you should be able to put your finger on *Bob* or *her husband* or *the garbage man* or a previous noun that the *he* is standing in for. If the pronoun is standing in for some concept or general idea that the reader is supposed to derive from the previous few paragraphs, you run the risk of the reader not getting the right idea. And if the reader can't tell whether the pronoun is supposed to substitute for *Juanita* or for *the surgeon* or for the general idea that one should usually administer anesthesia *before* beginning the operation, you run the risk of the reader choosing the wrong one and being horribly confused.

• *Keep the blocks unified.* You'll confuse readers if you jump around too much, flitting from one topic to another—and back again—like a butterfly in an overgrown meadow. Picture an article outline that looks like this:

1. History of Aboriginal society
2. The kangaroo
3. Bush foods used by the Aborigines
4. Aboriginal communication systems
5. The kangaroo
6. Aboriginal hunting techniques
7. More on the kangaroo
8. Aboriginal kangaroo stories
9. More on the kangaroo
10. More on Aboriginal communication systems

You can see that anyone trying to read an article whose structure follows this outline is going to have trouble following the bouncing kangaroo. The article offers a little bit of information about the kangaroo in a lot of different places, making it difficult to understand much about the poor animal. Far clearer would be a block about the kangaroo, placed where appropriate, and then blocks on the other topics.

• *Give readers clues, cues, and markers.* Readers like a confident guide, and they like knowing exactly where they are. Switches in direction, emphasis, or central point should be marked clearly:

> The new Mars landing craft is a bold departure, offering NASA a low-cost and reliable way of exploring the surface of the planet. The craft, built on time and below budget, shows what teamwork and innovation can do, even in a large bureaucracy like NASA. The landing craft has no chance of success. It has been cobbled together by too many different people, and not enough time and money have been spent to ensure that all the parts will work together well.

Hold it. Is this writer saying that the Mars craft is good, or that it's bad? It's too hard to tell in this paragraph. The problem is that the example offers two different opinions, but it doesn't signal to the reader when it's switching from one to the other. Just a few words would make all the difference:

> *Some people say that* the new Mars landing craft is a bold departure, offering NASA a low-cost and reliable way of exploring the surface of the planet. The craft, built on time and below budget, shows what

teamwork and innovation can do, even in a large bureaucracy like NASA. *Others, however, argue that* the landing craft has no chance of success. It has been cobbled together by too many different people, and not enough time and money have been spent to ensure that all the parts will work together well.

Other useful markers include *on the one hand...on the other hand, similarly, first...second...third...*, and so on. These markers let readers know when the path is taking a turn.

Speak Up!

Problems with voice don't technically violate any grammatical rules, but they can ruin an otherwise good article all the same. For example, picture a hypothetical article in the *New Yorker*. It is describing a village on the coast of the Amazon, as seen by the writer for the first time:

> The air hung thick and smoky around the thatched shacks that jealously ringed the tiny campfire, air tinged green from the light that wormed through a colander of thick leaves overhead. The shacks were shaggy monuments to the genius of their designers; cool air snaked through them, while warm air and dank odors swept upwards and whistled through a hole in the apex of the roof. A yellow dog, hobbled and scarred, lay in the shadow of the closest hut, staring as if trying to decide how much energy we were worth. That daggon lil' pup was jest about the orneriest flea-bitten ol' pile of bones I ever did see.
>
> Off in the wet and shady distance, the sounds of anxious conversation dripped through the air. We obviously had been seen, and I wasn't sure we were welcome.

On the whole, not a bad passage. But what the heck is going on with that "daggon lil' pup" sentence? It stands out like a train wreck. Even by itself, it would be awful. But in the context of the rest of the writing, it's even worse.

The problem is a change in voice. Throughout the first paragraph, the writer maintains a certain personality, a certain style, a certain manner by which he addresses the subject and the audience. Then, in that one pimple of a sentence, the voice changes dramatically, as though the writer were possessed for just a moment by the ghost of a backwoods bumpkin.

Writers are free to write in whatever voice suits them, and as long as editors find that voice appropriate for the topic and the magazine, articles will be published. The key, however, is consistency. Writers who change voice without any apparent reason will find that their work is so jarring, so distracting, and so annoying that editors will tend to toss back a "Dear Contributor" rejection slip and keep looking for good manuscripts.

Voice depends on several factors, including the choice of words, the use of jargon and slang, the person (first, second, third), the length and structure of sentences, and the writer's relationship to the topic and to the audience. Voice is built into the writing and cannot be changed with simple alterations, so problems in voice are effectively impossible for the editor to fix. Diving in here and there to fix the voice of an article is a lot like touching up the paint on your car—you can do a good job and get a pretty good match, but it will never look like the original paint. All voice problems should be sent back to the writer for reworking.

The Spice of Life

If sentences go on too long without variation, the effect can be monotonous, boring, and just plain annoying—even if no concrete grammatical rules have been broken. The effect is similar to a song that leans on the same note over and over again, without changing for long stretches of time.

Fortunately, writers have several techniques at their disposal to help them break this monotony.

• *Mix compound and simple sentences.* You don't want too many short sentences. They make the writing choppy. Choppy writing sounds stiff. It also sounds childish. It sounds like the writing in kids' books. Every sentence is the same. Same, same, same.

By mixing simple sentences with some compound sentences—sentences that link two independent clauses with a comma and a conjunction, with a semicolon, with a dash, or even with a colon—you can add variety and make the writing much more interesting.

Short sentences are fine. But so are long ones, and the longer ones can keep the short ones from becoming too choppy.

• *Use different clauses.* In addition to linking independent clauses in various ways, writers can use introductory clauses, subordinate clauses of several types, and so on to change the rhythm of their sentences. For example:

He likes to race fast cars. He prefers Mazeratis.

This passage is choppy, especially after a long string of simple sentences. This one is better:

Because he likes to race fast cars, he prefers Mazeratis.

In the second example, the first independent clause—"He likes to race fast cars"—has been subordinated and turned into an introductory clause through the addition of "Because." This technique delivers the same information as the two shorter sentences, but it does so without being quite so choppy.

Similarly, you can put clauses in the middle or at the end of sentences, altering the flow of a paragraph or a page.

Sometimes, of course, a strong rhythm is desirable. Sentences that use repetition to develop a pounding, predictable rhythm can be memorable and potent. Winston Churchill was a master of this approach:

Victory at all costs,
victory in spite of all terror,
victory however long and hard the road may be;
for without victory,
there is no survival.

Churchill's incessant repetition of "victory" drives his point home with power. But if long passages become overly riddled with short, sharp shots, like the drumming of fingers on a table, they can become annoying and distracting, losing their power instead of heightening it.

Sound Advice

Savvy writers—and editors—also listen to the sound of the words they are using. The deliberate use of alliteration, for example, and other sound techniques can add power and tone to sentences.

For example, alliteration is basically the repetition of initial sounds. Accidental alliteration can seem sloppy, but deliberate alliteration—especially in potent passages that command attention—can be stunning:

> Elle tossed the dried crab shell into the water and watched the waves pounding, pummeling, plastering the white carcass against the jagged sand.

That's better than watching the waves *pounding, beating, grinding* the shell. The repetition of the *p* sound—obviously with deliberate intention—gives the first example a tone and a power that the replacement words just couldn't match.

Similarly, writers can rely on rhyme and other aural techniques. (*Aural* means "pertaining to the ear.") Onomatopoeia—the use of words that sound like the thing they represent—also can give writing some punch:

> The car screeched across the parking lot and thumped into the light pole.

Even the repetition of inner vowel sounds can be used for effect:

> The pounding sound within the mound, like a drowned clown who...

Oops. All these techniques can be badly overdone as well.

Crossed Words

Now, for the chapter's Grand Finale, we'll look at several words that people seem to have trouble handling. The problem often stems from the fact that the English language is always changing. Not long ago, you would say that the house *burnt* to the ground. Some people still say that, especially in England. But just a couple of decades ago, in response to a general movement that's still under way to straighten out all the irregular verbs in American English, people started to say that the house *burned* to the ground. We still called charred bread *burnt toast*—and *burnt sienna* remains a Crayola favorite—but we'd say that the campfire *burned* all night. *Burned* became the now-straightened verb form, leaving *burnt* clinging on in the adjective slot.

And even that's pretty much gone, now, with some people referring to blackened slabs of whole wheat as *burned toast*. The adjective *burnt* is nearly gone, gasping for breath in a few pockets of our country, while the more regular form *burned* is taking over everything.

The same thing is happening with forms of the verb *to dive*. We used to say that she *dove* into the pool (*dove* rhyming with *grove*, not *glove*). But nowadays, more and more people are saying that she *dived* into the pool; we're regularizing verbs every chance we get.

Still, the shift to uniformly regular verbs doesn't account for all the difficulties that people face with certain words. Sometimes the problem is simply that too many words sound too much alike, and it's hard to hear the differences. Without hearing them well, we don't learn them well.

Here are some classics.

• *Lay* and *lie*. The granddaddy of messed-up verbs. The difference between *lay* and *lie* is relatively simple: you lay something down, and you lie down yourself. In other words, *lay* requires an indirect object (something that the action is being done to):

Lay that coat on the sofa.

Something is being put down on the sofa—the coat—so you would say *lay* because it takes a direct object.

But if you're not feeling well, you should *lie* down. We don't have to say *lie yourself down*, because lie doesn't require an indirect object. You can just lie down.

Another way of saying this is that *lay* is transitive, while *lie* is intransitive. The best way to think about the word *transitive* is to think about transition or transference: the action of the verb is transferred from the subject to the direct object. Consider this example:

Roberta lay the cup on the table.

In the sentence, the action is being transferred from Roberta to the cup. The word *lay* is used because the situation calls for a transitive verb.

But an intransitive verb has no direct object:

He lies down after every meal.

Because he isn't putting anything down except for his own sleepy self—in other words, because no direct object is involved—we use the intransitive verb *lie*.

• *Raise* and *rise*. The same distinction is made between *raise* and *rise* as between *lay* and *lie*. *Raise* is transitive; something (the direct object) must be raised:

Raise your glasses high!

But rise is intransitive; it does not take a direct object, so there is nothing for the action of the verb to transfer to:

Rise up and get going!

• *Sit* and *set*. *Sit* and *set* are the last pair on the transitive/intransitive theme. *Set* is transitive; something must be set. *Sit* is intransitive; just do it:

Set down your purse and sit on this chair.

• *Bad* and *badly*. If you eat too many under-ripe mulberries, do you feel *bad*, or do you feel *badly*? If your best friend gets the Perm from Hell on the afternoon of the prom, do you feel *bad* for her or *badly* for her? If you are wearing gloves and trying to tell by touch whether a coin is heads or tails—and failing—are you feeling *bad* or are you feeling *badly*?

The problem with these two words has to do with the difference between adjectives and adverbs. The blue-haired English teachers took an entire day in fifth grade to drill it into our heads: adjectives modify nouns, while adverbs modify verbs, adjectives, and other adverbs.

Great. Now I feel badly about skipping school that day.

Oops! I mean I feel *bad*. In this case, *bad* is an adjective; it is describing me. It's like saying *He is tall*. *Tall* is describing him. *I feel bad*. *Bad* is describing me.

If you say *I feel badly*, then *badly*—which is an adverb—is modifying *feel*; it's describing the manner in which your tactile senses are functioning. If I shoot my hand full of Novocain, I can pet a porcupine. Why? Because I feel badly. (It's that glove and coin thing from before.)

• *Good* and *well*. The same distinction is made between *good* and *well* as between *bad* and *badly*. *I feel well* means that I am perceiving the world tactilely in a successful manner. *I feel good* means that my heart is soaring—or that my stomach is settled.

• *Slow* and *slowly.* Same setup, different problem. In general, modern speakers of our language are taking a hatchet to adverbs and making them sound like adjectives. (It's probably because other people skipped that day in fifth grade, also.) The bottom line is that *He runs slow* is wrong. *Slow* is clearly supposed to be modifying *runs*, but it is written like an adjective.

I think that part of the problem can be traced to a few dysfunctional adverbs. Take *fast*, for instance:

He is a fast runner.

Terrific—*fast* is an adjective.

He runs fast.

Wrong—*fast* is an adjective. (Fine. You could say *The crustacean holds fast to the rock*, and *fast* would be an adverb. Duly noted. Back to the example.) But we can't say *He runs fastly*. There is no such word. So we have to chuck *fastly* and replace it with *rapidly*, *swiftly*, or *quickly*. And if there's no such thing as *fastly*, we begin to have doubts about *slowly* as well. In the end, we drop the whole thing and just say that cheetahs run fast and tortoises move slow. It's wrong—but it won't be for long. The anti-adverb tide is running strong these days, and your grandchildren probably will have no problem with *Juanita runs fast* and *Blake runs slow*.

The Never-Ending Glory of Grammar

If you take the tips in this book to heart, you'll know enough about grammar to get through most editing challenges. But, of course, grammar—like language itself—is infinite, and you will always encounter new situations that you hadn't thought about before.

As with other facets of editing, the key to success in those cases is to keep some good reference books nearby. That way, you can look up the grammatical rule in the privacy of your own office, without having to admit to anyone that you didn't know it.

If that doesn't work, it really doesn't hurt to admit that there are snippets of grammar that have escaped your otherwise excellent educational preparation. Your colleagues will actually think more highly of you if you confess that you're bewildered every now and then.

Besides, if you wander into the hallway and say to your co-workers, "Wow! I'm really stumped. I don't know whether the word *sensual* or the word *sensuous* is more appropriate in this sentence," the odds are good they won't know the answer either. And they'll be dazzled that it takes that kind of esoteric trivia to trip up your impressive grammatical mind.

13. Dots and Squiggles:

Spelling, Punctuation, and Other Proofreading Stuff

The writer who neglects punctuation, or mispunctuates, is liable to be misunderstood.... For the want of merely a comma, it often occurs that an axiom appears a paradox, or that a sarcasm is converted into a sermonoid.

Edgar Allan Poe

Proofreading is boring, mundane, tiresome, and vitally essential work. And while it has a very important place in the publishing industry, we would do well to keep the goal in mind. People who receive overwhelming joy from a beautifully clean manuscript probably are doomed to be proofreaders for the rest of their lives. But those who strive to correct every little flaw in an article because the flaws disrupt the dream, shatter the illusion, and destroy the magic of otherwise charming articles—those people will be great proofreaders and quickly promoted. The goal is to transport the reader into the writer's world, and errors in the grammar, spelling, and punctuation of the article will prevent that from happening.

Chapters 11 and 12 discussed grammar; now we're down to the spelling and punctuation part. We'll dispense with spelling quickly.

Spelling

The rules for spelling are numerous, intricate

I before *e* except after *c*, unless sounding like *a* as in *freight, sleigh,* or *weigh* and all that—and no one ever remembers them very well. We won't inflict them on you, but there are some reasonable suggestions we can offer that will help you correct the spelling of articles you edit.

• *Look at each word.* Checking each word in a manuscript is a lot more difficult than it sounds. When we read passages that make sense, that are familiar, or that are compelling, we tend to glide right along quickly, without stopping to consider each word. This is a perfectly reasonable approach to reading; *Moby-Dick* would take a lifetime to read if we first examined the word *Call*, then looked carefully at the word *me*, then scrutinized the word *Ishmael*, and so on.

But this way of reading means that a mispelled word can slide right by us. (Like the word *misspelled* in the previous sentence.) Proofreaders can't just glide along, enjoying the story. They have to stop, if for just an instant, on each word.

To do this, forget what your elementary-school teachers taught you: use your finger. Point to each word, check it with your mind, and move on. It doesn't really take all that long, and you'll improve your accuracy a great deal.

Another technique that some proofreaders use when checking spelling is to read the manuscript backward. That way, they don't get caught up in the drama, the humor, or the flow of the article. They just check sentences, one at a time.

• *Let computer spelling checkers help you, but don't count on them.* Wee all no that their good at catching sum errors, but there knot good at everything. The entire previous sentence, for example, looks just fine to my spelling checker. Homonyms—two or more words that sound alike but aren't—are a constant problem for spelling checkers, which, of course, can't help you if you inadvertently misspell one word by correctly spelling another.

So don't trust them. Use them, sure—if your spelling checker flags a word, take a good look at it. But an awful lot of misspelled words get past these simple programs.

(And for the record—don't bother with grammar checkers at all. They not only ignore mistakes, but also complain about perfectly decent sentences. If you follow their advice, you'll only make the writing worse. Some day, we'll have great grammar checkers on our computers, but that day has not yet come.)

• *Get to know the origins of words*. If you spend some time exploring etymology—the study of the roots and development of words—you'll have a better understanding of the sometimes strange and illogical spelling that curses the English language. Some charming and interesting books have been written on the subject—really!—and reading them for fun can help you with your spelling and your career as an editor.

• *Take care to pronounce words correctly.* Mispronunciation can lead to misspellings. If you pronounce the word *math-matics*, you'll likely spell it *mathmatics*—forgetting that it has an extra syllable: *mathematics*. If you pronounce the word *ath-e-lete*, you'll be inclined to spell it *athelete*—forgetting that it has just two syllables: *athlete*. Precision in speaking can lead to precision in spelling.

• *Learn problem words*. Everyone encounters words that just don't seem to stick well. If you always misspell *privilege*, *grievous*, or *mischievous*, or any other word, just follow this plan. First, write the word on a sticky note, with the proper spelling and the definition, if that would be helpful. Read it out loud, and spell the word out loud three or four times. Then put the sticky note on tomorrow's page of whatever calendar or time planner you use. Tomorrow, read it again out loud three or four times—and then move it ahead one week. When you reach it again, do the same thing: read it out loud three or four times, and then advance it one month. When you reach it again, same drill—but advance it one year. By this time, you will know the proper spelling, and you probably won't forget it for the rest of your life.

• *Remember the three-foot rule.* As always, keep a dictionary close at hand. When in doubt, check it out.

The biggest challenge, of course, lies in proofreading a manuscript in which the writer makes the same spelling mistakes that you do. Those are the hardest to detect, and so you'll have to conquer as many of them as you can.

With that, we will let you grapple with spelling on your own. Good editors take spelling seriously, and you'll get good at it after a while.

Punctuation, Period

Punctuation is essential for clarity without it messages however gracefully written otherwise become difficult if not impossible to decipher in addition all power charm and poise boil off in the heat of bad or missing punctuation.

And that's why we should punctuate our sentences and paragraphs well. Punctuation gives us rhythm, logic, passion, power, and poetry. Good editors spot badly punctuated sentences viscerally, even before their analytical brains have considered the offenses and the way to correct them. Good editors *feel* them and fix them with almost instinctive certainty.

This is not to say that editors have to know every little term, concept, and squiggle of punctuational minutiae. But a solid understanding of the basics allows editors to spot errors—especially errors that destroy meaning, shatter rhythm, or skew emphasis—without devoting entire afternoons to the scouring of stylebooks.

Because the basics are important, we'll cover them here.

And nothing is more basic than the period, so that's where we'll start.

I Said STOP!

As we all remember from our fifth-grade drills, periods do a lot of things. The main task of the period is to bring a sentence to a halt.

> Bob was skiing under the large overhang of snow he stopped to check his map the air was cold Bob blew his nose and the sound caused the snow to shake it fell and rolled Bob up into a giant snowball that careened down the hill

That example, of course, is hard to read and decipher. We have to work to figure out what is going on. The period allows us to divide streams of thoughts, actions, and words into chunks that make sense. By allowing just one main thought per chunk, we can keep the flow of language relatively clear:

> Bob was skiing under the large overhang of snow. he stopped to check his map. the air was cold. Bob blew his nose and the sound caused the snow to shake. it fell and rolled Bob up into a giant snowball that careened down the hill.

Even without commas, capital letters, and other important forms of guidance, we can begin to make better sense out of this jumble. The periods let us know when one main thought ends and the next begins.

But of course, that's just the primary task that periods tackle. They do a lot of other things as well.

For example, periods let us know when something has been abbreviated. Rather than writing out full names all the time—Hiram Puddlejumper Bartholomew—we often shorten them by abbreviating the middle name: Hiram P. Bartholomew. In general, the middle initial is all we need to identify old Hiram, so we don't bother with the whole thing. But to indicate that the poor guy's middle name really isn't P, we put a period after the initial. (Some people, of course, really do have single letters for their middle names. Harry S Truman, Michael J Fox, and Albert A Gore have had to go through life devoid of full middle names. Note that in strictly proper circles, no period would be used after the letter because it isn't an abbreviation for anything. The period is often added, however, just to make the name look right.)

Other common abbreviations (and their restrictions) include

Dr.   Doctor

This abbreviation should be used only immediately preceding names:

Dr. Lucretia Jimenez

Never use it by itself:

Quick! Somebody call the Dr.!

Mr.   Mister
Mrs.   Mistress (believe it or not)
Ms.   any woman

Ms. often is preferred over *Mrs.* or *Miss*, because men don't have courtesy titles that identify their marital status. Purists would argue that no period should follow *Ms*, because it really isn't short for anything; it's an invented title that parallels *Mr.* But most people think it looks odd without the period, and the absent period makes it parallel *Mr.* even less.

Ave.	Avenue
Blvd.	Boulevard
Ct.	Court
Dr.	Drive
Pl.	Place or Plaza
Rd.	Road
St.	Street

These abbreviations should be used only as part of addresses:

1234 Flippinworth Pl.
9876 Braggadocio Dr.

Never use them by themselves:

The armed suspect ran down the St.

| St. | Saint |

This abbreviation should be used only immediately preceding names:

St. Catherine's School
St. Louis, Missouri
St. Patrick's Day

Once again, never use it by itself:

She has the patience of a St.

Jan. Feb. Aug. Sept. Oct. Nov. Dec.

The abbreviations for the names of the months should be used only with dates, not by themselves.

B.C.	before Christ
B.C.E.	before the common era (refers to the same time frame as B.C.)
A.D.	*anno Domini* (in the year of the Lord)
A.H.	*anno Hegirae* (in the year of the Hegira (A.D. 622)

The abbreviations for eras should be used only with dates. Formally, they should be presented in small capital letters, with periods, and A.D. and A.H. precede the year:

4512 B.C.

A.D. 2020
A.H. 1421

A.M.   morning (*ante meridiem*)
P.M.   afternoon (*post meridiem*)

The abbreviations for the divisions of the day should be presented in small capital letters, with periods. They should be used only with numerals:

8:30 A.M.
11:45 P.M.

Never use them with spelled-out numbers or with *o'clock*.

Jr.   junior
Sr.   senior

These abbreviations are used with names to indicate the elder or younger person of the same name, and are set off from the names by commas:

Hank Williams, Sr.
Hank Williams, Jr.

e.g.   for example
etc.   and so on
i.e.   in other words

Many abbreviations become so familiar that we tend to write them without the periods. We do this for two reasons:

1. People already know what the abbreviation means. Most Americans, for example, know that the FBI is the Federal Bureau of Investigation, so we don't bother calling attention to the abbreviation.
2. People have come to know the abbreviation far better than the actual name of an organization. Most Americans can tell you that NASA is the agency that puts rockets into space, but not everyone can tell you that N.A.S.A. stands for the National Aeronautics and Space Administration. Similarly, a lot of people know that NASDAQ is a stock exchange, but very few could explain that the letters stand for National Association of Securities Dealers Automated Quotations.

Other common abbreviations that generally don't require periods include

CIA	Central Intelligence Agency
FAA	Federal Aviation Administration
FEMA	Federal Emergency Management Agency
MLB	Major League Baseball
NAACP	National Association for the Advancement of Colored People
NATO	North Atlantic Treaty Organization
NBA	National Basketball Association
NCAA	National Collegiate Athletics Association
NFL	National Football League
NHL	National Hockey League
OPEC	Organization of Petroleum Exporting Countries
USA	you get the idea

So we now have two uses for periods: ending sentences and indicating abbreviations.

Related abbreviations are acronyms. Technically, an acronym is a word (or at least something that can be pronounced like a word) formed by the first letter of each word in a key phrase, but acronyms can be lumped in with other kinds of abbreviations that form pronounceable words. These terms tend to not take periods. Here are some examples of both:

Botox	botulinum toxin
moped	motorized pedal power
motel	motor hotel
Nabisco	National Biscuit Company
radar	radio detecting and ranging
scuba	self-contained underwater breathing apparatus
snafu	situation normal all "fouled" up
sonar	sound navigation and ranging

Take a Break

The next most important piece of punctuation is the comma. We use commas to do a whole lot of different things for us, and commas are misused much more often than are periods.

The two main uses of the comma are to separate certain parts of a sentence and to separate the parts of a list. We'll start with the first.

When two sentences (independent clauses) are joined to form one complex sentence, the joining has to follow certain rules. If you don't follow these rules, you'll end up with a run-on sentence:

Nancy vaulted over the tiger, she landed safely on the other side.

This is also called a *comma splice*. One of the ways to avoid a run-on is to join the two independent clauses with a comma and a *conjunction* (*and, but, or,* and so on):

Nancy vaulted over the tiger, and she landed safely on the other side.

So one important use of the comma is to work with a conjunction to link two independent clauses.

You'll also get a run-on if you link two independent clauses with a conjunction but leave out the comma:

The tiger was not amused and Nancy practiced her sprinting skills.

The other main use, separating the items in a list, is somewhat less precise. The main problem is that newspaper editors and magazine editors disagree over the details.

In a basic list, the items are generally separated by commas:

human, Klingon, Romulan, Cardassian

This separation allows for additional words without causing confusion about the items themselves:

bold humans, valiant Klingons, conniving Romulans, devious Cardassians

Even with the addition of four words, we still obviously have just four items.

The disagreement between newsfolk and magfolk comes with that last comma, and it stems from the old-fashioned approach to the printing process. The old-timey presses required an elaborate procedure for the creation of characters—letters, punctuation marks, and so on. For each character, some old guy named Gus would have to take out a metal mold—say, for the letter Q—and pour hot lead into it. Once the lead cooled, Gus would take the letter and place it upside down and backward in a large frame, following the handwritten text that was gathering dust on the table next to him. He would do this for every character in the manuscript: every letter, every period, every comma. As you might imagine, this procedure took a lot of time, and the lead fumes caused old Gus to talk to himself in the back. For magazines, this was not a problem. The long deadlines allowed the process to churn along, and Gus probably talked to himself when he was hired in the first place. But for newspapers, which were trying to meet tight deadlines, the process was agonizingly slow. So anything that could be done to speed things up was appreciated.

One way that the process could be accelerated involved the elimination of any unnecessary character. In a list, newspaper people reasoned, we already have the word *and* separating the last two items:

humans, Klingons, Romulans, and Cardassians

So why stick in that comma? If we cut out those commas, we could save Gus a good twenty minutes per newspaper.

So they did. In newspapers, even to this day, you'll see no comma in such lists:

The Tribbles destroyed the humans, the Klingons, the Romulans and the Cardassians.

But magazines worked under easier deadlines, and magazine editors pitched their wares to elite readers who felt that newspapers were tawdry and common. In fact, that last comma, which is usually called the *serial comma*, is also called the *Harvard comma*, complete with all the upper-crust airs that the term implies. Magazines tried to look more formal, more refined, and more exclusive than newspapers, so magazine editors kept the serial comma to show that they weren't bound by such mundane concerns as short deadlines and Gus's mental capacity.

So except for the news magazines—*Time, Newsweek, U.S. News & World Report*—magazines tend to use the serial comma.

We now have two good uses for commas. They separate independent clauses (when used with conjunctions), and they separate items in a list. But these versatile little squiggles are good for much more than that.

• *Set off nonessential clauses and phrases.* If a clause or phrase isn't critical to the meaning of the sentence, it should be set off with commas:

> Karen Goldsmith, who is only a sophomore, pitched a perfect game against Arch Rival High.

The basic point of the sentence is that Karen Goldsmith pitched a perfect game. The fact that she is a sophomore is offered as an aside, like "by the way" information:

> Karen Goldsmith, who by the way is only a sophomore, pitched a perfect game against Arch Rival High.

These clauses are inserted to provide additional information to the curious reader, but they don't directly affect the main meaning of the sentence. If you flop the clauses, you change the basic point of the sentence:

> Karen Goldsmith, who pitched a perfect game against Arch Rival High, is only a sophomore.

In this sentence, the main point is that Karen is a sophomore. The fact that she pitched a perfect game is offered as "by the way," "in case you happen to care" information.

These "aside" clauses are often called parentheticals, which really does refer to parentheses. You could even write the sentences that way:

> Karen Goldsmith (who is only a sophomore) pitched a perfect game against Arch Rival High.

Clauses like these are also set off with commas if they come at the beginning or the end of a sentence:

> Full of felons and devil worshipers, Arch Rival High hasn't won a game this season.

The main point is that ARH hasn't won a game; the nature of its student body is offered as "in case you happen to care" information. Similarly:

> The losing players set fire to the bleachers, which is the fourth time they've done that this season.

The main point: they set fire to the bleachers. "In case you happen to care": this is the fourth time they've done that.

- *Set off introductory phrases.* An introductory phrase also represents "aside" information and should be set off by a comma:

> While the bleachers were burning, the ARH pitcher roasted marshmallows.

What really matters in this sentence is that the pitcher was roasting marshmallows.

- *Set off appositives.* We all know what *opposite* means. Well, appositives are the opposites of opposites. *Opposite* means something that is exactly *not* like the main thing. *Apposite* means something that *is* exactly like the main thing:

> The ARH pitcher, Mortitia Darkshadow, seems attracted to large fires.

In this sentence, "The ARH pitcher" and "Mortitia Darkshadow" are one and the same person; "Mortitia Darkshadow" is simply another way of naming the ARH pitcher. Those two terms are apposites, so the second one is set off with commas.

It is important to point out that when a name or term is used to indicate precisely which person or thing we're talking about, it is not set off with commas. If Mortitia (through some miracle) had three friends, we would not write:

> Mortitia's friend, Lepra, joined in the roast.

This sentence would imply that "Lepra" and "Mortitia's friend" were one and the same. But if Mortitia had three friends, that would not be the case. So because "Lepra" tells us which of Mortitia's friends joined in the roast, it is essential information, not just an appositive. It would be written without commas:

> Mortitia's friend Lepra joined in the roast.

- *Set off words used in direct address.* This is where you insert a direct reference to the person you are talking to:

> Frankly, my dear, I don't give a hoot.
> Nancy, would you please get your foot off my ear?
> What do you think of that, Hank?

- *Set off elements of dates and addresses*

July 4, 1776
Meet me on August 4, 2004, at the elephant cage.
I live at 10000003 Far End Boulevard, Anchorage, Alaska.

- *Set off the salutation of a friendly letter (formal letters take colons) and the closing of all letters*

Dear John,
The last three hours have been the happiest of my life. But somehow, we've drifted apart since we first met over by the popcorn stand. I must end it now, before we ruin the entire evening.
 I hope you'll come to understand someday.
    Hugs and kisses,
    Frederica

- *Set off titles and other designations after names*

Marissa Gonzalez, Ph.D.
Frederick Rutherford Pinth-Sebastian, Jr.
Freddie Pinth, Sr.

Semicolons: The When-you-want-to-indicate-a-break-but-not-as-big-a-break-as-a-period-indicates Punctuation Mark

Semicolons serve two useful purposes in this world. That's it. Just two. After the comma and the period, this comes as welcome news.

- *Gimme a kinder, gentler break.* The first role for semicolons is to indicate a closer break between sentences than a period signals. In other words, if two sentences are closely linked in meaning, a semicolon can be used to show that linkage:

Kenny pulled the pin on the hand grenade; he quickly regretted that decision.

Because the decision that Kenny regretted was described in the first independent clause, a writer might choose to link the two clauses with a semicolon. A period, while technically correct, would insert a jarringly firm break.

Note that the writer could have linked the sentences another way:

Kenny pulled the pin on the hand grenade, and he quickly regretted that decision.

Linking independent clauses with a comma and a conjunction works just fine and indicates a closer relationship than does the semicolon. The semicolon, then, serves as a sign that the linkage between the independent clauses is closer than that offered by a period but not as close as that offered by a comma and a conjunction.

Along these lines, a semicolon might be advisable as a way to break up the patterns of sentences. If a writer writes a paragraph filled with independent clauses linked by commas and conjunctions—or filled with independent clauses standing alone, set off by periods— then a semicolon might be just the thing to vary that rhythm.

• *Faster than a speeding comma.* The other use for semicolons is as a kind of "supercomma." There are two situations when the supercomma can be helpful.

The first is when you have a list of things—and there are already commas in the things:

It's going to be a fun party. I've invited Hoon, his sister, Li, the Abington twins, Karen, and Leslie.

How many people have been invited to the party? One possible answer is seven:

1. Hoon
2. Hoon's sister
3. Li
4. The Abington twins
5. Karen
6. Leslie

But the right answer also could be four:

1. Hoon
2. Hoon's sister, Li
3. The Abington twins, Karen and Leslie

Subtle clues can help the poor reader who has to decipher this mess; the comma after "Karen," for example, indicates that Karen and Leslie are not the Abington twins. But if you make a reader work that hard to figure things out, the next sound you'll hear will be the turning of the page.

Supercommas to the rescue. By using semicolons to indicate the big breaks between items in the list, we can make the sentence unshakably clear:

> I've invited Hoon; his sister, Li; the Abington twins; Karen; and Leslie.

It turns out that the number of guests is six, and the improved sentence allows for no other interpretation.

The other supercomma situation involves a similar problem: sentences that contain commas, linked together in a potentially confusing way:

> Old Man Jenkins owns four German shepherds, three Great Danes, two Chihuahuas, and a dachshund, and his cat, Nellie, is nervous.

The sentence is correctly punctuated, but it's awfully hard to figure out. By the time the beleaguered reader has figured out that the comma after "dachshund" is supposed to indicate a division between two independent clauses—and does not indicate a continuation of the list of canines—she's probably ready to give up on Old Man Jenkins and turn on a *Gilligan's Island* rerun. The addition of a simple semicolon saves the day by indicating that this break is not just another break like all the other breaks in the sentence:

> Old Man Jenkins owns four German shepherds, three Great Danes, two Chihuahuas, and a dachshund; his cat, Nellie, is nervous.

And This Is What I Mean

Winding down now, we pay a cordial visit to the colon. (Yes, we could make a lot of jokes, but we won't. It would be too much like snickering about the planet Uranus.)

The colon has one big job: to introduce things. It introduces lists:

> Five states currently outlaw snickering at legitimate statements about colons: Louisiana, Alaska, Maine, Rhode Island, and Wyoming.

In that example, the colon introduces the list that the previous sentence was describing.

It is important to note that you shouldn't use a colon when the list flows naturally as part of the main sentence itself:

The five states that outlaw snickering are Louisiana, Alaska, Maine, Rhode Island, and Wyoming.

A colon should *not* be placed after *are.*

Similarly, colons can introduce restatements of something that was indicated in the main sentence:

After dropping the rock on his foot, Colin had just one thing to say: Ouch!

Because the "Ouch!" serves as a restatement of "just one thing to say," we use a colon to introduce it.

We also use colons in a handful of routine little ways:

• Between the hour and the minute when writing the time

8:32 A.M.

• Between the volume number and the issue number of citations in academic writing

Podiatric Journal of Gravity and Large Rocks 12:2

• After the salutation in formal letters

Dear Mr. Rebeboth:
I'm sorry to hear about your foot.

• Between the chapter and the verse of biblical citations

Romans 8:38–39

Otherwise, this chapter notwithstanding, you shouldn't overdo colons. They're rather stuffy and abrupt, so use them only when necessary.

Dashing Through the Snow...

Dashes are controversial.

I know—it's a little hard to imagine a controversial piece of punctuation. But dashes do seem to bring out passionate positions in some people.

On the one side, there's the "Dashes Are a Sign of the Downfall of Civilization as We Know It" group. These people feel that dashes take the place of more proper forms of punctuation, that they reflect laziness on the part of the writer. "We have perfectly good colons and semicolons, not to mention periods and commas," they say. "Why toss all that into the rubbish bin in favor of a one-size-fits-all horizontal line?"

On the other side, there's the "If It Helps You Make Your Point or Set the Right Rhythm, What's the Problem?" camp. These people are more concerned with meaning and poetry than they are with tradition and a close adherence to the English of Shakespeare and Milton.

Where you fall is up to you, but you should at least know how dashes work and what they're good for. Then you can decide whether to banish them from your writers' repertoire or embrace them like a casually dressed friend.

First things first. A dash is, indeed, a horizontal line, but it's not just any horizontal line. It's technically called an *em dash*, meaning that the horizontal line takes up the same amount of space as a lower-case letter *m* in the font you're using.

If you hit the key near the upper-right of your keyboard—the one with the little horizontal lines on it—you won't get a dash. You'll get a hyphen: -. Compare that with the dashes in the previous sentence, and you'll see the difference.

Back in the typewriter days, you typed a dash by typing two hyphens next to each other: --. Today, if you do that, many computers will automatically convert them into one proper dash.

To get an em dash, you'll probably have to hit a combination of keys. On most Macintosh computers, it's shift-option-hyphen. On PCs, though, the em dash can be found in the "Symbol" section of the "Insert" menu on the toolbar.

Now that you know how to make one, we should figure out what dashes good for. The dash has several handy uses.

• *To set off an aside or to indicate an abrupt change in thought.* In this way, the dashes act a bit like parentheses:

He jumped—or, I should say, he belly-flopped—into the pool.

Sir—and I use that term loosely—I must ask you to leave.

- *To add emphasis*

To defuse the bomb, clip the yellow wire and—without touching the blue wire at all—press the red button.

- *To introduce a passage that explains something that came before.* In this way, dashes act like colons, standing for such phrases as *that is, namely,* or *in other words*:

There was only one thing left to do—run!

Then he made his move—he kissed her.

And then there's the lowly *en dash.* The en dash, so named because it's about as wide as a lower-case letter *n,* lacks the omnipresence of the hyphen and the power of the em dash. In fact, the en dash is used for only rather special and fussy typographical purposes.

- *To separate numbers in a range*

Please read pages 12–54.

The en dash is useful here because the numbers aren't linked, as a hyphen would suggest, and the sentence is not being set off in parentheses-like ways, as an em dash would suggest. The en dash indicates a connection that is different from that of its cousins, substituting for the word *through.*

You also use the en dash with variations on the theme, such as a range of dates:

January–May 2004

or ages:

SM seeks SF, 32–64, for fishing and romantic dinners.

- *To substitute for the word* to

The spy caught the Prague–Budapest train.

- *To replace the hyphen in some two-word, or compound, adjectives.* When one or both parts of a compound adjective are open or are separated by a hyphen, an en dash makes the adjective clearer than a hyphen would:

The artist took the San Francisco–Paris flight.
The architect had to deal with the private-sector–public-sector debate.

Hyphens

Hyphens, the shortest of the horizontal lines, come in handy in a few situations.

• *To indicate an adjectival phrase.* To be sure, *adjectival phrase* sounds a bit heavy. But all it means is that if you have two related adjectives modifying a noun, those adjectives should be linked with a hyphen.

The key word here is *related*. Two distinct adjectives describing something should be separated by commas:

the large, muddy hippopotamus
the long, scaly crocodile
the fierce, bloody battle
the sleepy, satisfied hippo

But if the adjectives form a phrase, and that phrase—as a unit—modifies the noun, then they should be connected with hyphens:

The blue-green parrot flew over the high-school band and swooped
past the French-horn player.

There actually is a good reason for this. Take the parrot, for example. It isn't a green parrot that happens to be blue, which is what you might infer if you read the "blue, green parrot." Without the hyphen, each of the adjectives applies to the noun separately. (To make the point more bluntly, he's not a horn player who happens to be French, and it's certainly not a school band that happens to be high.)

The hyphen in these cases becomes somewhat optional if the adjectives are so commonly linked that few people would read them as separate terms:

the Junior Miss Pageant
the ice cream cone

(Note that we don't hyphenate adjectival phrases if they follow the noun they modify. So we would write *the first-place runner,* but drop the hyphen in *The runner took first place.*)

(Also note that we don't use hyphens for adverbial phrases, for reasons that no one knows. So *the partially blocked punt, the awkwardly running boy, the happily married man*—all these are fine without hyphens.)

• *To connect written-out numbers from twenty-one through ninety-nine*

seventy-six trombones

but

one hundred ten cornets

although often it is better to use figures for exact numbers above one hundred. Follow this rule even if the number is part of a larger number (although often it is better to use figures for larger, exact numbers):

five thousand, two hundred, fifty-eight people

• *To separate the prefixes* all-, ex-, quasi-, *and* self-, *and the suffix* -elect, *from the main word*

all-inclusive roster
ex-football player
quasi-intellectual
self-made millionaire
president-elect

Also, use a hyphen after any prefix that comes before a proper noun or proper adjective:

un-American slogans
anti-British protestors
pro-Canadian voters

- *To prevent awkwardness or misreading*

re-creation   to create again

but

recreation   to have fun

and, to avoid the awkwardness of *reex*

re-examine

- *To divide a word at the end of a line.* In the computer age, this is rarely necessary. Most manuscript guides suggest that you set your margins to "flush left," meaning a straight line down the left side of the page, and "rag right," which is short for "ragged right" and means that the right-hand side of the page will not be straight. With "rag right," the lines break between words at the spot closest to the end of the line. Rag right, also known as "align left" and other terms, is generally considered easier to read than fully justified text:

Full justify,
not rag right →

To divide a word at the end of a line. In the computer age, this is rarely necessary. Most manuscript guides suggest that you set your margins to "flush left," meaning a straight line down the left side of the page, and "rag right," which is short for "ragged right" and means that the righthand side of the page will not be straight. With "rag right," the lines break between words at the spot closest to the end of the line.

Rag right →

To divide a word at the end of a line. In the computer age, this is rarely necessary. Most manuscript guides suggest that you set your margins to "flush left," meaning a straight line down the left side of the page, and "rag right," which is short for "ragged right" and means that the righthand side of the page will not be straight. With "rag right," the lines break between words at the spot closest to the end of the line.

If you toss in some long words, though, you might find yourself wanting to break some of them to make the lines look better:

same often words here find quite under throughout opinion antidisestablishmentarianism order it is where place even result wrong run find ever wind use firm day event worth delay fears wait rays films to have also truth now.

With a hyphen, we can break the big word and make the lines fall better:

same often words here find quite under throughout opinion antidis-establishmentarianism order it is where place even result wrong run find ever wind use firm day event worth delay fears wait rays films to have also truth now.

Of course, some rules apply when breaking words:

• Divide the word between properly pronounceable syllables

gener-ate
mag-nify

If a word has only one syllable, do not break it:

stayed (not stay-ed)

• Don't break words so that only one or two letters are stranded

e-normous
identi-fy
a-ppropriate

• For words with prefixes or suffixes, try to break between the root and the prefix or suffix

happi-ness
toss-ing
pre-amble

- Without violating the previous rule, generally try to break words between double consonants

recom-mend
al-locate

but, to adhere to the preceding rule:

fulfill-ment

Don't do this if you doubled the consonant because you added the ending:

regret-table
swim-ming

- When in doubt, grab a dictionary.

High Marks

We've talked about the comma. Now we're going to give it a raise—and talk about apostrophes and double and single quotation marks.

We'll start with the apostrophe. The basics are easy.

- *Possessives.* To make a word possessive, add an apostrophe and an *s*:

Tom's walrus
Jill's dogsled
the iceberg's color

No problem. Learned it in fifth grade, haven't forgotten it since.

Twist 1. To make a noun both plural and possessive, add an *s* (or whatever else you need to do to make it plural), and then add an apostrophe:

the cars' colors
the planets' rotations
the gardens' flowers

This also means that you stick to this pattern even if the word already ends in *s*:

kiss → *plural:* kisses → *plural possessive:* the kisses' effect

This gets especially tricky when it comes to things like names. If five people named Jones own a car, how would you write that?

Jones → *plural:* Joneses → *plural possessive:* the Joneses' car

Some people just toss an apostrophe on the end of such names, like the Evans' house. But this form of the possessive suggests that several people named Evan own a house:

Evan → Evans → Evans'

In fact, if the house is owned by several people named Evans, you would do the same thing you did with Jones:

Evans → *plural:* Evanses → *plural possessive:* the Evanses' house

(Ah, the strange-but-true world of English punctuation!)

One last point: for words that are made plural in strange ways, follow the same pattern—first make them plural, and then make them possessive:

child → children → children's
moose → moose → moose's
woman → women → women's

Twist 2. If two or more people (or things) possess something, you have to decide whether they possess it separately or together. If the two own something separately, you put the possessive on both owners:

Jane's and Janika's answers
the rhino's and the dolphin's teeth

But if they own it together, you put the possessive on the final one, to indicate that they are a team and the team possesses the thing:

Tom and Li's car
Jane and Janika's answers

Twist 3. Use apostrophes when writing phrases that technically are possessive adjectives:

a day's work
five minutes' worth

• *Missing letters.* Use an apostrophe when a word or term is contracted, to show where the missing letters used to be:

can't

it's

they're

For quotation marks, things are a bit simpler. For starters, the difference between single and double quotations marks. In this country, we start with the double marks, and then—if we have to put something in quotation marks *inside* the first set—we use single:

"He said, 'Frankly, my dear, I don't give a hoot,'" she said.

Note that both sets of quotation marks have to be closed when they're done; that's why we ended up with three after "hoot." (The qualification "In this country" is key; in England, they do this the other way around.)

From now on, we'll pay attention to the more common double marks. Here are some useful rules.

• *Sentence capitalization.* If the quote contains a complete sentence, capitalize it normally:

The woman said, "Eat your beans, Frank."

If *she said* or the equivalent breaks a sentence, don't capitalize the second part:

"I called you Frank," she said, "because I confused you with my first husband."

If the break comes between sentences, capitalize the second one normally:

"You had a first husband!" he said. "I didn't know that."

If the quote is a phrase that flows directly from the sentence, don't add any punctuation except the quotation marks:

Don't you believe in "love at second sight"?

• *Commas and periods.* Put commas and periods inside the quotation marks:

"I'm not sure," he said, "whether I believe in love at all."

• *Semicolons and colons.* Put semicolons and colons outside the quotation marks:

> She said she was "shocked"; he had never talked like this before. He had only ever talked about his three "favorite things": football, *Star Trek*, and his model railroad set.

• *Question marks and exclamation points.* Put question marks and exclamation points inside the quotation marks if the quoted material is a question or an exclamation:

> "Do you still love me?" she asked.
>
> "Of course I do!" he replied.

But put them outside the quotation marks if the quoted material is not:

> But did he really believe in this thing called "love"?
>
> As we know, "only time will tell"!

Never put more than one ending punctuation mark on any given sentence. For example, do *not* write:

> Did he say, "Ouch!"?

• *With each new speaker, start a new paragraph*
• *Titles.* Put quotation marks around the titles of book chapters, magazine articles, short stories, poems, songs, and other short works. In other words, if the thing is part of a larger unit, put it in quotation marks:

> You can skip chapter 7: "How to Write a Soap Opera."
>
> I love that new song, "Eat Your Beans with Frank."

Titles of the larger units themselves—books, magazines, CDs—are printed in italics.

Side by Side

Last but not least: the side things. Parentheses and brackets.

Parentheses are used to indicate information that is not essential to the main point. Asides. "By the way" information. The same kinds of situations in which commas and dashes can often be used:

Eat your lunch. (But don't eat the dessert. It's awful!)

The information (see the chart on page 12) shows that we are losing money.

Put punctuation inside the parentheses if it's part of the "aside" material. Otherwise, put it outside.

Note that *parentheses* is the plural form of the word. The singular is *parenthesis*.

Outside of mathematics, brackets are good for just two things. They show that words have been added to quotes:

He said, "I am amused by it [the prank]."

They also are used as parentheses within parentheses:

The Tribbles destroyed the Klingons, the Romulans, the Cardassians, and the humans (whose mission ["To boldly go where no one has gone before"] thus suffered a serious setback).

Armed with these rules—and a good reference book, so you don't have to remember them all—you should be able to detect errors in punctuation and know how to fix them. In fact, the process will become rather automatic. You'll develop a sixth sense about improperly built sentences, and you'll fix them quickly and easily.

And then, you'll do a brilliant job, earn a promotion quickly, and begin working your way up to the higher ranks of editing, where you can grapple with loftier considerations—like what to do when someone hands you $250,000.

14. The Supporting Cast:

The Other Little Things that Editors Do

The human tendency to regard little things as important has produced very many great things.

G. C. (Georg Christoph) Lichtenberg

It's odd, when you think about it. Every single word in every single issue of a magazine had to be written by someone and edited by someone.

The articles, of course, are obvious; we've been talking about them throughout this book. But other elements abound in a typical magazine, and editors either create or edit all of them.

One big area is advertising. People have to conceive the ads, design them, take the photos, make the artwork, do the layout, and put them into the magazine.

We won't worry about all that right now. The triumphs and pitfalls of ad work are best left to another book.

Besides, we have plenty left to think about. When I first became an editor, I was surprised at all the little things that had to be done—things that readers typically don't think about. But editors *have* to think about them, and they have to do them well. At times, they can make or break the success of an issue.

Some of these items are significant, and we'll address them first. We'll leave the really little things to the end of the chapter.

Big Words

Few readers realize it, but writers don't write the headlines for their articles. Readers tend to assume that writers create their own headlines, and writers often have been chastised in restaurants and at bus stops for some lousy titles they wrote. The writer always protests, "I didn't write it! Really! An editor did that—and I hate it, too!" The protests are never successful, but you have to try.

The reason that editors write the headlines is simple: when a writer is working on a story, she has no idea how that story will be laid out in the magazine. Will it begin on one page or on a two-page spread? Will it be accompanied by a large photo, a lot of little photos, a background photo? How big will the headline type be? what font?

All these questions affect how many words a headline can allow. A headline that will cover one line across one page, in a large font, can have just a few words. (Good luck if you have to work *Afghanistan* or *Mozambique* into the headline! It's at times like this that you hope the article is about Peru or Ohio.) A headline that can stretch across two pages, taking two or even three lines, can be much more descriptive and complete.

Because writers can't anticipate the page design, they are not in a position to write their own headlines. Most do anyway, if for no other reason than to put something across the top of their manuscripts. Sometimes, editors use the writer's suggestion or try to come up with something similar. Most of the time, the writer's version won't work in the layout and has to be scrapped.

Typically, the graphic designer for the magazine has been hard at work on the article's design while the writer is doing the research and writing the article. That is at least a good goal for editors to hold; graphic designers like to be brought into the picture early so they can get the photos and artwork they want.

Once a preliminary design has been developed for an article, the editor will have some idea of the headline parameters. The graphic designer might say that you have four or five words at most. Or you might get eight or nine on a good day. Then it's your job to come up with a headline that fits those parameters and that meets all the requirements of a good headline.

What are those requirements? In general, they are some of the same requirements that apply to good leads.

- *Introduce the topic.* Obviously, readers won't decide to invest time in an article if they can't figure out what the article is about. The headline should give them at least a general idea. Is this about politics? art? sports? football, baseball, soccer? quarterbacks, running backs, linebackers? Peyton Manning, Tom Brady, Brett Favre? Peyton Manning's throwing style, his leadership, his career? The headline should reflect the topic and indicate the degree of specificity that the article will offer. "The NFL's New Quarterbacks" is obviously a very different article from "Manning's Quest for the Super Bowl." The headline should mirror the article as much as possible.

- *Set the tone.* Your writer drinks gallons of coffee, eats doughnuts by the box, destroys his love life, and plunges into the depths of sleep deprivation—all just to deliver the funniest article he has ever written. It would be the height of cruelty to top that article with a bland, serious, or otherwise out-of-step headline.

Readers assume that the tone reflected in the headline will resemble the tone reflected in the article. It is imperative, then, that the headline introduce the tone of the article. Got a sarcastic article? Hit readers with a biting headline. Got a tearjerker of a story? Give readers a headline that will have them sobbing before they reach the lead.

But whatever you do, don't kill an article's tone with a headline that projects the wrong tone—or no tone at all.

- *Engage the reader's interest.* As mentioned previously, readers tend to look at the photos first, then the captions, then the headline. So if they've made it to the headline, they are at least not bored or repulsed by the topic suggested by the photos and captions. Now it's the headline's turn. With those few words, you have to pique their curiosity, excite their minds, and inspire them to head on over to the lead for a deeper look. If you've done your job well, they'll settle in for a long, pleasant read.

In addition to those goals, there is one thing a headline must *not* do: it must not steal the lead's thunder. If the lead relies on suspense, the headline mustn't give away the ending. If it relies on humor, the headline mustn't blow the joke. If it relies on a puzzle, the headline mustn't throw out the answer in advance.

Mercifully for editors who have the opportunity to write headlines, they have more to work with than just the main string of a few words. Headlines have several different parts that can be used to create an effect.

• *Main head.* The main head is just what it sounds like: the main words, usually offered in large type, that carry the primary weight. Some are relatively straightforward:

Get Rich by Raising Ostriches

or

Ostrich Ranching—Not Just for Feathers Anymore

They also might be less obvious, more playful, or more enigmatic:

Big Birds, Big Bucks

or

Don't Drop the Eggs

The more playful or clever headlines tend to be less clear; it's harder for readers to grasp what the article is about. That's where some of the other parts of headlines can come to the rescue.

• *Deck head.* The deck head usually is a phrase or short sentence that runs under the main head, explaining the topic or setting the tone more completely. For straightforward headlines, a deck head might not be necessary. But for short, playful headlines, a deck head is almost essential:

Big Birds, Big Bucks

You can feather your nest nicely by raising ostriches in your spare time

The deck head, which often is presented in a relatively straightforward manner, tells readers what the headline means and gives them a sense of the article to come. It can be invaluable if the main head is too short to allow much explanation.

• *Kicker.* I've also heard kickers referred to as hammers, headers, and other things. Kickers are short labels that appear over the main head. They often indicate the department—"Finance" or "Health," say—but they also can be used to offer a bit of additional information or make the headline clearer:

$2,000 gets you started

Big Birds, Big Bucks

You can feather your nest nicely
by raising ostriches in your spare time

The graphic designer will tell you what tools you have to work with: main head, deck head, kicker. As with everything else, of course, this is negotiable, especially early in the design process. If the designer tells you that you have room for a one-line, one-page main head, two or three words max, with no room for a deck head or kicker, I'd say it's time to talk things over.

And when you sit down to write some headlines, keep in mind the things that separate the good from the great. If appropriate, you want to write these with humor, suspense, surprise, or cleverness, and you should try to get action verbs in there whenever possible.

Picture This

Writers rarely see the photographs that will be used with their articles; it isn't until the article comes out in print that they find out how the whole package looks. It typically falls to the editor, then, to write the captions that run beneath the photos.

Captions—also called cutlines—have the same responsibilities as all the other parts: to inform, and to inspire the reader to read the article. The inspiration should come through the topic, the wording, and the content itself. That leaves the informational part of the challenge.

Good captions go beyond merely identifying the people and actions in the photo. If you see a photo of the president shaking hands with the vice president, you probably don't need a caption that reads: "This is the president shaking hands with the vice president." What you want to know is *why* they are shaking hands.

Even if you didn't know the people in the picture, you'd want more than simple identification and description. For a photo of a man planting corn, you would be unimpressed with a caption that explained: "Rich Loam plants corn in his field."

And yet you also would be unimpressed if the basics were left out. If you saw the hand-shaking picture with the caption "The budget bill passed by a 62–38 vote," you'd wonder what was going on with the hand-shaking. Similarly, if you saw the corn-planting photo with the caption "Forecasters predict record rainfall this summer," you'd wonder what that has to do with this guy standing in his field.

So good captions do both. They identify the people in the photo and describe what those people are doing, *and* they add information that explains some of the significance or context that makes the photo meaningful:

> President Smith and Vice President Jones congratulate each other after the budget bill passed in the Senate by a 62–38 vote. Both leaders considered the bill a top priority for their administration.

> Farmer Rich Loam planted corn early this year because forecasters are predicting a record rainfall this summer. The extra rain could jeopardize late-summer crops.

It is important to note that as the editor, it is your job to make sure that the credit for the photo appears in some logical place. Many magazines put it at the end of the caption:

> Farmer Rich Loam planted corn early this year because forecasters are predicting a record rainfall this summer. The extra rain could jeopardize late-summer crops. (Photo by Josh Weedstomper)

Others make the credit a separate element, running it immediately beneath the photo or even up one side. Publishing a photo without proper credit is a major blunder, though, so editors get in the habit of checking to make sure that all the credits are properly in place.

Blow 'Em Up

If you look at almost any major magazine article, you'll see some quotes or passages copied, "blown up"—printed in larger type—and scattered in strategic places throughout the pages. These large-type passages are called pull quotes or call outs.

Pull quotes provide another means by which the attention of the readers may be enticed. They are yet another element that might inspire readers to point their eyes at the lead and start reading in earnest.

when the obvious needs often requires the holders a major demographic add a who demand required and shift in textured analysis all valuable services to begin a long and arduous process an often-overlooked advance easily be considered in the extensively leveraged views but sketchy preliminary or that many competitors are significant way, according most major branding and significant undertaking a design element that can't absence of wide-ranging or that articulate a thorough advance informative role a unable to command in any to the financial officers of service organizations that fail to consider the kind of goods and services firms or overarching long view that

"He was murdered?" she asked.

manufacturing outfits long is typical of the majority

They also can steer readers to the beginnings of articles. According to some studies, nearly half of all readers flip through magazines from the back to the front, so they reach the last page of an article first. If the photos have been used early in the article, which is typical, the last page might be nothing but gray, lifeless text. Editors figure that the photos have to run early to catch readers' attention, but by the time readers reach the last page, they're going to press on to the end no matter what. So if readers hit the last page first, and they see this ocean of drab text; nothing leaps off the page that might make them care about the article. That's where pull quotes come in. They jump off the page with provocative text, causing the reader to stop and think, "Wow. That sounds interesting. What's this article about, anyway?" Then they flip to the first page of the article, where the headlines and photos can do their jobs.

Because of their attention-getting role, pull quotes have to be punchy. They contain just a few words—most consist of a single, short sentence or even a part of a sentence—and they have to make the reader stop flipping and start reading.

Beyond that, there are a few additional considerations.

• *Quote or text?* The name pull quote implies that the words that are enlarged come from actual quoted text—from passages with quotation marks around them. Some editors take the term literally, insisting that using actual quotes is the best approach. That way, you are highlighting something a source said, rather than blowing your own horn by highlighting your writer's writing.

Other editors, however, disagree, arguing that pull quotes should represent the liveliest, zippiest, sexiest, most potent phrases you can find, regardless of how they were created. If the goal is to attract attention, you should use your most attention-attracting stuff.

• *To thine own self be true?* Another debate surrounding pull quotes has to do with the accuracy of the quote. Once a phrase or sentence has been chosen for a pull quote, is the editor obligated to reproduce it verbatim? Or can the editor rewrite it a bit to add zest and sizzle?

Some editors feel that because the pull quote is reproducing printed text that readers can find in the article, it should present the exact wording of the text. Others argue that because the function of the pull quote is to capture readers' attention, a little strategic massaging of the wording is acceptable.

Prominent magazines have taken both sides of this issue, so once again—it boils down to your call.

• *Whence comest thou?* The other debate centers on the physical placement of the original quote. Some editors maintain that the pull quote can come from anywhere in the article; just grab your best material and find good places to put it.

Other editors insist that the pull quote should come from the same page on which the text it is quoting appears. This way, readers who notice the pull quote can scan the page to find the original, in the hopes of getting some context or more information (*Who* was murdered?). The choice, of course, is yours, although I tend to side with the latter camp. I think that readers find it frustrating to see an engaging pull quote and then have trouble finding the actual passage on the page.

Bombshells

Pull quotes are short and punchy, but they're nothing compared with cover blurbs. Cover blurbs are the short phrases that appear on a magazine's cover, and they serve one purpose only: to get newsstand browsers to pick up the magazine.

Because cover space is at a premium—and because you don't want to block too much of the cover photo—the blurbs have to be extremely short:

Tom Cruise—
Up Close

Lose 10 lbs.
by Saturday!

Can War
Be Stopped?

Bald Eagles
Stage Comeback

Sometimes, a blurb can carry its own deck head, a short explanatory phrase in smaller type below:

Kick Back!

The Tae-Bo workout that really works!

The key, of course, is high power in a short space.

The location of the blurbs on a magazine cover is very important. If you scan the magazine rack at your favorite bookstore, you'll notice that most of the cover blurbs appear along the left side of the cover and across the top. That's because shelf space on most newsstands is tight, and magazines are placed overlapping each other, with the folded (left) side sticking out from behind another magazine. So browsers in the bookstore won't see anything you put on the right-hand side of the cover until they pick it up. Because the purpose of cover blurbs is to get browsers to pick up your magazine, the blurbs have to be on the left or across the top, where they might peek out over a shorter magazine on the shelf.

Hello Out There!

The purpose of pull quotes, cover blurbs, and the like is to entice readers' attention. But magazines have other tools that serve other purposes as well, and all must be written or edited by editors.

One such tool is the letter from the editor in chief. Not all magazines have such a feature; some editors feel that the space can be better used for advertising, articles, or some other material. The magazines that publish a letter from the editor do so because the editors feel that it makes the magazine more personal, more homey, more friendly. It's a chance for the editor to speak directly to readers—an opportunity not found elsewhere in the magazine—and it lets the editor explain some of the thinking behind the editorial decisions represented in the issue.

There are no rules for these letters. They often are written by the editor in chief, but they are occasionally ghostwritten by someone else on the staff. They usually are informal, conversational, and cheerful, but they also can be thoroughly researched presentations advocating a particular position or making a particular argument. (For an example, see the pieces that Louis Lapham writes in *Harper's*.)

I think the only major considerations for these letters are that they not be too hokey—not overdone with the "aw, shucks," "hey y'all" informality that reeks of affectation—and that they not be overly self-serving, trying to make the magazine look like a cutting-edge player in the international sphere of modern communication. Readers are savvy enough to know that the editor's letter is not un-biased, and laying it on too thick only inspires them to roll their eyes and put the magazine down.

Return Fire

Just as the editor may, if she wishes, write a letter to readers, most magazines also publish letters *from* readers.

The reasons for the "Letters" department are strong. Letters from readers can bring about a dialogue—or even a debate—that the rest of the readership will find interesting. They bring fresh voices and perspectives into the magazine. They give readers a chance at the last word. And they offer solid proof that the magazine is being read and that it is provoking thought and initiating discussions.

Most editors, if they don't start out with a policy about letters to the editor, develop one quickly. The opportunity for problems and headaches is big, and a clear, consistent policy can prevent a lot of hassles.

Several key points should be addressed in a good letters policy.

• *Length.* Without a limit on the length of letters from readers, you run the risk—which will become a reality—of readers sending in enormous missives, diatribes, rants, position papers, dissertations, and other documents. These submissions are almost always highly biased, weakly supported, and of little interest to your readership.

If you put a cap on the length of letters—say, 150 words or so—you can reject the manifestoes and keep the "Letters" department lively and engaging.

• *Factual accuracy.* Most magazines want to inform and enlighten their readers, and this can't be done unless the information being printed is accurate. Even though the material in the "Letters" department did not originate with the magazine's writers and editors, the magazine has a responsibility to its readers to print the truth.

On the surface, this restriction seems easy. If a reader sends in a letter arguing that Canada is actually part of the Asian continent, you can dismiss it rather quickly.

But it can get sticky in a hurry. If a reader submits a letter that insists that Mars is populated by creatures who keep shooting down the rockets and probes we send there, the situation is a bit dicey. The reader probably can't offer any proof that these creatures exist, but you can't offer any proof that they don't. In the absence of contrary evidence, can you say that a letter is factually incorrect?

The solution, of course, is to require letter writers to support their claims when challenged. If they can't back up their statements, then you decline to run the letter.

Stickier still are issues of interpretation. Several organizations still insist that the Holocaust never happened, and they send letters to editors at a staggering rate. These people "support" their claims with "evidence" that they say is valid, and they won't be dissuaded by any evidence that you produce to the contrary. Now you're in a clash of views. The Holocaust did happen, of course, and we all know that—but these revisionists won't back down.

Bottom line: there will be times when your decision to reject a letter will be met with screams of anger and accusations of bias, censorship, and even conspiracy.

And the only proper response is to hang up the phone, toss the letter in the recycling bin, and move on. There are worse things in this world than upsetting a bunch of Holocaust deniers.

• *Tone.* Good policies include a statement in which the editors reserve the right to edit letters to remove offensive language or comments. The off-limits comments can—and probably should—include personal attacks against anyone at the magazine, another letter writer, and anyone mentioned in the articles. The debates should be focused on the issues and should not be allowed to devolve into name-calling sessions.

• *Style*. This catch-all term allows editors to correct spelling and punctuation, fix bad grammar, and make other mechanical alterations without the letter writers complaining that the editors changed their letters without permission.

• *Topic/content*. Some magazines also insist that the letters they publish relate to an article or a letter that previously appeared in the magazine. In other words, readers can't send in material that introduces a new topic just because it's on their minds.

Other magazines deliberately dismiss such a rule, on the theory that readers who want to write in with a particular question or comment should feel free to do so—the more, the merrier.

Roll Out the Barrel

Another common task for editors is overseeing the section of the magazine I like to call the accordion. This section is filled with short, funny or punchy mini-articles on a wide range of often offbeat topics.

These sections go by many names. *Yankee* calls its accordion section "Quips, Quotes & Queries." I've also seen "Etc.," "Miscellanea," and other titles.

I refer to these sections as accordions because they provide a valuable service for editors: they can expand or contract at the last minute.

So if the three-page article you were planning comes in at a solid four pages—and it's worth every word—no problem. You just take a page out of the accordion section. If the three-pager comes in at two pages, and it covers the topic well, that's fine too. Just add a page to the accordion section, and you're in good shape.

A brief discussion about the printing process will make the significance of this adjustment clearer. Most magazines are printed in *signatures*. A signature is a set of pages—typically eight or sixteen—that comes off the press. The pages are printed this way because the rollers that ink the paper can hold four or eight pages at a time. Printing on both sides of the paper, then, gets you eight or sixteen pages from just two rollers. If you added even one page to the set, you'd need an additional pair of rollers.

This means that editors can't add or subtract just one page whenever they want to. They have to hit multiples of eight or sixteen; the whole magazine has to be thirty-two, forty, forty-eight, fifty-six, sixty-four (you get the point) pages long to be cost effective. So when an article comes in too long or too short, either it must be adjusted to fit the space or something else in the magazine has to give.

Hence the beauty of the accordion section. You can't easily hack off a page from some other article, but you can drop a page from "Quips, Quotes & Queries" with ease—you just save that handful of mini-articles for the next issue.

But, of course, someone has to create all those mini-articles, and it's usually the editor's job to either write them or assign the writing to staffers and freelancers. It's a bit of a chore; with so many little topics, the amount of work per word actually goes *up* compared with a long article.

Stand Aside

Sometimes, an article needs a little company. If some facet of the topic requires a bit of extra explanation, or if some tangent is worth exploring but isn't appropriate for the main article, a sidebar might be in order.

Sidebars are small companion articles that are printed—usually in a special box, or with a larger typeface—next to the actual article.

The article

The reason that our unmanned spacecraft keep on "vanishing" when they reach Mars is that aliens on the planet's surface are shooting them down. These aliens—who, of course, aren't considered aliens on Mars itself—possess sophisticated technology that enables them to track and destroy incoming spacecraft with ease. They allowed the first few spacecraft to land and roam around because they were curious about our civilization and our intent. Now that they know that we have a history of conquering any new territory we find, these Martians are determined to keep us off their planet.

The sidebar

Can We Talk with the Martians?

We have made several efforts to communicate with aliens in the past. Two of the *Voyager* spacecraft left . . .

Readers who are interested in the sidebar can read it easily, but the information in the sidebar doesn't get in the way of the main article. Sidebars are especially useful if an article topic carries a lot of "heavy cargo": history, background, technical explanations, statistics, and the like. That material can be shunted off into a sidebar, leaving the main article uncluttered and easy to read.

Often, the writer of the main article is asked to write any necessary sidebars as part of the original assignment. But sometimes, the idea for the sidebar comes later, after the writer has completed and submitted the article. Then the editor has to ask the writer to create the sidebar (usually for an additional amount of money), assign it to another writer, or write it herself.

Sneak Preview

The last major part of magazines that we'll discuss here is the table of contents. The "ToC" is more than just a guide to the page numbers; it represents yet another opportunity for the magazine to entice readers to buy—and spend time with—the magazine.

So the contents should go beyond just a rundown of headlines and their starting pages. The entries on this page should make the articles sound as appealing and intriguing as possible.

Often, the table of contents is broken into sections—Features and Departments offer a logical division—with the sections even published on separate pages if necessary. (Because the front of the magazine is valuable "real estate" for advertising, printing the parts of the table of contents on separate pages can make financial sense as well. Doing so expands the front section, creating more pages for expensive ads.)

Within each section, editors usually include each article's title and a brief teaser to draw readers inward:

Features

I Was Trapped in Quicksand, by Myron Reynolds

Mired up to his neck in slimy, oozing quicksand—knowing that at any moment he could be swallowed up and lost forever—Myron Reynolds had to struggle against the urge to struggle . . . . page 24

Identify Poisonous Snakes by Their Bites, by Wilma Dunwitty
If the snake that bit you slithered off before you got a good look at it, you
can still tell the ER doctors what kind it was . . . . page 30

Out on a Limb, by Frank Barclay
Chased up a tree by a large grizzly, Frank Barclay held on for dear life until
help arrived thirty-six long hours later . . . . page 34

One point of debate among editors has to do with the wording of
an article's title. Some editors insist that the title listed in the table of
contents be the same as the one on the opening page of the article.
That way, they reason, readers can be sure they've found the right article.

Others maintain that by making the wording different, you create
two different opportunities to capture a reader's attention. If "Out on
a Limb" on the contents page didn't appeal to a particular reader,
perhaps "A Grizzly Chewed My Shoes" on page 34 will inspire him to
read.

One additional small note: the top of the table of contents page
should read "Contents," not "Table of Contents." It's presenting the
contents themselves, and the format—the table—is not what's important.

The Small Stuff

Editors have to concoct a handful of other, very small items that appear in the magazine. These don't take a whole lot of creative
thought, but they do require accuracy.

• *Masthead.* The masthead is the rundown of the people who
work for the magazine. It lists everyone from the editor in chief
down to the interns. Mastheads often include the publishing and
business people, too, but not always.

• *Contributors' bios.* Some magazines put small descriptions of
their writers—background, education, interests, previous articles in
the magazine, and other biographical information—on a special
contributors' page; some put the appropriate description on the
first page of each article; some don't run them at all. The key with

these, which are often written by the writers themselves, is to make sure you don't introduce any errors. Contributors hate it when you describe them incorrectly.

• *Teasers.* On the last page, on the table of contents page, or at some other designated point, some magazines print teasers about articles coming in future issues. The point of teasers is to encourage people to buy the next issue—or to subscribe, so they don't have to worry about missing any of the cool stuff. Editors write them, and they have to conjure up their most sizzling promotional voice to do them well.

• *Legal.* The legal is the small-type paragraph that tells the world who publishes the magazine, how often it comes out, where to write for subscription or circulation problems, and other information required by law to appear in magazines.. Incredibly boring copy, but someone has to write it and make sure it's correct.

• *Jump lines.* Now we're down to the truly small stuff, but it's important anyway. Jump lines are the little phrases that indicate when an article is "jumping" to another page—in other words, when it is continued on a page later in the magazine. No one ever won a Pulitzer for writing great jump lines—they're pretty much "continued on page 42" and "continued from page 28," sometimes with a little mini-title attached—but readers get really ticked when the jump line says "continued on page 42" and they discover that page 42 is nothing but an ad for hair coloring. Once again, accuracy is the key—they have to be written and checked just before printing.

• *Folios.* Folios are the page numbers. If they have words next to them—the name of the magazine, a keyword from the article's title—they are known as running heads or feet, depending on whether they appear at the top or the bottom of the page.

• *Bylines.* Get a writer's byline wrong, and you've probably just lost a writer.

All these parts of a magazine—from the grand to the tiny—are either written or assigned (and checked) by editors, and the quality of a magazine often can be gauged by the quality of these fine details.

The best editors remember that it's the little things that can get you, and so they take the time and annoying trouble to make sure that all these items are strong.

15. The Business of Editing:
How to Recognize Success Without
Looking Overly Surprised

I never know for sure [whether we're doing a good job]. I get
some idea from the mail, and from noticing how many good
writers want to be in our pages.

William Whitworth, editor, *The Atlantic*

Bottom-line reality time: magazine publishing is a business. Sure,
some magazines are published by not-for-profit groups that support
them through dues and other means, but the vast majority of magazines have to bring in more money than they spend—or they shut
down. Publishing is a profit-based business, for the most part, and
wise editors take that reality to heart.

This does not mean that publishing is necessarily cold-blooded.
Making a profit is a simple and relatively harmless by-product of functioning in the modern world. And magazines with the best intentions—magazines that were created to help alleviate world hunger,
for example, to reduce the number of highway-traffic fatalities, to
bring comfort and healing to victims of child abuse, or to promote
the ethical treatment of animals—cannot continue to publish if they
cannot pay for ink, paper, electricity, office space, editors, writers, and
designers. One way or another, magazines have to earn money to remain alive, and they can't bring about positive and much-needed
change in this world if they can't publish the next issue.

Typically, magazines are run by publishers, and publishers are
(one hopes) insightful business thinkers. These people watch the bottom line, they make decisions about expenditures based on the benefit that spending will bring to the corporation, and they work hard

> Magazines are in the biz of making money. If you don't sell 40 percent
> of your newsstand copies, you won't last. So you have to make the
> coverlines compelling, the cover image sell a promise. If you don't
> have enough ads in your magazine, you'll fold hard and fast. So, you
> have to deliver the readers. And you deliver the readers by giving them
> what they want. Editorial, Advertising, and Circulation are the three
> legs of the magazine stool. Can't have one without the others.
>
> **Jeff Csatari, executive editor, *Men's Health***

to find new streams of revenue to ease the constant financial pinch
that most magazines feel. Sound, solid magazines have good publishers at the helm.

The publisher, responsible, as always, for the financial health of
the magazine, hires the editor in chief. Some magazines, especially
small ones, combine the publishing and editing jobs into one position. This is usually a bad idea, however, because the skills necessary
to run a successful business and the skills necessary to edit a good
magazine are rarely found in one person. In fact, the two positions
are somewhat at odds, making their harmonious union a long-odds
proposition.

The publisher also hires an advertising manager, which gives the
magazine its initial breakdown: editorial on one side, and advertising
on the other. The heads of both departments report to the publisher;
the advertising manager typically does not (as many people think)
answer to the editor.

Then the publisher hires the third member of the triumvirate: the
circulation manager. Sometimes, this job is farmed out to an external
company, but one way or another, someone has to be responsible for
selling subscriptions, getting the magazine onto the newsstand
shelves, and making sure that every subscriber receives the magazine
promptly every month. (Sometimes, this job is broken down even
further, with the circulation manager working to increase subscriptions and newsstand sales, and the distribution manager working to
get every copy of the magazine into the right hands efficiently.)

Editorial, advertising, circulation/distribution—these are the major
departments at most magazines. This book focuses on just one of
those departments, but no editor can afford to ignore the other two.

> The business side has virtually no effect on the editorial of *American Archaeology*. But I have worked for magazines where there was virtually no separation between the advertising and editorial departments.
>
> **Michael Bawaya, editor, *American Archaeology***

Savvy editors pay close attention to advertising and circulation, working steadily to make the product (bizspeak for the "magazine") desirable and successful for a specific audience.

The Great Wall

Many editors are quick to point out the Great Wall that separates advertising from editorial. This wall allows the editorial side of the magazine to make decisions and choose stories and angles without worrying about what the advertisers might think.

This separation has both ethical and practical sides. On the ethical side, we have to remember that readers count on us for unbiased, honest information. If we promoted the products and services of the highest bidder—regardless of quality, safety, or value—we would be betraying that trust.

On the practical side, readers would figure out pretty quickly that the magazine was just a mouthpiece for a handful of wealthy corporations. Once that happened, they would go elsewhere for their information—and then those audiences that the advertisers wanted so badly would be gone. And the magazine would be gone as well, abandoned by the very advertisers we were trying to serve.

While the Great Wall that separates advertising and editorial exists for the good of the magazine, some magazines have higher walls than others. Those whose walls are easily scaled have made that choice for several reasons.

For one thing, editors want to know what the advertising people are doing. If, for example, a company bought space in the magazine

> The business side and the editorial side are church and state here. The ad guys are not even in the same town. They sell ads, we produce editorial, and we never do stories in conjunction with advertisers.
>
> **Steve Spence, managing editor, *Car and Driver***

and planned to run an ad that would be thoroughly offensive to the readers, violate the magazine's mission, or make fun of things that the magazine holds dear, the editor wants to know about it—and you can bet that she'll be in the publisher's office in a heartbeat screaming about the horrific lapse of judgment that took place on the other side of the wall. But it's far better to have a showdown in the publisher's office than to open the magazine and find, right next to the brilliant article about the dangers of alcoholism, a full-page ad for single-malt Scotch. So editors might thump on their sturdy wall with satisfaction, but they peek over the top all the time.

And, in turn, the advertising people want to know what the editors are up to. If the editor decides to publish a cluster of articles about great vacation spots on the Florida beaches, the ad gang would like to know that, so they can ring up the folks selling Teva sandals, Coppertone sunscreen, Florida condos, New York–Miami airplane flights, itsy-bitsy-teeny-weenie bikinis, and (probably) tequila and the mixes

This is a very fine line to walk for any publication, but it is especially so for a special-interest magazine like ours. We want very much to publish a certain kind of material, but some of our advertisers would like us to publish things more supportive of their goals.

This is the first and most complex dilemma that any publisher faces, and it amounts in its worst form to a kind of media bribery. The advertisers basically say: "If you write something on X, we'll advertise in your magazine."

The pressure on advertising space salespeople, who make their living selling space to these companies, is unbelievable. And pretty soon they have difficulty distinguishing between making a living and preserving their magazine's journalistic integrity.

And here is why the editorial and the advertising departments tend to be in conflict with each other. They both want different things, and they both feel their objectives are legitimate.

In fact, most magazines, including ours, could not get along without advertising. But we make a distinction between commerce and editorial integrity. We have to. If we started publishing puff pieces for our advertisers, our circulation base would shrink fast.

Jon Wilson, editor, *WoodenBoat*

for margaritas. The editorial idea presents a big opportunity for the advertising people, and they hate to miss big opportunities.

So some magazines maintain a wall that keeps pressures on one side from overly affecting operations on the other—but that is low enough to let the two sides peek over every now and then.

For some magazines, the wall is even less than solid in the most sacred of areas: advertising influence over editorial decisions. More and more, advertising does influence the editorial content at certain publications, mainly because of financial pressures. Imagine it: Coca-Cola rings up your magazine. If you agree to print a guide to great summer beverages in your next issue, and you promise to say nice things about Coke products and leave Pepsi completely out of the picture, Coca-Cola will not only take out a long-term advertising contract, but pay your very top rates.

To an editor, this is financial blackmail. An outrage! Horrific! "Not a chance," we say to the publisher. "Our readers would never forgive us."

"The readers wouldn't even notice," the ad manager shoots back. "No one is going to say, 'Hey, where are the Pepsi products?' They'll just enjoy a nice article about good drinks—and we'll land a huge ad contract."

The publisher sighs. The cost of printing has been going through the roof, driven upward by zooming paper costs. All the editors want raises. All the writers want raises. The computers are getting old and cranky, and the microwave in the employees' lounge just burst into flames when Harold tried to nuke a foil-wrapped TV dinner in it. That ad contract starts to look awfully tempting, and the "harm" to readers seems to be pretty minimal.

And so it goes. Increasingly, advertising is calling the shots at some magazines. Not entirely, you understand; the arguments about the loss of readers are valid. Few people are willing to pay to sub-scribe to a catalog of products. But some magazines are gearing their editorial content more and more to suit the desires of their major ad-vertisers, rather than the desires of their readers.

Does this mean that good-quality editing is doomed? Are editors being reduced to hucksters for big corporations? Not entirely. What it does mean is that editors must sharpen their arguments for why the wall is a good thing—and then use those arguments as often as necessary to keep the wall from crumbling.

Truth on Advertising

Editors don't have to know about every little corner of the advertising world, but some key aspects of the business are worth learning about.

• *Tough come, easy go.* Editors always feel that they are the heart and soul of the magazine, but when viewed from a business perspective, things change a bit. The business reality is that the advertising side of a magazine brings in money, and the editorial side spends it.

Editors get paid. Editors pay writers, copy editors, proofreaders, and others. The editorial side of a magazine costs a lot of money—and it doesn't directly bring in a dime. All it does, as some advertising people see it, is fill up the space between the important parts of the magazine: the ads.

The advertising people, however, get paid only if they bring in the bucks. Some positions are salaried; others are commissioned. Either way, if the advertising people don't bring in a lot more money than they require for themselves, they all get fired or the magazine goes under. To the advertising staff, the real game is played on their side of the wall. The editorial side is just the cleverness that gets the readers to open the magazine and see the ads in the first place.

• *Size matters.* If you ask people why some magazines are thick and others aren't, many of them will tell you that some editors have more material to publish than do others. It's simple enough: more stuff to publish = bigger magazine.

It's simple, but it's wrong. Editors always have more ideas, more submissions, and more suggestions than they know what to do with. Part of an editor's job is to filter through all that material to find the very best articles and ideas for their magazines.

So it's not the case that editors of those thin magazines don't have enough articles. Thanks to a nation full of eager freelancers, they have a near-infinite amount of material at their disposal.

Magazines are thick or thin because of their advertising. In general, most magazines want at least 50 percent of their total acreage devoted to ads. So if the ad people sell 24 pages of advertising for the June issue, that issue will be 48 pages long. If the ad gang sells 80 pages of ads, the poor postal carriers will be delivering a bunch of 160-page magazines that month.

This relationship between ad sales and magazine size has direct implications for editors. The more space the ad people sell, the more space the editors have to fill—and more space is good. Editors have a lot of great stuff they want to publish, and heartbreak happens when you have to kill a fantastic article because you just don't have room for it.

So smart editors are rooting for their advertising counterparts. When the ad people do well, the magazine gets more money and the editors get more space. Everyone is happy.

That Great Wall between advertising and editorial, then, is not always an impenetrable barrier. Editors don't want to be affected by advertising pressures, but do want the ad people to do well.

Of course, the best way editors can help the advertising side is to produce a fascinating, can't-put-it-down magazine each month. With a great editorial product comes a large readership. With a large readership come higher advertising rates *and* more companies eager to advertise in the magazine. With soaring ad revenue comes better pay for editors, better pay for writers, better pay for photographers, and for everyone else who puts together the magazine.

It's all good.

• *The thrill of the chase.* Later in this chapter, we'll talk about how editors know whether they're doing a good job. It can be tricky, sometimes, to tell.

For the advertising people, it isn't tricky at all. More money = good. Less money = bad. It's a simple and very clear report card.

This reality is one of the main reasons that editors and ad people don't always understand each other. To editors, the thrill lies in coming up with a great article idea, finding a terrific writer to do it, managing that writer well, and winding up with a piece in the magazine that brings tears to readers' eyes and makes them flood the mailboxes with passionate and resounding letters.

To the ad folk, that's all a bit flaky. The thrill on this side of the wall lies in developing a relationship with a major corporation, convincing the right people that advertising in your magazine will help their business efforts, and closing the deal with a contract that brings in a pile of cash to the magazine.

Editors have to declare victory. Advertising people can prove it.

• *Real effects.* More on that commission point: wise editors never forget that for many of the ad folks, their income is directly linked to their sales. In other words, if they land a lot of big contracts, they make a lot of money. If they don't, their paychecks shrink immediately—and eventually they are replaced by people who are better able to make some dough.

There's no point in being maudlin about the situation; they chose to take those jobs. But it is useful to remember that editorial decisions can have very real consequences for the advertising people. When Coke makes its dramatic offer of a large ad contract in exchange for a cheerful (and exclusive) focus in an article about summer drinks, that contract means more than just another pipeline of cash for the company. It also means that Karen over in ad sales will get the money she needs to repaint her house, pay off a credit card, or help send her kids to college.

Again, no weeping for Karen. But if you take a stand against the Coke deal—as most editors would—don't expect flowers and chocolates from Karen for a while.

Please, Don't Go!

The circulation leg of the magazine tripod matters enormously as well, and smart editors pay attention to the people in this department, too.

The reality on this side of the equation is that magazines will always lose readers: they die, their finances change, they go through periods of upheaval that make them cancel or drop all magazines, and so on.. So the circulation manager has to continually bring in new readers.

That's a tough job. For every reader who bids a magazine farewell, the circulation manager has to find more than one reader who agrees to subscribe. And every month, the circulation manager is expected to find more newsstands and convince them to carry the magazine, to display it well, to prop up little cardboard promotional figures, to stick special signs in their windows, and generally to help convince readers that they have to have this magazine.

Circulation managers—and their staffs—go about trying to get new readers in several ways.

• *Freebies.* Studies have shown that once someone subscribes to a magazine, he usually keeps the subscription for a while. That means that the real goal is to get readers to subscribe in the first place.

So the circulation people come up with rewards to entice readers to subscribe to the magazine. Sign up now, and we'll give you 50 percent off our regular subscription price. (Of course, that offer won't apply when you renew your subscription—but by then, they hope, you'll be hooked.) Sign up now, and we'll give you a free tote bag (or book, sweatshirt, or pair of sunglasses). Sign up now, and we'll give you a chance to win a new car, a trip to Florida, a big bag of cash.

These promotions work reasonably well—that's why you keep seeing them. But they also shift the focus a bit. Ideally, editors want readers to subscribe because the magazine is so compelling that they have no other choice. But if that doesn't work, the occasional tote bag can sometimes get the job done.

• *Direct-mail appeals.* Direct mail includes the postcards, letters, and other come-ons that arrive unannounced in your mailbox, urging you to take advantage of an incredible offer to subscribe to this incredible magazine right now! Direct mail is used because it is relatively inexpensive and can cover a large number of potential subscribers. Its success rate, however, is depressingly low: if you mail 100,000 pitches, you'll be lucky to get 2,000 people to subscribe. That means that 98,000 people took a look at that materials that you slaved over and paid for—and tossed them into the recycling bin.

Still, 2,000 subscribers is a pretty decent number, and they can help replace the ones you lost to attrition.

One of the side effects of the direct-mail advertising business is the creation of targeted lists. How do you find the 100,000 people to mail to in the first place? If you are trying to get people to subscribe to a magazine about mountain biking, you probably don't want to waste your time and money on certain types of people: the elderly, the sedentary, and others unlikely to participate in this sport. So how do you increase the chances that your mailing will end up in the hands of someone who might actually be interested?

Quite a few companies exist just to create these targeted lists. For a (hefty) fee, they will provide you with the names and addresses of

100,000 people who can reasonably be assumed to be true potential subscribers. Some of them might be subscribers to other outdoor, action-oriented magazines. Some of them might have entered a sweepstakes to win a new mountain bike (or four-wheel-drive SUV, camping gear, or a trip to the Grand Tetons). Some of them recently purchased backpacks, scuba gear, or fanny-pack hydration systems. Some of them recently reserved rooms at lodges in Yellowstone, seats on a flight to Machu Picchu, or the services of a bush pilot on the North Slope.

These companies use this information to provide lists to a wide range of businesses, including magazines. And as a result, the envelope ends up in the hands of 100,000 somewhat predisposed potential subscribers, 2 percent of whom (on a good day) actually say yes.

• *On-air advertising.* On-air advertising is not the most cost-effective option, but it can make a splash. This approach involves creating a commercial for broadcast on television or radio. Such an advertisement is expensive to make, and air time is expensive to buy—although radio is substantially cheaper than television—and the results are varied. But a broadcast campaign can liven up a magazine's marketing effort significantly.

• *Newspaper advertising.* Newspaper ads are cheaper to make and run than are broadcast ads, and you have the added advantage of being able to track the campaign's effectiveness carefully. You could, for example, offer a coupon in a major metropolitan daily, and then see how many of the coupons are actually mailed back to you by people wanting to subscribe. You can then be confident of the response that the ad generated. (Of course, the actual response will be a bit higher; some people will subscribe without bothering with the coupon, some people will lose the coupon but go ahead and subscribe anyway, some people will retain a positive impression of the magazine and then respond to a later campaign, and such). You also can create phantom mailing addresses—you'll often see them listed as "Department WP" or "Suite SFB." These lines in the addresses mean nothing to the post office, but they signal to the magazine that the reader was responding to the ad in the *Washington Post* or the *Sacramento Bee.*

• *In-magazine advertising.* One of the best ways to convert newsstand buyers into subscribers is through advertising in your own magazine. The potential subscriber already has demonstrated an interest in the magazine—she's holding it in her hands—and she probably is thinking that it just might be easier and cheaper to go ahead and subscribe.

In-magazine advertising takes several forms. One kind is the simple one-page ad, touting the virtues of the magazine and offering new subscribers an irresistible discount. But anyone inspired by that ad is going to have to dig out her checkbook, find an envelope somewhere, fish a stamp out from the bottom of the junk drawer in the kitchen, cut out the subscription form from the magazine page, and put it all together and mail it. (Or—she'll have to fire up the computer, navigate to your Web site, dig out a credit card, worry that hackers are going to steal her number, send it anyway, and hope that it all went through.) That might be too much trouble; she'll do it "some other time."

That's why magazines use subscription cards. These cards are preaddressed to the subscription department of the magazine's business office, they are postage paid, and they need only a name and an address. The customer will be billed later, so there's no need for checkbooks or credit cards. Just a name and an address—and drop it in the mail. Subscribing with these cards is much easier than mailing off a standard form, and so more potential customers follow through.

But how do you get readers to notice the cards? The cards are somewhat attention getting because the magazine tends to fall open to them; their stiffness acts as a marketing tool. But readers might just ignore the cards and read the magazine without paying attention to the delicious deal being offered to new subscribers. Now what do you do?

Enter the blow-in machine. Most major printers have a device that blows loose cards into the pages of a magazine; these are the cards that flutter out when you skim through the pages. You turn the page, a card falls to the floor, you bend down to pick it up, you hunt around for the nearest recycling bin, you toss the card into the bin, another card falls to the floor—the cards are annoying, but that's part of the point. Studies have shown that the more time you spend with that card in your hand, the more likely you are to read it. And when you read it, and see that you can get the magazine you already like for 85 percent off the cover price, you figure it's worth it and put your name down.

• *Phone banks.* Phone banks are staffed by the dreaded telemarketers, who call during dinner and never seem to get your name right.

Telemarketers actually deliver a relatively high percentage of sales, compared with some of the other options. So even though people find them irritating, some magazines use them to build a subscription base. They are even more effective when linked with a freebie promotion: "Subscribe to *Cottonballs and QTips* now, Mrs. Henderson, and we'll send you a free *Cottonballs and QTips* spatula!"

The reason telemarketers call during the dinner hour, of course, is that most people are home then. It costs money to have two dozen people just sitting at phones and dialing numbers when no one answers, so they time the calls for the greatest odds. They don't much care that they annoy people. What they want is the chance to pitch their spiel.

Telemarketing might be on the decline in the coming years, as more and more people take steps to fight the intrusive calls. People are letting their answering machines pick up calls during dinner, for example, or they're using caller ID to find out if the call is from a friend or relative.

And some states—Indiana and New York, for example—are instituting laws that allow people to sign up for "no call" lists, meaning that telemarketers are forbidden from calling these numbers. The federal version, the Do-Not-Call Implementation Act, has been challenged but is being refined by Congress, so telemarketing might begin to fade into history.

• *Subscription houses.* You might already have won! The Publishers Clearing House and other companies offer subscription services for magazines. These services put the magazine's pitch in front of people in exchange for a percentage of the subscription price.

And to get people to open the envelope, they offer sweepstakes that give people a chance to win $10 million, a new car, or some other great prize. The odds of winning are often very similar to the odds of winning one of the multistate lottery games—in other words, *very small*—but people send in their entries and hope for the best anyway.

Many of the subscription houses make their contests difficult to enter. They don't mind if you enter; in fact, your entry gives them a confirmed name and address for future marketing efforts. The reason that these contests make you find and tear out stamps, lick them, put them in certain places, scratch the coating off little cards to reveal special numbers, and scores of other gimmicks is the same as the reason for the blow-in subscription cards: the more time you spend with the subscription materials, the more likely you are to actually subscribe to a magazine.

Stop Where You Are!

Replacing a steady exodus of subscribers can be difficult, and, of course, the real job is to bring in readers *faster* than you lose them. So in addition to bringing in new subscribers, circulation managers are constantly trying to hang onto the subscribers they have.

The main tool for keeping subscribers, of course, is a great magazine. If people love the magazine, they'll renew their subscriptions no matter what. But circulation managers have to do all they can to keep the numbers moving ever upward, so they take several active steps.

• *Push continually for renewal.* Often, just a few weeks after you subscribe to a magazine, you'll get a letter that says something like "The time is NOW to renew your subscription to *Goldfish and Guppies!*" The writers of that letter, of course, don't mean that your subscription is about to expire. That won't happen for months. What they mean is that they would really, really like it if you would hand over another chunk of money and extend your subscription by another year. This obviously works, at least to a small degree, because circulation managers continue to do it.

• *Offer multiyear subscriptions.* Many of the subscription offers you'll see give you an extra break if you sign up for more than one year. The logic is obvious: if they can get you for two years, that's one more person they won't have to replace in twelve months.

• *Offer continual subscriptions.* Some circulation managers even offer continual renewals. The deal is that you give the magazine your credit card number, and the business folk whack it each year

> We have one report card we watch: our renewal rate. With the exception of the effect of the *Enola Gay* controversy, which caused some cancellations, we have been happily pulling in a composite renewal rate of roughly 70 to 75 percent.
>
> **George C. Larson, editor, *Air & Space***

until you tell them to stop. Of course, they'll whack it at the highest rate that the magazine charges, unless you have some agreement worked out in advance. The advantage to the subscribers, though, is that they get the magazine without interruption and don't have to worry about renewing each year just to keep the magazine coming to their doors.

• *Listen to the customers.* Circulation people often get the letters that say, "How dare you publish something that scandalous / offensive / outrageous / liberal / conservative / masculine / feminine / whatever! Cancel my subscription immediately!" Smart circulation managers relay that information to the editors, to make sure that decisions about content are made with the understanding that some choices result in the loss of subscribers.

Editorial Report Card

The advertising and circulation people have pretty simple measures of success—they can look at revenue and readership. But how do editors know when they're doing a good job? How can we be confident that we are on the right track?

It's difficult to determine how successful you are as an editor, but there are at least two good reasons for making sure you do it. First, your dreams for the magazine depend on it. If your goal for your magazine is to achieve some major social change, help people

> I would say, first and foremost, if I'm meeting my own standards, I believe I'm doing a good job. And if readers are writing a lot of complimentary letters to the editor, my boss gives me a fat raise, and the magazine is winning awards, I'm probably doing OK.
>
> **Michael Bawaya, editor, *American Archaeology***

> We know we're doing a good job when a good number of readers write to tell us they liked the articles that didn't turn out as well as we hoped they would. We also know we're doing a good job when we get great joy and satisfaction from what we do.
>
> **Gerry Bishop, editor, *Ranger Rick***

through difficult times, educate children, or make retirement easier to manage—you obviously won't accomplish those goals if you aren't doing a good job as editor.

And there's another strong reason for creating a way to measure your own success. Publishers are responsible for the financial success of the company—primarily, it involves looking at the profit margin and seeing whether it is rising or falling—and should the trend move in the wrong direction, you can expect an unpleasant meeting to take place. Editors who are caught off guard by this downturn can find themselves "promoted out of the organization." Editors who can determine for themselves whether they are doing well can see negative trends coming and can take actions—in advance of calamity—to correct problems.

If a magazine's revenues are waning, for example, and the publisher wants an explanation, a prepared editor will be able to acknowledge the problems and describe the solutions that *she already has put in place* to get the magazine on track. These solutions might include a redesign, a shift in editorial focus, a change in tone, or another alteration that the editor believes will correct the slide. Armed with information and a plan, she will be in much better shape than if she simply said to her boss, "Gee, I didn't realize things were that bad. I guess I'll have to look into it." An editor who responds that

> You know you're doing a good job when you read your own magazine and you are proud of what you've done. You know you are *not* doing a good job when you wish your name wasn't on the article or the masthead. Another way of knowing you are doing well is when you get a letter from a reader that says you've made his life better through something you've written or edited.
>
> **Jeff Csatari, executive editor, *Men's Health***

To be honest, we don't always know if we are truly, or completely, serving our readership. A group of 950,000 people is bound to have a pretty broad base, and we could never hope to please them all. We get letters of support as well as letters of condemnation. But it isn't our goal or, if I can speak for myself, my goal to please them all. My goal is to use as much creative energy as possible to introduce our readership to the world at large, to increase their understanding of travel and its possibilities for adventure, and to provide thoughtful, well-written editorials. That, I believe, is ultimately my responsibility as an editor.

Jackson Mahaney, associate editor, *Endless Vacation*

weakly probably *won't* have to look into it; instead, she'll have to look into the help-wanted section of the *New York Times*.

Before you can determine whether you're being successful as an editor, you have to define success. For some people, it means BMWs and summer cottages and trophy spouses. For others, it means eternal happiness. Still others might regard it as the completion of specific tasks or goals.

For most magazines, we can define success in two ways. One is the ability to keep the magazine alive. Whatever other goals the magazine might have, nothing will be accomplished by going out of business.

The other is the accomplishment of some outside objectives. Some magazines exist to entertain readers and bring riches to their publishers, for example, while others exist to serve a social good. Either way, they have to have some measurable means for gauging whether they are accomplishing those goals.

At many editors' conferences, I've frequently heard editors say: "If I haven't offended or upset a reader, government official, or company in the past six months, I haven't been doing my job well." I think there's some truth in that. When our company lawyers are concerned about a story we're about to publish, or a legal threat or outside complaint, we search our souls and our backup research files and sometimes make some changes, but that's also when we know we probably have a damn good story and are fulfilling our editorial mission.

Susan Ungaro, editor, *Family Circle*

You know you are doing a good job when you set specific goals for the magazine, and then meet them. You must continually improve the magazine. As to how you are doing, you must make this assessment yourself. Comments from others can be comforting or disturbing, but it is you who must evaluate. Work with other people, not for them or in spite of them.

John McDonald, editor, *Woodwork*

If you decide that your magazine will attempt to reduce the incidence of divorce among American couples, for example, one of your objectives should be the actual—and measurable—reduction in that statistic. Your mission statement might read, "We at *Keep It Together* feel that divorce is a nationwide tragedy. It is our goal to shrink the percentage of marriages that end in divorce by 2 percent each year until more than 75 percent of all American marriages remain intact."

If you hold such a goal as central to the reason you chose to publish a magazine, you should regularly take steps to determine whether you are meeting that goal. Objective, measurable targets allow you to assess your progress and make changes if the outcome is less than you desired.

So editors develop a clear set of objectives:

• Keep the magazine alive.
• Bring in a good return on the publisher's (or the stockholders') investment.
• Reduce the divorce rate in America by 2 percent a year until 75 percent of all American marriages remain intact (or reduce hunger, increase child safety, enhance the pleasure and interest in competitive skiing, or...).
• Offer solid information and useful advice to readers in an interesting and engaging format.
• Provide a good working environment for employees.

Not bad. Those are good objectives. But good objectives aren't enough by themselves. If they were, students could begin each semester with a great objective—"I'm going to get all *A*s this term"—and it would magically happen. Good objectives don't become reality without hard work.

> There are different levels of whether it's been a successful day, whether it's been a great day. On one level, if I see reporters and editors excited about what they're doing, and we have this smooth-running operation where people really feel as if they've produced the best they can—when I see people producing their personal best—it's a real high. When I see a story in the magazine and I realize that we are giving consumers valuable information they can't get anywhere else—it's a real high. When I see a story in the magazine and I realize that we are giving consumers valuable information they can't get anywhere else—it's a real high. Then I can go home and say that "this is a five-blob day," to use *Consumer Reports* vernacular. This is excellent.
>
> **Margot Slade, editor, *Consumer Reports***

One way to gauge success is to trust our own instincts, telling ourselves: "If we think we're doing a good job, we probably are. After all, we're supposed to be the experts. We're supposed to be the professionals. If we can't trust ourselves, who can we trust?"

But personal self-reflection is a dangerous siren. We might be fooled by our own egos, our high hopes, and our flattering friends. Publication of the magazine might mean a small degree of celebrity, with people suddenly interested in what we have to say. We might feel important; we might feel triumphant; we might feel *visionary*. But none of that will necessarily translate into long-term success. To achieve a lasting impact, we have to be able to determine whether our magazine is having the desired effect.

Fortunately, the bright and circumspective editor has several tools at his disposal for gauging his performance.

• *Build an objective measure into the mission statement.* As discussed previously, mission statements are at their best when they offer concrete measures of success. If part of the mission of *Hamster Racing Weekly* is "to promote the sport of hamster racing so that every state in the country has at least two active Hamster Racing Clubs," you'll know whether you're getting the job done. Year 1: hamster-racing clubs only in California and Massachusetts. Year 5: hamster-racing clubs in twenty-two states. Year 10: hamster-racing clubs in thirty-four states. With that trend, you'll know that your publication is at least part of a growing movement—and that the

How do you know when you're doing a good job? Readers will tell you. They will send you "love" mail. They will send you presents (no kidding—I've gotten photos, plastic animals, a handmade disc holder, persimmons, chocolate, a beanie baby and a bunch of other items in thanks).

Cheryl England, founding editor, *MacAddict*

Making sure that *Military History* meets the readers' needs is simple—I read the questionnaires and letters, and if the issues they address are reasonable, I respond to them, both in the Letters column or in the format of future issues. I know how I'm doing by the magazine's sales in proportion to those printed, and from the feedback I get from the readers. My subscribers tend to be a thinking and highly opinionated lot, and they don't hold back when they've a comment to make, pro or con.

Jon Guttman, editor, *Military History*

Sometimes we hear from readers when they especially like or don't like something we publish, and we try to be responsive to their comments. For example, we have received criticism lately for publishing too many sad stories, and we are making an effort to stay away from sad stories for a while.

Gerry Mandel, editor, *Stone Soup*

magazine probably is helping that movement. In fact, it would be safe to assume that the magazine is contributing to the sport's expansion. The editors don't have to guess whether they are doing a good job. The numbers spell success.

• *Get reader feedback.* The readers are the final judges. If they like the magazine, you win. If they don't, you lose. So a lot of editors make sure they have ways of finding out what the readers think of the publication.

Letters to the editor make up an important link between readers' attitudes and editors' minds. As long as letters are coming in, editors are happy. If the letters are full of praise and compliments, that's great. If the letters are full of disagreement and objection, that's not as great—but it's not entirely bad, either. At least people are reading the magazine and responding to its content. If the letters are full of

Reader response through letters, surveys, phone calls. Sometimes we include environmental action postcards in the magazine, asking the reader to take action to protect an area discussed. If many of these are sent, we assume readers responded to the article that accompanied the cards.

Joan Hamilton, editor, *Sierra*

How do I know if the magazine is doing its job? In a word, feedback. Obviously, I hear from my superiors if they are displeased, but I also hear from rank-and-file members. I suspect I get rather more mail than a secular publication editor might receive principally because my magazine serves a special interest and therefore assumes a high level of commitment from its readers than a secular publication might assume.

Richard McMunn, editor, *Columbia*

If you're not doing a good job, readers let you know. Your numbers go down. If you're lucky, they write and tell you what they don't like—and if there are enough of them, it's the tip of an iceberg you'd better watch out for.

Mimi Handler, editor, *Early American Life*

corrections and information that your writers should have included, that's bad—readers will soon turn their attention to a more reliable source of information. Worst of all, though, is when the letters stop coming altogether. If readers don't care enough to write a note or send a quick e-mail, your magazine doesn't matter in their lives. And if it doesn't matter, they'll stop subscribing.

Some magazines also conduct formal surveys, done by phone or mail, in which readers are asked questions about the magazine. One

We know when we're doing a good job by the tenor of the mail we receive. If we get complaints about errors in fact, we know we should have done a better job at fact checking. If we receive commentary from both sides of a controversial issue in equal amounts, we know we've done a reasonably good job of presenting a story.

Fred L. Schultz, editor in chief, *Naval History*

We do not edit by poll, but after each edition appears, we poll by mail, asking our readers to rate each piece. The queries include a question concerning the "faith content" of the issue, i.e. whether it is too weak, too strong or about right. This gives us one good measure of the magazine's health. But nothing beats the renewal rate, which for *Guideposts* is 80 percent or above.

Fulton Oursler, Jr., editor in chief, *Guideposts*

We are strong believers in reader research, and we make sure we are fulfilling our audience's needs through in-magazine surveys, open-ended requests for opinions, focus groups and periodic questionnaires mailed to random samplings of our circulation list. Fortunately, we find that our readers are a very communicative group more than happy to share their thoughts.

Peggy S. Person, associate editor, *Mature Outlook*

of the most common questions is: Which articles from the last issue do you remember? What do you remember about them? If readers can't remember much of the content of the magazine, they obviously aren't paying much attention—and before long, they'll begin to wonder why they're paying for it. Surveys can be formal or informal, tabulated and tallied or simply looked over for a general sense of the situation. However they are done, they can tell editors a great deal about the overall mood of the readership.

Every month, we tabulate readers' opinions concerning articles by looking at the number and nature of their comments, criticisms and commendations. This unsolicited feedback is received in the mail, by phone, and over America Online. Also, after each month's issue is sent out, 800 members, chosen at random, are surveyed for their reactions to the issue's contents. Readers are asked how much of each article they read, whether the coverage left them wanting more (or less). They are also asked to write their impressions—general and specific—of the articles and the magazine in general. We keep a keen eye on this valuable feedback when determining the content of future issues.

Patrick J. McGeehan, research correspondence, *National Geographic*

I know I'm doing a good job because I meet my readers and they tell me how much reading *Entrepreneur* has done for them.

Rieva Lesonsky, vice president and editorial director, Entrepreneur Media Inc.

As a magazine that's primarily controlled circulation, we can't use newsstand sales as a means of determining how well we're doing our job. The focus groups and informal calls, however, do give us a good idea of how we're received by our target demographic.

Brad Pearson, editor, *Heartland USA*

It's gratifying when I get responses from kids (and from parents). It could be 300+ entries to a contest (not bad for a circulation of 6,000), or enthusiastic book reviewers, or a Christmas card from a reader. Often kids will add a line to their Find the Line contest entries: "I love your magazine. Keep up the good work!" or "I liked the Horse Sports in Sports Line" or "I read the whole magazine on the first day—as SOON as I get it in the mail." Thank heavens for e-mail, too—it makes keeping in touch with readers a lot easier!

Mary Clemens Meyer, editor, *On the Line*

Another tool for editors is simple personal contact. Editors do like to get out of the office every now and then—to conferences, to parties, to meetings of various sorts—and readers are rarely shy about offering their opinions no matter what the setting. This steady stream of commentary can be a bit draining, but editors take comfort in the fact that the opinions mean that people are reading and thinking about the magazine. And sometimes, the comments can be quite helpful. Every now and then, an insightful reader will offer a suggestion that makes a lot of sense, and editors rush back to the office eager to try out the new idea. The comments also carry weight when they gang up on editors. The first three people who tell you that they hated that article about tapioca can be ignored; just chalk up their response to personal tastes. But when fifty or a hundred people, one at a time, tell you that the article was awful, it's time to start paying attention.

• *Use focus groups.* As you've probably noticed, gauging your audience's reaction to your magazine is a lot like researching the readers' interests, and focus groups play a role in both tasks. The con-

> We measure our success by the circulation, the results of readership preference studies—focus groups, surveys, and interviews conducted by an independent research company—and reports on readership trends conducted by a major syndicated research firm.
>
> **Cele G. Lalli, editor in chief, *Modern Bride***

cept remains the same, with only a few modifications: gather a small group of randomly selected people—all readers of your magazine—in a comfortable room equipped with video cameras. The moderator engages the members of the group in conversation about the magazine, asking them what they like, what they don't like, what they would like to see, and so on. The conversation is free-flowing, although the moderator guides it toward key questions about the magazine and the readers' reactions to it.

When the session is over and the participants are rewarded and sent home, the videos are studied and the conversation is examined for indications of changes that should be made.

Focus groups are potent tools, but they also are subject to problems. The randomly chosen group might turn out to have one particular bias or another, for example, or a dominant person in the group might steer the conversation in support of his own position. Still, editors can learn a lot from these sessions, and many magazines conduct them.

• *Conduct postmortems.* This rather gruesome-sounding operation involves the editors of the magazine gathering to talk over the issue that just was published. What problems did we run into? What could we have done better? What opportunities did we miss?

> Readers let us know whether we're doing a good job or not. Plus we have regular postmortems to review stories and design, always asking what we could have done better, what did we leave out, etc. If the staff is well versed in the subject matter of the magazine, beyond being good writers or editors, it's fairly clear what kind of job it's done. And we read other magazines—scores of them. Occasionally, we ask outside editors to review our last few issues with us.
>
> **Karan Davis Cutler, managing editor, *Harrowsmith Country Life***

We schedule periodic brainstorming sessions for the editorial and design staffs. In these freewheeling meetings, we critique our own magazine and share examples of things we think other publications are doing right or wrong. The goal is to avoid falling into a *rut by constantly refining* our product and keeping up with current editorial and design trends.

Peggy S. Person, associate editor, *Mature Outlook*

How do you know when you're doing a good job? By monitoring newsstand sales, subscriber renewals, and reviews in the industry press. Also, by listening to each other in critiques following each issue.

Craig Cox, editor, *Utne Reader*

The advantage of a postmortem is that editors can draw on the skills, insights, and expertise of their peers at the magazine. When conducted well, postmortems can offer quick, clear, and honest evaluations of an editor's performance.

But, of course, they also present dangers. If the editors at a magazine don't get along all that well, postmortems can become opportunities for finger-pointing and unpleasant personal attacks. When the sessions devolve in that way, everyone puts up their defensive shields, and no true listening gets done.

Postmortems also run the opposite risk, in which everyone in the room heaps praise and flattery on everyone else. The meeting becomes a back-patting celebration, rather than a critical review of the previous issue.

In short, personal dynamics color the atmosphere of postmortems, and it takes a skilled and astute leader to keep them on the

You should critique issues of all magazines in your subject area to make sure your magazine is a worthy competitor. You should routinely be a magazine reader, studying as many of them as you can, to add to your general knowledge of current magazine style, format, graphics, content.

Bonnie Leman, editor, *Quilter's Newsletter Magazine, Quiltmaker,* and *Quilts and Other Comforts*

right track. When they work properly, however, they can both unify the editorial staff and sharpen the magazine's future issues.

• *Keep an eye on the competition.* Editors also pore over their competitors' magazines, looking for stories or angles or themes that should be pursued (or avoided) and for mimicry or other tip-offs that they're on the right track. If you run something in your April issue, and then you see the same approach or idea in your competitor's July issue, you can be pretty confident that you hit an important target. Imitation really is the sincerest form of flattery.

• *Monitor renewal rates.* One of the most consistent and reliable gauges that editors watch is the renewal rate: How many of our current subscribers are happy enough with the magazine to renew their subscriptions for another year?

This tool is valuable for several reasons. First, subscribers who are happy with the magazine tend to resubscribe. Pretty simple. Give them what they want and expect, and they'll keep on coming back. So the renewal rate is a fairly decent measure of how happy the subscribers are.

The renewal rate is also rather uncluttered. Keeping the readers happy is the editor's job, and the renewal rate will reflect that. The number of people who subscribe to the magazine for the first time might also be a reflection of how interesting or compelling or essential the magazine is; if someone reads it in the dentist's office and loves what she sees, she might go home and subscribe. But the first-

We have four forms of readers research: *Reader mail* is one of our best barometers of how we're doing. Our editor in chief can often predict a best-selling issue by the volume of mail we receive. From time to time, we also conduct *focus groups* of people who are reading *Family Circle* to find out how we're doing, or focus groups of people we wish were reading our magazine, to find out why they are not. *We also use [a private research firm].* This company conducts a reader satisfaction poll for us on every issue. It tells us how interesting our readers found each article, sidebar, and even photo in the magazine. And, although it doesn't lead our editorial decisions, it helps us spot trends in interest and also know what works best and what didn't work at all. We also have a *Family Circle Consumer Panel*, which is a revolving group of about 1,000 readers who volunteer to fill out 100-page surveys twice a year. They provide us with answers to questions about everything from their purchasing habits (which is used for marketing and sales research) to telling us how they feel about important social and family issues (which is used by the editors).

Susan Ungaro, editor, *Family Circle*

time subscribers' rate can also be affected by the marketing efforts that the magazines puts forth. If the marketing campaign is powerful—if the promise of T-shirts and tote bags, the offer of dramatic savings, the entry into fantastic sweepstakes, or the lure of sexy stories and photos gets people to subscribe—the number of people who sign up will not really reflect how well the editor is doing. Those new subscribers might be delighted with the tote bags, but they might also become bored or annoyed with the magazine and decide not to re-up. So the renewal rate is a clearer reflection of the editor's success than is the initial subscription rate.

The renewal rate also reflects a serious desire to keep receiving the magazine. Typically, subscribers pay more to renew than they did to sign up in the first place. (And few subscribers can be bothered with canceling their subscriptions and then signing up again, just to save a few bucks.) So the decision to renew indicates a belief that the magazine is worth the current price, even if it's higher than the introductory price—a strong sign of support for the editor.

• *All of the above.* Most editors, of course, want to watch several indicators that will show them when they're on track and when they are straying. Through a subjective blending of these signs, editors can take comfort that they are doing well—or begin to think about changes that have to be made. These editors have multipart answers to the question: How do you know whether you're doing a good job?

• Edward Kosner, editor in chief, *Esquire*: "The audience has grown in syndicated research, renewals are up and so are new-sub sales."

• Jill Benz, reader service editor, *Ladies' Home Journal*: "How do you know if you're doing a good job? The answer is simple: newsstand sales and renewals, as well as the 'letters to the editor' letters that we receive."

• Frances Huffman, editor and publisher, *U. Magazine*: "We generally judge this on response rates to the magazine and letters to the editor. At one point we created a peer council of journalism students to critique the magazine, which gave us a lot of insight."

• David J. Eicher, managing editor, *Astronomy*, and editor, *Explore the Universe*: "When the anecdotal response from readers is very upbeat, circulation is up, lots of articles are getting done that bring new ideas and great images to the readership, and the profitability of the product is solid.

• Beth Renaud, managing editor, *National Gardening*: "Circulation numbers, reader letters, and follow-up surveys."

• John H. Johnson, founder, publisher, and editor, *Ebony*: "First of all, our readers write and call us to express their enjoyment in what we are doing. Secondly, the fact that over

We know we're doing a good job when

(a) we see reaction to what we write in government or reflected in the media,

(b) our subscription rate is high, and

(c) the mail is prolific, but not necessarily, although as we would prefer it, positive.

Matthew Carolan, executive editor, *National Review*

As for how you know you're doing a good job—you never know. That's what makes it interesting and challenging.

Casey Winfrey, editor in chief, American Health

11 million readers give *Ebony* their stamp of approval each month, making *Ebony* the world's largest and most successful Black-owned and oriented magazine, speaks for itself."

• Roanne P. Goldfein, editor, *American Indian Art Magazine*: "I feel that we've done a good job when certain criteria are met: The articles contain more truth than falsehoods and/or more truth than vacuous generalizations; we've kept clear of all political and/or commercial influences; the articles have been reviewed and corrected by as many researchers as possible; when each article has been edited to be as clear as possible and as accessible as possible to as many readers as possible without undermining the author's own idiosyncratic style (no small feat); and when we've been able to protect the article, if you will, from the dangers facing them prior to publication: errors of fact, troublesome organization, bad design or photo selection, bad negatives, bad printing....I think I'd say that it is the publisher who probably feels that happy subscribers are a sign of a job well done. I myself probably judge our success or failure in terms of how much truth is published per issue, whether or not the artwork and authors have been presented to best advantage."

• Bonnie Leman, editor, *Quilter's Newsletter Magazine*, *Quiltmaker*, and *Quilts and Other Comforts*: "It is certainly one of the most important parts of a magazine editor's job to pay close attention to what the readers say. Beyond reading their letters, and in my opinion no editor should fail to do this, doing a yearly readers' survey and studying renewal rates monthly are two major ways of keeping in touch with whether readers think the magazine is meeting their needs. I tell my staff that our renewal rate is our ultimate report card and our readers letters are its lifeblood."

• Tom Slayton, editor, *Vermont Life*: "As long as the magazine remains the best-selling magazine in Vermont (after *TV Guide*) and our renewal rate stays above 70 percent, I'll be pretty sure we are meeting our readers' needs. I'd actually like to try doing some focus groups to make it more appealing to resident Vermonters, especially younger Vermonters. Also, we enter contests with other regional magazines and are one of the consistent winners, having won more than 50 national awards for excellence in the past 10 years. Our professional group, the International Regional Magazine Association (IRMA), is a great help in maintaining and increasing quality. It helps us stay abreast of what our peers in the regional magazine field are doing."

Those perspectives are real and valid, but not everyone insists that gauging success is easy.

16. Final Thoughts:
A Great Job and How to Get It

Magazines, after all, are living creatures—at least those that possess a soul—and they struggle to thrive in a changing and often hostile environment. Sometimes the gene pool is exhausted and a magazine fades away, sometimes a magazine has to suffer a near-death experience in order to be reborn. And it's beyond dispute that great magazines have to be reinvented every decade or so—perhaps even more frequently these days.

Edward Kosner, editor in chief, *Esquire*

Editors will forever be burdened with the public perception that they are grammar nerds, cocktail-schmoozing glitterati, or tough-nosed autocrats.

Such is life.

But as you now know, editing is more than these things—and even more than these things put together.

Editors work with ideas, grappling with concepts that must prove themselves to be fascinating, enlightening, valuable, or necessary—or risk dismissal as the editor plows on in search of better ones.

Editors work with words, making them inform, making them amuse, making them sing.

But most of all, editors work with people. We work with readers, first and foremost. We work with writers a lot. We work with designers, publishers, circulation managers, and artists. We work with sources: presidents, janitors, movie stars, prostitutes, CEOs, victims, teachers, and everyone else we can find who will tell us great stories and make us *feel* something.

We spend too much time in the office, but we get out when we can: to parties, to conferences, to gatherings of people who might give us the next great story to tell.

Magazines are so powerful as a medium. You can have so much influence on the way people think about things, even though you can't make them think one way or the other. You can watch small ideas grow into great realities through the power of the printed word. And it is very exciting, no matter what your field is. There's not much glamour in it, although there is some glory, if your communication mission is successful. And there's pretty good money in it for the skilled and talented who apply themselves.

Jon Wilson, editor, *WoodenBoat*

We worry—more than we admit. We worry about budgets. We worry about deadlines. We worry about where our next great idea is coming from. But mainly we worry about making our readers so happy that they decide to spend more time with our magazines. We really do care about them, and we don't want to let them down.

Editing allows you to meet interesting people. Editing allows you to meet famous people. Some of the famous people are even interesting—although it's kind of rare. Editing allows you to travel. Editing allows you to see things that other people don't get to see. But mainly editing allows you to think. You're paid to think and create and work with teams to build something new each month.

It's a great job.

How to Get This Great Job

If any of this interests you, and you'd like to become an editor someday, I have good news for you. Becoming an editor isn't really all that hard—and the rewards can be potent.

The business of editing is a process of learning that never ends. There is always so much more to know—more about the topics being covered in each issue; and more about a multitude of skills relating to good writing, editing, printing, the use of graphics, new computer technologies, etc. And that makes editing an intensely interesting profession.

Ed Holm, editor, *American History*

College graduates get editing jobs as they always have—they usually select three or four magazines by subject material that appeals to them, and they apply at the bottom rung, possibly starting as a summer intern, etc. I personally think the best education is to start at a "good" daily, a small paper. (And avoid the "bad" daily, as that's where a lot of young people can learn bad habits and think they are the correct habits. An example would be a paper that writes stories in return for ads, and so forth.) There is nothing like the small paper for someone just starting out. I have a journalism degree from a very good J school, and yet I learned more in six months at the *Monrovia Daily News-Post* than I learned in four years of my major in college. A lot of that was me—I was fooling around, and no one was paying me to work on the college paper.

Steve Spence, managing editor, *Car and Driver*

To position yourself well for a career in magazine editing, you should take several steps before you graduate. People who wrap up their college careers with decent grades and a long history of working at McDonald's might want to consider graduate school as a way of buying time and gaining opportunities to acquire some skills and show them off. But if you start now, while you're still in college, you'll be able to apply for jobs at magazines and have a good chance of getting them.

• *Freelance now*. There is nothing keeping you from freelancing for major magazines right now. The key to getting published as a

You really have to love what you are doing, because the job market has never been fabulous in journalism. You're in it because you're committed to the conviction that people need certain information to be able to make cogent decisions in their lives and that you're in a position to present that information. Journalism is the one profession that is actually protected by the Constitution of the United States. It is really something to be safeguarded, and I think you enter this profession because you have the absolute conviction that people need information to function and to make the important decisions in their lives.

Margot Slade, editor, *Consumer Reports*

freelancer is to come up with the right idea for the right magazine. Then you send a persuasive letter about the idea to the editor of that magazine. If she says yes, you're on your way. If she says no, you send your letter to another magazine that might be interested. If you have good ideas and some stoic patience, you'll get published.

Freelancing is a powerful tool for the eventual acquisition of jobs because many editors would rather die than advertise an opening. Here's the standard scenario: Jamal has an opening for a writer (or a copy editor, an editor, or whatever) at his magazine. He rings up *Editor & Publisher*, *Folio:*, the *New York Times*, and he places the smallest ad he can write: "Writer wanted. 1234 North Main, New York, NY 10000."

The next sound Jamal hears is the groaning of the stairs as an army of postal carriers haul bag after bloated bag of résumés to his office. Jamal had planned to go golfing this weekend—but those plans have just been changed. He has a few billion applications to consider.

He starts digging through the piles. Every applicant assures him that she would be perfect for the job. But in letter after letter, résumé after résumé, he spots typos, grammatical mistakes, garish exaggerations, lame writing, and outright lies. He opens manila envelopes, magenta envelopes, Mylar envelopes. He sees every screaming amateurish letterhead imaginable:

Bob Franklin, Wordsmith!

TIA RAMON, CEO OF THE WRITERS' ENTERPRISE

Reginald Rutherford Bartholomew III, Writer Extraordinaire

Melinda Meganthorpe, Painter of Words

He reads underwhelming claim after claim: "My writing is so good, my mother has kept ever letter I've ever sent to her!" "I can write three first-rate articles a day!" "I know how to form the plural of every word in the English language!"

He finally weeds out the noise and the junk, and he settles on five finalists. Then he brings them to New York, one at a time, for interviews—only to find that most of them aren't nearly as impressive as they seemed on paper.

Eventually, because he has to fill the position somehow, he chooses one and offers the job. But he can't shake the feeling that he's hiring a stranger who might just make the office a miserable place for the foreseeable future.

Or

Jamal has an opening, and he thinks, "You know. That freelancer, Bonnie Penn, has been doing some great work for us. I like her writing, she does thorough research, and she's pleasant to talk with on the phone. She even mentioned that she'd be interested in full-time work some day. I think I'll give her a call."

The latter option is far less time-consuming, far less aggravating, and far more likely to succeed. Rather than going through a laborious process and then hiring a stranger, he'll cut right to the chase and hire someone who has already demonstrated that she knows how to write for this magazine.

And for Bonnie, that handful of freelance articles that she squeezed out between classes, parties, and practices with the cross-country team just resulted in a full-time job at a major magazine.

So freelance now to increase your chances of a good job later. But keep in mind that some editors do advertise openings in the *New York Times*—so read the classifieds early and often.

• *Seek out internships.* Editors want to hire people who have some real-world experience. Class work is great, but there is no substitute for gathering information, writing articles, and making decisions under deadline pressure for real audiences.

Internships can help convince prospective employers that you have such experience. As an intern, you'll pitch in to help a magazine or newspaper (or an advertising agency, or...) get its work done each day.

It's true that some internships are much better than others. Some interns have the honor of fetching doughnuts for the "real" workers. But some interns write articles for publication, edit copy, participate in issue-planning discussions, and gain a strong sense of what it's like to work as an editor. These interns also get the chance to show off their enthusiasm, style, flexibility, adaptability, and skill to people who might write letters of recommendation for them someday.

Desktop publishing is part of the challenge of a small, nonprofit, membership-based publication. The editor must be able to do everything: negotiate with vendors, use the software, process the paperwork. If everyone drops off the face of the Earth, the book must still come out.

Sandra Bowles, editor, *Shuttle, Spindle & Dyepot*

Most companies post internship information on the Web. It's usually easy to find out what you need and get your applications in.

• *Take appropriate classes.* Courses in journalism (especially magazine writing and editing), creative writing, and literature can help you understand the basics of good writing. Courses in marketing, management, and economics can impress potential employers because they show an interest in the real-world, business side of publishing. And courses in the topic you're interested in can help. If you want to work for a fashion magazine, take courses in fashion design and marketing. If you want to work for a science magazine, take courses in physics and astronomy. If you want to work for a music magazine, take courses in music theory and popular culture.

• *Embrace newspapers.* When I graduated from college, I met with the editors of *The Atlantic* and *Smithsonian*, two of my favorite magazines. Both editors encouraged me to do "hard time" at a daily newspaper. In the newspaper business, you'll write and edit more articles in a month than you will all year at most magazines. You'll also deal with a wide range of people—from the charming to the miserable—and you'll sharpen your people skills. You'll get good at gathering information quickly, asking tough questions, and writing articles efficiently.

I like to see newspaper experience. It tells me this applicant busted some hump, learned to write tight on deadline, and isn't afraid of hard work and long hours. Work an internship at a magazine. It's the best way to get hands-on experience. Work like a dog for an editor, and he or she will want to keep you around.

Jeff Csatari, executive editor, *Men's Health*

You should definitely do internships—we have six interns here this summer. You should work for your school newspaper or magazine. You should be working toward your goal the whole time. I think that's important.

Leslie Heilbrunn, senior editor, *Cosmo Girl*

And, as the *Smithsonian* editor said, "If you work at a daily paper for a while, you'll never have to explain why you didn't."

• *Write and edit on campus.* Nearly every college and university in the country has a newspaper, a yearbook, newsletters, alumni magazines, and other publications. Writing and editing for them will give you experience, credentials, references, and confidence. You also will be able to demonstrate to prospective employers that you have many of the skills they want: You can work under deadline pressure. You can gather information quickly and thoroughly. You can write in the midst of a noisy office, even though you have three term papers and a group project due this week. You can meet the parameters of an assignment. And you can keep editors happy enough to give you additional assignments.

So even if no one outside your school has ever heard of the *Campus Spleen*, write for it anyway. It's experience you want. Fame will come later.

• *Don't be afraid to start small.* Along those lines, don't turn up your nose at opportunities at small publications—for employment or internships. Sure, you'd rather work for *Cosmo* or *Esquire*, and the offices of *Terrycloth Retailer Monthly* aren't exactly located in the heart of Manhattan, but experience is experience. And smaller publications often offer interns and new recruits better opportunities for writing and editing quickly, getting you out of the doughnut-fetching stage more rapidly than you might if you went straight to a big magazine. You might not want to spend your entire career at a small publication in Nowhere, but cutting your teeth and paying your dues are always useful. You'll learn a lot, and you can move on from there.

Along similar lines, don't dismiss small jobs at big publications, either. Sure, you want to be a major assignment editor at *Vanity Fair* or *Esquire*. But you won't start there, no matter how bright or hardworking you are. If a magazine you love has an opening for an editorial assistant, a fact checker, a copy editor, or another position, apply with enthusiasm. You can work your way up later.

• *Master the art of cheerful persistence.* I'm a big fan of cheerful persistence. People who master this art are never afraid to pick up the phone and call that editor again. They aren't shy about meeting with people and talking about their plans and their work. And they are unerringly upbeat about it—that's why people pay attention to them. This attitude goes much farther than do Impatient Whining or Sullen Silence.

After positioning yourself well by freelancing, taking important courses, and following these other steps, the time will come for you to begin applying for jobs. Of course, you should send personal letters and polished résumés to the editors you have worked with as a freelancer. I'd also recommend a three-part strategy for the rest of the applications.

First, apply for every opening you can find. Read *Editor & Publisher, Folio:,* and the other trade publications that cover the magazine industry. Every time you see an opening on a magazine staff, get your materials to the right person promptly. I'm a huge fan of wasting postage. For the cost of a few stamps, you can put yourself in the running for a lot of jobs.

Second, look through *Writer's Market,* the *Standard Periodical Directory,* or the magazine shelf at your local bookstore, and come up with a list of ten magazines that you think would be perfect for you (be-

People who want to pursue magazine writing/editing careers should *do* editing as a means of learning how to do it. They should get in the habit of editing in their heads everything they read and checking a stylebook or another resource when they are uncertain about how they might make a sentence or section clearer. They need to develop an eye for mistakes in print, a discernment for what makes this article interesting, that story compelling, this paragraph weak. There is plenty of poor writing for them to improve as well as good writing for them to emulate, and if they practice thinking like editors they will learn a lot about writing and how to fix it.

Bonnie Leman, editor, *Quilter's Newsletter Magazine, Quiltmaker,* and *Quilts and Other Comforts*

yond any that you have been freelancing for already). Then call these magazines and ask the receptionist for the name of the person to whom you should send your materials.

Send your materials to these people and ask for a chance to meet with them to talk about magazines, the publishing industry, careers, and other pertinent matters. Asking for a pleasant conversation over lunch is much easier—and much more likely to succeed—than asking for a job. And the request is sincere; talking with people in the business will help you get ready for a job down the road. In the meantime, of course, these conversations translate into contacts—and after the meeting, you should send each of them a thank-you letter and your latest résumé. If you impress any of them, doors can open for you.

Third, it's shotgun time. Choose 100 magazines that you can imagine working for and send them your résumé—whether they have posted job openings or not. Most job openings are never publicly advertised, so getting your materials into the right hands might just line you up for a job that you don't even know is available.

Then, once all these manila envelopes have been sealed and mailed, don't be shy about making cheerful phone calls to further your cause—and don't stop freelancing. Your next assignment might be the one that turns into a full-time job.

Enjoy

Magazine editing is a lively, important, absorbing, and cool career. Those of you who stand at the beginning of such a career can look forward to decades in which today is never the same as yesterday, in which people admire you for what you do, and in which you stand a decent chance of making a difference in the world.

To the best of our knowledge, we get only one life to spend on Earth. People who tolerate boredom and drudgery for a big paycheck are wasting the most precious gift they will ever receive. Follow your heart—and if your heart leads you to the offices of a magazine somewhere, I'm sure you'll have some fun along the way.

> So. A woman marches into the room. She looks vaguely familiar.
>
> "You're late," you say, barely looking up. "I've been editing *Focused and Fabulous* for twelve years now. I was beginning to think you weren't going to show up."

The woman says nothing. You gesture to a briefcase in the corner of the room. Inside it is $400,000. "I believe that's yours," you say.

The woman takes the briefcase. She counts the money and snaps the case shut.

"Who are you, anyway?" you ask.

The woman looks you in the eye. She smiles.

And with that, she turns and walks out the door.

I guess there's one common characteristic among people who are involved in this business: They either believe passionately in their subject, or they believe strongly in the process—the art and the science of communication. If you like ideas, and if you like to hear the ideas of others, the magazine business is a wonderful place to be.

Jon Wilson, editor, *WoodenBoat*

Say What?
Some Important Terms and What They Mean

absolute privilege The right to make certain claims without legal reprisal. Many government officials and members of the legal profession, while carrying out their appointed duties, are free to speak openly without fear of a lawsuit. *See also* **qualified privilege**.

appearance of impropriety The situation in which it looks like you're doing something wrong. If you appear to be doing something wrong, you can damage your credibility even though you're not actually behaving improperly.

average Precisely, the number you get when you add the values of several items and divide by the total number of items. For example, let's say you have five watermelons of the following weights: 1 pound, 1 pound, 2 pounds, 3 pounds, and 3 pounds. The total weight is 10 pounds. Divide that number by the five watermelons you have, and you come up with an average weight of 2 pounds.

It is important to remember the distinction between the average and the mean. *See also* **mean**.

brainstorming The act of bouncing ideas off one another. A good brainstorming session focuses on a specific goal. The participants toss out any idea that occurs to them, even if it seems goofy or dangerous or bizarre. All ideas are written down. Then, at a later time, you can go through the list of ideas and sort out the weird from the wonderful.

burden of proof The responsibility for proving something in court. If the person who has the burden of proof fails to meet it—meaning that he fails to present convincing evidence or testimony that proves his claims—the other side doesn't have to do anything at all.

byline   The name of the author of an article. Increasingly, designers and editors are getting bylines as well.

call out   *See* **pull quote**

categorical imperative   An ethical decision-making model, developed by Immanuel Kant, by which we can discern good actions from bad ones—at least, according to him. *See also* **communitarianism, Golden Mean,** *and* **utilitarianism.**

chart   A table or similar grid in which information can be displayed simply and easily. *See also* **graph** *and* **infographic.**

circulation   The actual number of magazines delivered to readers. *Road Kill Weekly* might have a circulation of 10,000, but its readership might be higher. *See also* **readership.**

cliché   A trite, overworked expression. Clichés typically draw on some kind of comparison or metaphor, but the literal meaning has long been leached out of them, leaving behind dry, empty linguistic shells.

clips   Copies of your previously published work. *See also* **tear sheet.**

communitarianism   An ethical decision-making model that seeks to provide for the good of the group before all else. *See also* **categorical imperative, Golden Mean,** *and* **utilitarianism.**

copy editing   Paragraph-, sentence-, or word-level editing in which an editor checks for grammar, spelling, punctuation, good transitions, and stylistic details. The precise definition varies, but copy editors are not charged with evaluating the quality of a manuscript as a whole.

cover blurb   A short, punchy teaser that runs on the cover of a magazine. Cover blurbs give readers a sense of what's inside the magazine, and they try to inspire newsstand shoppers to buy the issue. *See also* **teaser.**

cutline   The caption that runs with a photo.

deck head   The headline that appears under the main head of an article. The deck head usually is longer than the main head, and it offers additional information about the article's content, the meaning of the main head, the rationale for the article, and the like. *See also* **kicker** *and* **main head.**

demographics   The breakdown of an audience into categories: sex, age, income, and other characteristics. Demographics can give editors valuable information that helps them shape the content of their magazines.

departments   The regular "slots" that a magazine offers in each issue. Departments sometimes run in the very front of the magazine, before the features, and sometimes run in the back. (Or sometimes they run in both places.) Departments tend to be shorter than features, and they focus on consistent themes from issue to issue. Typical departments for commercial magazines are "Health," "Politics," "Business," "Education," "Fashion," "Family," and so on. Departments can also be service-oriented pieces, such as an activities calendar, or hodgepodge collections of small items, which often are given such titles as "Grab Bag," "Quips, Quotes & Queries," "Potpourri," and "Miscellanea." *See also* **features**.

dilemma   Precisely, a situation in which you face either two equally good choices or two equally bad ones, with no room for compromise or alternatives.

dingbat   A small symbol, typically a squiggle or a box, that is used as a decorative element or a divider in text. In magazines, dingbats often are used to indicate the end of an article. Some common dingbats are ❏❈❀▲❖❂■○☆❖✦★✪●. Many magazines design their own dingbats from their logos or initials.

editing   *See entire book*

ethics   Precisely, the study of morality. In more conversational use, ethics refers to knowing the difference between right and wrong and acting accordingly.

fact checker   A member of a magazine staff who devotes much of her time to verifying the information that writers include in their articles.

features   The longer, more in-depth articles that typically fill the front half of a magazine. Features are "one-shot" pieces; they don't recur from issue to issue. *See also* **departments**.

features well   The section of a magazine in which the features typically appear. In many magazines, the features well begins after the table of contents and some of the departments, and continues until the middle of the magazine or beyond.

focus group   A group of people, carefully selected, who are called together to discuss a product—in our case, a magazine or potential magazine. These people are asked about their likes and dislikes, the likelihood that they would buy a particular kind of magazine, and other such questions. The information provided by focus groups is used to help magazines understand and meet their readers' needs.

folio   The page number. *See also* **running head**.

font   Generally, a particular typeface, such as Times Roman or Garamond. Some fonts take up more horizontal space than do others, and some take up more vertical space. Fonts affect the readability, the character, and the feel of a magazine.

free press   Generally, the operation of the news media without interference from the government. Freedom of the press is one of the fundamental characteristics of American democracy, guaranteed in the First Amendment of the Constitution, although the government has, over the years, passed several laws that restrict that freedom to a certain extent.

freelancer A writer who works for magazines without joining the actual staff.

Golden Mean An ethical decision-making model, developed by Aristotle, according to which any extreme action is bad—hence the best option is the one that lies closest to the center of any spectrum. *See also* **categorical imperative, communitarianism,** *and* **utilitarianism.**

graph A diagram that shows the relationship of two or more things. Various kinds of graphs include bar graphs, line graphs, and pie charts. *See also* **chart** and **infographic.**

harassment The unreasonable bothering of a person for no valid reason. Reporters can be guilty of harassment if they call a source every five minutes, trying to get him to give up and offer a quote.

infinitive The *to* form of a verb: *to run, to jump, to throw, to eat,* and so on.

infographic A kind of chart or graph that uses colorful symbols, often related to the theme of the article, to convey information. An infographic about snowfall totals in Colorado resorts might convert a line graph into a ski slope, with little skiers schussing along the lines. *See also* **chart** *and* **graph.**

invasion of privacy The unreasonable intrusion into someone's private life, especially in the absence of any newsworthy goal.

jump line The little note that indicates when an article is "continued on page 36" or "continued from page 13." Jump lines also might carry key words from the article's title, to help readers make sure that they are reading the right piece.

kicker A short phrase that appears above the main head of an article. The kicker often labels the department or offers a small bit of interesting information about the article. *See also* **deck head** *and* **main head.**

kill fee Money that is paid to a writer when an assigned article is rejected through no fault of the writer's. The article is fine and fulfills the assignment well, but the editor might have changed her mind, the magazine published something after the assignment that makes this article less desirable, and the like. The kill fee usually is a prestated percentage of the total amount promised, often 25 or 33 percent.

lawsuit A grievance that is filed in court. The requirements for filing a lawsuit are pretty generous; almost anyone can file a suit for almost any reason. When we say, "You could be sued," we really mean that you could *lose* a lawsuit.

lead or **leed** The beginning section of an article. For most magazine pieces, the lead is anywhere from one to six or seven paragraphs long. It is typically followed by the nut graf. *See also* **nut graf.**

lead time   The time a magazine needs between the planning-and-idea stage and the final printing. This time is necessary for the assigning and writing of articles, the editing, the photography, the design and layout, and the printing.

legal   The small-type description, required by law, that lists the publisher of a magazine and the addresses of the publication and advertising offices as well as other facets of the operation.

libel   Specifically, damage to reputation through the publication of false information. *See also* **slander.**

main head   The main headline for an article. *See also* **deck head** *and* **kicker.**

malice   The publication of damaging information, even though you knew it was false or did not bother to determine its validity.

masthead   The list of editors, writers, graphic artists, and other people who put a magazine together as well as the addresses of the magazine's offices and other useful information. The masthead usually is near the front of the magazine, often in a single column. Savvy freelancers check mastheads before they send out manuscripts, just to make sure that the editor hasn't changed recently.

mean   Precisely, the number that occupies the middle position in a series, with as many numbers above as below. It is important to remember the distinction between the average and the mean. For example, let's say that there are seven children, and each child has a handful of coins. Their totals look like this:

Abby	25 cents
Barney	50 cents
Chloe	$2
Daphne	$1
Evie	25 cents
Frankie	10 cents
Gigi	$2

The average of their savings is just over 87 cents (610 cents divided by seven children). But to get the mean, order the children by wealth:

Chloe	$2
Gigi	$2
Daphne	$1
Barney	50 cents
Abby	25 cents
Evie	25 cents
Frankie	10 cents

The mean of this series is 50 cents. Three children have more than Barney's 50 cents, and three have less. *See also* **average**.

mission The reason a magazine exists.

mission statement A short, clear statement summarizing the magazine's mission.

morality Rightness and wrongness. We can discuss the morality of a situation in an effort to determine whether it is right or wrong. Loosely, morality also refers to rightness; this is moral, but that is immoral.

negligence The failure to act with the prudence that a reasonable person would have shown.

nut graf The paragraph that tells readers, in a "nutshell," what an article is all about and why they should read it. *See also* **lead**.

private individual A person who is not a public official or public figure. Private individuals are protected from libel and invasion of privacy to a greater extent than are public figures and officials. *See also* **public figure** *and* **public official**.

pseudonym A fictitious name used to hide the identity of a source or subject.

public figure A person who thrusts himself into the public eye through his work or actions. Movie stars, corporate CEOs, and similar people typically are public figures. *See also* **private individual** *and* **public official**.

public official A person who holds an elected or appointed public position. Mayors, sheriffs, and similar people are public officials. *See also* **private individual** *and* **public figure**.

pull quote A bits of text from an article, copied and blown up to a larger size. Pull quotes are used to break up a text-heavy page and to inspire readers to read the article.

qualified privilege The right to use material from a privileged source. *See also* **absolute privilege**.

readership The people who actually read a magazine. One common formula says that for every copy of a magazine that is distributed, three people read it. (This takes into account several members of a family, patients in waiting rooms, and the like.) So a magazine with a circulation of 20,000 might have a readership of 60,000. *See also* **circulation**.

reckless disregard for the truth Steaming ahead to the publication of possibly false information.

release date The date on which a magazine will hit the newsstands and mailboxes.

running head or foot The words printed next to the page numbers, often the name of the magazine or a keyword from the title of the article.

shield law A law that protects journalists from certain types of lawsuits.

sidebar A small companion article that conveys information not in-cluded in the main piece. Sidebars can appear in paragraph form, or they can offer lists or other brief formats.

signature The grouping of magazine pages—typically eight or sixteen pages at a time—that is necessary for efficient printing. The way most presses work, printing a set of eight pages is actually less expensive than printing seven pages. So most editors make their magazines' page count work out to a multiple of eight or sixteen, because doing so gives them the greatest number of pages at the lowest cost.

slander Specifically, damage to reputation through the spoken word. *See also* **libel**.

subhead A single word or short phrase used to mark the beginning of new narrative blocks. In magazines, subheads often are centered on the page and printed in boldface type:

Therefore, the management issues inherent in top–down global imple-mentations cannot be understated with regard to circulation on a general operating system consisting primarily of elements regarded as outdated.

Sex

In order to properly conceive and articulate these central variables, an acquisition portfolio outlining the structural components, leading to a re-consideration of harmony across the generic landscape, is an opportu-nity without precedent.

sue *See* **lawsuit**.

target audience The readers that a magazine wants to attract.

tear sheets Actual examples of your previously published articles, "torn" out of the magazines in which they appeared. *See also* **clips**.

teaser A preview of articles that will appear in future issues of a maga-zine. Often run on the last page of the magazine, teasers serve to en-tice readers to buy the next issue and perhaps even to subscribe to the magazine. *See also* **cover blurb**.

undercover work The use of deception to get information for a story. Undercover work includes posing as an employee to get information about a company, pretending to be a phone-company worker to gain access to a building, or even just striking up a conversation with someone without telling her that you are gathering information for publication.

utilitarianism An ethical decision-making model that seeks to provide the greatest good for the greatest number of people. *See also* **categori-cal imperative**, **communitarianism**, *and* **Golden Mean**.

voice The personality of an article.

A Brief Bibliography

Those of you who just can't get enough information about editing—which I imagine means those of you who intend to become editors, and a few additional zealots whose self-worth is far too tightly linked to the sense that your understanding of language exceeds that of all others—might find these books useful as well.

The Chicago Manual of Style. 15th ed. Chicago: University of Chicago Press, 2003.

This monster stylebook covers nearly every writing question imaginable. It is terrific as a resource, but no one in his or her right mind would actually sit down and read it cover to cover.

Gardner, John. *On Becoming a Novelist.* Foreword by Raymond Carver. New York: Norton, 1999.

Off the topic a bit, but this book is fantastic for inspiration and a general sense of "I can do that."

Goldstein, Norm, ed. *The Associated Press Stylebook and Libel Manual: Including Guidelines on Photo Captions, Filing the Wire, Proofreaders' Marks, Copyright.* Reading, Mass.: Addison-Wesley, 1998.

This style manual is great for solid information about how to handle myriad writing problems, but be aware that it is geared to newspaper reporters and editors. Not all the advice applies to magazine editing.

Jacobi, Peter P. *The Magazine Article: How to Think It, Plan It, Write It.*
Bloomington: Indiana University Press, 1997.

This outstanding book by an outstanding writer and educator offers
a special combination of hard information and uplifting prose.

Kovach, Bill, and Tom Rosenstiel. *The Elements of Journalism: What
Newspeople Should Know and the Public Should Expect.* New York:
Crown, 2001.

This book raises worthwhile questions about the role of journalism
in today's society.

Merrill, John C. *Existential Journalism.* Ames: Iowa State University Press,
1996.

This insightful approach to journalism invigorates the mind and
challenges assumptions.

Rowse, Arthur E. *Drive-by Journalism: The Assault on Your Need to Know.*
Monroe, Maine: Common Courage Press, 2000.

This study explores the sensationalist anemia that is plaguing the
communications industry.

Strunk, William, Jr., and E. B. White. *The Elements of Style.* 4th ed.
Boston: Allyn and Bacon, 2000.

This classic is a must-have for every serious magazine person, who
should put it in the bathroom and read it often.

Wright, John W. *The New York Times Almanac.* New York: Penguin, an-
nual.

This reference offers tons of information that every editor will need
someday.

Index

absolute privilege, 75–76, 339
"accordion" section, 292–93
adspeak, 148–50
advertising, 299–304; to attract sub-
    scribers, 305–9
African-American, as preferred term,
    101
Air & Space, 10, 34, 159, 310
American Archaeology, 8, 16, 124,
    129, 171, 299, 310
American Health, xiii, 324
American History, ix, 35, 45, 58, 327
American Indian Art Magazine, 100,
    324
anecdote, as lead, 182–83
apostrophe, 276–78
appearance of impropriety, 339
Arizona Highways, 60
Arts Indiana, 46
Astronomy, 16, 24, 27, 43, 323
Atlantic, The, 34, 40, 117, 297
audience, 8–11, 18–39, 125, 155,
    163–64
average, 339

bad and *badly*, distinction between,
    251
Barthold, Charles, 18, 24
Bawaya, Michael, 8, 16, 124, 129,
    171, 299, 310
Belt, Don, 132

Benz, Jill, 19, 323
Better Homes and Gardens, 11, 32, 55,
    321
biographies, of contributors, 295–96
Bishop, Gerry, 35, 36–37, 61, 311
Bok, Sissela, 89
Bowles, Sandra, x, 331
brackets, 280
brainstorming, 113–15, 339
burden of proof, 66, 339–40
byline, 296, 340

call out, 286–88, 340
caption, 285–86
Car and Driver, 9, 33, 114, 115, 180,
    299, 328
Carolan, Matthew, 18, 56, 323
categorical imperative, 90–92, 340
chart, 340
Chasan, Alice, 51, 95, 96
chronological structure, of an article,
    177–78
Churchill, Winston, 248
circulation, 304–9, 340
Cliburn, Greg, 49
cliché, 226–28, 340
clip, 340
colon, 268–69
colored, as derogatory term, 101
Columbia, 316
comma, 261–66

communitarianism, 93–94, 340
competition, among magazines, 58–61, 321
conceptualization, of a magazine, 3–17
conclusion, of an article, 188–90
Consumer Reports, 1, 21, 133, 148, 314, 328
contributors, biographies of, 295–96
copy editing, 340
corrections, 207–8
Cosmo Girl, 23, 107, 130, 160, 332
cover blurb, 288–89, 340
Cox, Craig, 12, 24, 44, 320
Csatari, Jeff, 36, 41, 131, 153, 169, 298, 311, 331
curiosity, 112
Curtis, Mike, 117
Cutler, Karan Davis, 50, 117, 119, 310
cutline, 340

dangling modifier, 237–39
Daniels, Scott, 20, 58, 123
dashes, 269–72
DeChristina, Mariette, 42, 60–61, 62, 125
deck head, 284, 340
defamation, 72–73
demographics, 38, 340
departments, 340–41
dilemma, 341
dingbat, 341
direct-mail marketing, 305
Do-Not-Call Implementation Act, 308

e structure, of an article, 180
E/The Environmental Magazine, 36, 57
Early American Life, 15, 316
Ebony, 11, 323
editor, as Reader Number One, xiv
editorial team, 50–53
Eicher, David J., 16, 24, 27, 43, 323
Endless Vacation, 29, 49–50, 116, 312
England, Cheryl, 12–13, 24, 35–36, 52, 315
Entrepreneur, 24, 29, 111, 318

Esquire, 40, 44–46, 109, 323, 326
Essence, 25, 44, 52
ethics, 83–106, 341
etymology, 256
Explore the Universe, 16, 323
Exploring, 20, 58, 123

facts, checking of, 193–208, 341
fair comment, 73
Family Circle, 16, 147, 312, 322
features, 341
features well, 341
Field & Stream, 20, 24
fit, of an article, 153–59
Florida Sportsman, 60
focus group, 30–33, 318–19, 341
folio, 296, 341
font, 341
foreign terms, use of, 144
fragments, sentence, 215–16
framing structure, of an article, 179
free press, 341–42
freebies, to attract subscribers, 305
freelance writers: choosing and hiring, 121–23; nurturing, 123–32
freelancers, 56, 342
freelancing, to launch career, 328–30

Gambling Times, 55–56
geographical structure, of an article, 179
geographical/regional magazines, 13–14
gifts and favors, 97
Golden Mean, 88–89, 342
Golden Rule, 86, 88
Goldfein, Roanne P., 100, 324
grammar, 209–53
graph, 342
Great Wall, between advertising and editorial, 299–301
Guideposts, 317
Guttman, Jon, 27, 63, 315

Hamilton, Joan, 12, 26–27, 46, 316
Handler, Mimi, 15, 316
harassment, 81–82, 342
Harr, Jonathan, 5

Harrowsmith Country Life, 50, 117, 119, 319
headline, 282–85
Heartland USA, 30, 34, 51, 318
Heilbrunn, Leslie, 23, 107, 130, 160, 332
hobbies, as magazine topics, 12–13
Holm, Ed, ix, 35, 45, 58, 327
Huffman, Frances, 10, 33, 323
hyphen, 272–76

ideas for articles, 112–17
Indian, as disputed term, 101–2
infinitive, 342
infographic, 147–48, 342
International Wildlife, 37, 142, 173
internships, 330–31
invasion of privacy, 78–80, 342
inverted-pyramid structure, of an article, 179

jargon, 142–44
Johnson, John H., 11, 323
jump line, 296, 342

Kant, Immanuel, 90–92
kicker, 284, 342
kill fee, 342
Kosner, Edward, 40, 109, 323, 326

Ladies' Home Journal, 19, 323
Lake Superior Magazine, 49
Lalli, Cele G., 47, 319
Larson, George, 10, 34, 159, 310
law, 64–82
law enforcement, cooperation with, 99
lawsuit, 65, 342, 345
lay and *lie*, distinction between, 250
lead, of an article, 181–88, 342
lead time, 343
legal, 296, 343
Leman, Bonnie, 110, 320, 324, 333
LemMon, Jean, 11, 32, 55, 321
Lesonsky, Rieva, 24, 111, 318
letter from the editor, 289–90
letter to the editor, 21, 22–24, 290–92

libel, 65, 68–78, 343
Lichtenberg, G. C. (Georg Christoph), 281
Life, 7
logic, 145–47, 150–52
Look, 7
Lutz, Diane, xiv, 15, 24, 130

MacAddict, 12–13, 24, 35–36, 52, 315
Mahaney, Jackson, 29, 49–50, 116, 312
mailing lists, for surveys, 28
main head, 284, 343
malice, 66–67, 343
Mandel, Gerry, 315
masthead, 295, 343
mathematics, 144–45, 201–2
Mature Outlook, 47, 59, 317, 320
McDonald, John, 156, 313
McGeehan, Patrick J., 116, 157, 317
McMunn, Richard, 316
McPhee, John, 180
mean, 343
Men's Health, 36, 41, 131, 153, 169, 298, 311, 331
Men's Journal, 9
Meyer, Mary Clemens, 13, 50, 318
Meyer, Scott, 21, 25, 43, 100, 120
Military History, 27, 63, 315
mission, 40–63, 110, 117–18, 344
mission statement, 46–50, 314–15, 344
mix, of articles in a magazine, 119–20
Modern Bride, 47, 319
Moment, 60
morality, 344
Moss, Doug, 36–37, 57
Muse, xiv, 15, 24, 130

Nation, The, 83, 95, 106, 121, 193, 200
National Association for the Advancement of Colored People (NAACP), 101
National Gardening, 26, 323
National Geographic, 6, 30, 34, 116, 120, 132, 157, 158, 209, 317

National Geographic Traveler, 47–49
National Review, 18, 56, 323
National Wildlife, 34
Native American, as disputed term, 101–2
Naval History, 13, 27, 53, 316
Navasky, Victor, 83, 95, 106, 121, 193, 200
negligence, 67, 344
New England Monthly, 5
noun–pronoun agreement, 220–22
noun–verb agreement, 222–23
nut graf, 187–88, 344
Nuwer, Hank, 46

Okrent, Dan, 5
On the Line, 13, 33–34, 50, 318
Organic Gardening, 21, 25, 43, 100, 120
organization, of an article, 138–40, 169–81
Oursler, Fulton, Jr., 317
Outside, 49

parallel construction, 239–42
parentheses, 280
passive voice, 223–25
payment, for interviews, 98–99
Pearson, Brad, 30, 51, 318
period, 257–61
Person, Peggy S., 47, 59, 317, 320
Petzal, David E., 20, 24
planning, 109–32
Poe, Edgar Allan, 254; "The Bells," 211
police. *See* law enforcement
Popular Science, 42, 60–61, 62, 125
Porteous, Peter, 6, 30
postmortem, 319–21
Poynter Institute, 100
press release, 56–57
private individuals, 77–78, 344
privilege, 75–76
pronoun, antecedent of, 217–20, 244
pseudonym, 95–96, 344
public figures, 77, 344
public officials, 76, 344
publishers, 297–98

pull quote, 286–88, 344
punctuation, 257–80

qualified privilege, 73, 76, 344
Quilter's Newsletter Magazine, 110, 320, 324, 333
quotation marks, 278–80
quote, as lead, 184

raise and *rise*, distinction between, 251
Ranger Rick, 35, 36–37, 61, 311
readership, 344
reckless disregard for the truth, 67, 344
release date, 344
Renaud, Beth, 26, 323
renewals: rates of, 321–22; by subscribers, 309–10
rewriting, 129–30, 135–36
Rogers, Leslie, 209
Rosen, Jay, xvii
running head or foot, 344
run-on, sentence, 216–17

Sail Magazine, 19, 23, 321
Schultz, Fred L., 13, 27, 53, 316
Scouting, 20, 58, 123
semicolon, 266–68
sense, of an article, 133–52
sentence, structure of, 212–17
Seventeen, 20, 55
shield laws, 82, 344
Shuttle, Spindle & Dyepot, ix, 331
sidebar, 148, 293–94, 345
Sierra, 12, 26–27, 46, 316
signature, 345
sit and *set*, distinction between, 251
Slade, Margot, 1, 21, 133, 148, 314, 328
slander, 66, 345
Slayton, Tom, 27, 325
slow and *slowly*, distinction between, 252
Smithsonian, 113
social causes, as magazine topics, 11–12

Society of Professional Journalists, 100
sources, for fact checking, 202–6
spelling, 254–57
Spence, Steve, 9, 33, 114, 115, 180, 299, 328
spine structure, of an article, 179–80
spirituality, as magazine topic, 13
split infinitives, 225–26
step-by-step structure, of an article, 178–79
Stone Soup, 127, 315
structure, of an article, 138–40, 169–81; of a sentence, 212–17
subhead, 345
success, as an editor, 310–25
surveys, of readers, 26–30, 316–17
symbolic logic, 150–52

table of contents, 294–95
T'ai Chi, 60
target audience, 345
tear sheet, 345
teaser, 296, 345
telephone solicitations, for surveys, 28–29
thesaurus, 143–44

tone, 159–68
topics, of magazines, 11–15
trespass, 80–81
truth, as libel defense, 73

U. Magazine, 10, 33, 323
Ulrich, Amy, 19, 23, 321
undercover work, 96–97, 345
Ungaro, Susan, 16, 147, 312, 322
utilitarianism, 92–93, 345
Utne Reader, 12, 14, 44, 320

Vermont Life, 27, 325
Villarosa, Linda, 25, 44, 52
voice, 246–47, 345

Wenner, Jann, 9
Whitworth, William, 34, 40, 297
Wilson, Jon, ii, 4, 300, 327, 337
Winfrey, Casey, xiii, 324
WoodenBoat, ii, 4, 300, 327, 337
Woodwork, 156, 313
words, choice of, 228–36
World Press Review, 51, 95, 96
writers, as sources for ideas, 115–17

Yachting, 18, 24